THE BIG
"LITTLE GTO"
BOOK

Albert Drake

Motorbooks International
Publishers & Wholesalers Inc
Osceola, Wisconsin 54020, USA

© Albert Drake, 1982
ISBN: 0-87938-112-4
Library of Congress Number: 81-14224

Printed and bound in the United States of America
Book and cover design by William F. Kosfeld
Cover illustration by Robert Straub

Motorbooks International is a certified trademark, regis-
tered with the United States Patent Office.

7   8   9   10

Motorbooks International books are also available in bulk
quantity for industrial or sales-promotional use. For details
write to Marketing Manager, Motorbooks International,
P.O. Box 2, Osceola, Wisconsin 54020.

Library of Congress Cataloging in Publication Data

Drake, Albert.
    The big "Little GTO" book.

    1. GTO automobile.   I. Title.
TL215.G27D7   629.2'222   81-14224
ISBN 0-87938-112-4 (pbk.)   AACR2

For
Jim Wangers
Big Daddy of the GTO

ACKNOWLEDGMENTS

To say that this book could not have been finished without the help of many is an understatement.

I'm especially grateful to those people who are GTO authorities for taking time to talk with me, often at length, about the development of the GTO; these primary sources include Roger Huntington, George DeLorean, Michelle Peters, Jim Wangers and Jeff Tillman.

Others whose help was invaluable are Dennis Bornhorst, Dick Thompson of Pontiac Motor Division, Tony Bastien (president) and Paul Rader (vice president) of the GTO Association of America, Donald A. Bougher of the Pontiac-Oakland Club International, Incorporated, and Edward Morehouse.

I'm grateful to everyone who responded to my questionnaire and who sent photographs. My special thanks to R. Chris Halla, Gordy Cowan, Richard and Constance Buss, Mike DeFazio and Lester Crabtree.

Thanks to Randall L. Grider for obtaining some of the photos in this book. Thanks also to Ms. Barbara Woolf of the *Detroit Free Press* Action Line for locating a photo of Ted's Drive-in as it appeared in the 1960's, and to Ms. Nancy Jenkins for allowing me to copy it.

Two others to whom I owe much are Ed Reavie, who supplied incentive as well as information, and my friend Ernst 'Ernie' Lucas, whose enthusiasm for American automobiles of the past thirty years is exceeded only by his detailed knowledge of them.

INTRODUCTION

GTO: Gran Turismo Omologato. The name was unpronounceable for most Americans, and its meaning was unknown to three out of four Pontiac owners. While the name seemed to be akin to other Pontiac lines, such as the LeMans and the Grand Prix, it quickly touched off a controversy because it implied that this car was in the same class as that other GTO, the Ferrari. Pontiac did not try to prove or dispel this notion, but it did try to simplify the name by translating it as 'ready,' indicating that the foreign name was attached to an all-American product which was ready in both senses of the word: readily available and ready to *go.*

The name was appropriate, in a way, since the GTO was described by the manufacturer as a "sports car," and such cars had always had foreign roots. The GTO *was* a sports car, an Americanized grand touring version, and indeed it was the sports car that thousands of American drivers had yearned for since the early 1950's. It had the trappings associated with sports cars—bucket seats, tachometer, floor shift—and it handled reasonably well. Most of all, it had *power*—enough power to scare the bejeezus out of drivers accustomed to four doors and several inches of undercoating! Moreover, unlike foreign two-seaters, the GTO had plenty of room and was designed to do double-duty: You could run it at the Saturday-night stoplight burnouts or at the legal drags, and on Sunday morning you could load up the whole family and drive to church without having to change anything but the rear tires.

Such is the stuff of the GTO legend. Today it's considered the archetypal muscle car: immortalized in song, remembered as the hero in an unending saga of memories of Woodward Avenue axle-twisters, drive-ins, Saturday-night dates where love was wrapped around a car capable of spinning its tires in every gear and traveling the quarter mile at 105 mph, factory exhausts roaring.

Today the GTO continues to be sought out for those same qualities, but it is seen as the knight errant of the Golden Age of Detroit and time has increased the intensity of its heroic glow: It is the kind of car that could be built by people who *cared* about cars. It represents the product of an industry unfettered by federal safety and emission limitations, and it represents what many see as the epitome of what we have lost, namely freedom of choice, uncrowded streets, an unlimited supply of twenty-five-cent-a-gallon gasoline and an eighty-mph speed limit.

The GTO is easily mythicized because it was that kind of a car—a true supercar—but it's important to remember the origins of the myth. Here are the three things that made the GTO unique:

1) The GTO was first with the big V-8 engine in an intermediate-size body and chassis. As such, it was the first muscle car, and godfather of those that followed.

2) The GTO was a personalized car built on an assembly-line basis. It was originally an option on the Tempest series, but in addition the factory offered the buyer an extensive list of other options; some installed at the factory, some installed by the dealer. Because of the many performance and trim options, a buyer could, as the factory suggested, "tailor-make" his own car.

3) The GTO was heavily promoted in the media through advertisements and spinoffs; its image was clearly established, and the importance of image must be emphasized.

The sum of the three features is that the GTO was and is an outstanding car; it was well-made, it was fast, it enjoyed great popularity and, without a doubt, it is a historical artifact—the machine that symbolized the car culture of the sixties.

CONTENTS

CHAPTER ONE

Origins

*T*he birth of the GTO was a miracle, an immaculate conception achieved almost entirely by three wise men: an advertising man who was struck by divine revelation and two executive engineers who recognized the meaning of his prophecy. Or, in the language of board rooms, the GTO was conceived "to meet a marketing need," a car which would help Pontiac maintain the hold it had on the youth market and help maintain Pontiac sales in general. And that is exactly what it did.

But the amazing thing about the GTO story is that the car happened at all.

Although at that time there were few federal mandates limiting what a car maker could or could not do and little pressure from outside the industry other than public opinion, there were pressures being exerted from within the various corporations to end the horsepower race which had begun in the early 1950's. There were auto makers who believed that cars sold for any number of reasons—quality workmanship, appearance, styling triumphs, accessories, even gimmicks and gadgets —but not because of horsepower ratings or how well a particular make did in competition. And even if cars were sold because they were fast, some auto makers believed that was the wrong kind of appeal to make to the public. These were not the voices of isolated individuals crying in the wilderness; in many cases their status quo opinions carried authority. It was the exceptional auto maker who worked, always against the grain, to carry out plans to build an innovative machine.

This was especially true at Pontiac, where many of the decision-makers could remember the cars they had built only ten years earlier—cars characterized by wide swaths of chrome, illuminated Indian heads on the hood and rows of silver stars on the fenders. These were the men who raised strong objections to the development of a car like the GTO. In spite of the styling and engineering revolution that had taken place at Pontiac in the late 1950's and early 1960's, and would continue with amazing consistency throughout the decade, certain key executives yearned to see Pontiac return to what it had been earlier: a company which produced a solid, dependable, non-controversial and very slow car.

It was the kind of car that a father drove but the son rejected; it was a visible definition of the phrase, the generation gap. A gaudy car, but otherwise unremarkable. If you stood on a busy street corner in the early 1950's and closed your eyes you could easily identify the Pontiacs as they passed because of the high-pitched whine of the Timkin rear axle bearings protesting in their races.

A definite and dramatic difference between the 1964 GTO and the Pontiac of ten years earlier had to do with a media term which took on increasing importance during that decade: *image*. The GTO had a clear image; the Pontiac of the 1950's did not. In the late 1940's and early 1950's it was hard to say who preferred Pontiacs, because the company had been building cars for anybody and everybody. If there was a projected market it seemed to be the middle-aged, middle-class family that aspired toward success and saw its movement from a Chevrolet to a Pontiac as a sign of upward mobility. But perhaps buyer motivations were not even that clear. In the book, *On A Clear Day You Can See General Motors*, John DeLorean mentions the lack of image that Pontiac suffered during the early 1950's, and cites a survey the company took. "The results showed that the Pontiac had no distinctive image at all among its owners and potential customers. It was a solid, reliable and sturdy car which evoked no discernable emotion one way or the other."

Part of the lack of image had to do with the company's attempt to blend the old with the new—although the car had the new envelope body design, Pontiac still used the L-head straight-six and straight-eight engines. There was, many people felt, something fundamentally wrong with a car built at mid-century which continued to use an engine that dated from the 1930's, an engine with obvious weight and design handicaps. The old Chevrolet six could be hopped-up, and even Hudson supplied optional speed equipment for the Twin H-Power engines, but no one tried to coax an extra horse out of a Pontiac! What the car needed, of course, was a new ohv V-8. Oldsmobile and Cadillac had had their ohv V-8 engines since 1949, and Buick had had one since 1953. When General Motors built nine futuristic cars for the important 1954 Motorama show, the Oldsmobile Cutlass and F-88; the Buick Wildcat; and the Cadillac El Camino, Espada and Park Avenue all had modern V-8 engines; but the Pontiac Strato-Streak and Bonneville—a sleek coupe with open wheels and gullwing doors, which looked like a rocket sled ready to blast off —still had the old straight-eight engines.

Road tests of Pontiacs made during the years 1950-54 didn't even mention performance because that factor, like white noise, was difficult to discuss. One frustrated Pontiac owner, who spoke for many, wrote to *Motor Trend*: "I am driving my eighth Pontiac, but cannot wait any longer for them to come out with their V-8. Would it be practical to install a Cadillac V-8 engine in it?"

Due to this poor image and feeble hardware, the company began going downhill rapidly. Pontiac sales declined to a distant sixth place and, of its plants, only the foundry showed a profit; there was a strong chance that General Motors would

In early 1960's, Pontiacs were unbeatable at drag strips all over the country.

phase out the line. As John DeLorean noted, "In 1956 . . . the auto industry and the city of Pontiac, Michigan, were full of rumors that GM was going to shut down this troubled car division. Annual sales were a paltry 233,000 units. Management morale was low and dropping lower each day. The once proud [company] was losing money, and the word around the division was that GM would assign the Pontiac name to another car division to let the Pontiac dealers down slowly."

Because Pontiac did not aim its projected sales toward a particular segment of the motoring public, the real question, one upon which the very fate of the company hung, was: Who would buy a Pontiac? This problem was compounded by the fact that Pontiac had to compete with other GM cars. Various people, for various reasons, might buy a Chevrolet; when they wanted something different within the GM line they often skipped Pontiac, because it was too similar to the Chevrolet they had just got rid of, and moved to an Oldsmobile or a Buick. DeLorean summed up the situation neatly: "Pontiac was too small an operation to have any complicated problems. The problems were basic and twofold: Its management was old and entrenched, and its products were dull and therefore not accepted by the public." So the changes that needed to be made if the company was to survive concerned the car's *raison d'être*: Why should there be a Pontiac?

Two major changes occurred in the company to help answer this question. The first change occurred in 1955 with the introduction of Pontiac's all-new ohv V-8 engine. Called the Strato-Streak, it had a displacement of 287 ci and was rated at 180 hp at 4600 rpm. Although the announcement of this engine was overshadowed by the new Chevrolet ohv V-8, *Motor Trend* was able to say that "the new Pontiac moves out like no other Pontiac ever has." The magazine's test car went from 0-60 mph in thirteen seconds, turned a top speed of 103 mph and got 20.2 mpg at a constant 30 mph. Not bad for a car whose intended owners simply wanted to get to the store and back!

This engine featured a wedge-shaped combustion chamber, similar to that found in the 1954 Oldsmobile, with the chamber machined rather than rough-cast. This limited the variation between cylinders and achieved a more symmetrical cylinder design, which produced more identical compression ratios, and it also helped to control turbulence in a manner not possible with cast chambers. A unique feature was the use of offset cylinder banks, with the right bank forward of the left, which allowed a simplified distributor installation on the right side of the engine accepting the upward force on the distributor gear. The engine had excellent lubrication qualities, including a Quad-gallery system where four main passages carried oil to the moving parts. This car introduced two engineering firsts, setting an engineering trend that would continue for Pontiac during the 1960's: It was the first American production car to have the reverse-flow gusher cooling system, and the first production V-8 to use a harmonic balancer on the crankshaft.

The introduction of the V-8 was an important event. Equally important was the arrival of Semon E. 'Bunkie' Knudsen in 1956 as general manager of the company. His mission was to turn Pontiac around, to change, as he put it, "the image of Pontiac from a schoolteacher type of car to something a lot more vigorous . . . Pontiac had been associated in the public mind with a prosaic family-toting sedan from the time Pontiacs were first built." If he could turn Pontiac around he just might be able to attain his ultimate goal: to get Pontiac from sixth to third place in sales, right behind Ford and Chevrolet.

This was an ambitious task; to some it seemed impossible. Even with the new V-8 engine, as DeLorean noted, "Pontiac's sales penetration had fallen from 7.4 percent to 6.0 percent in just one year, from 1955 to 1956." To effect the dramatic changes Knudsen hoped for, he brought in bright, young engineers, men like Pete Estes and John DeLorean; they understood engineering, they understood marketing techniques, they *cared* about cars and they had new ideas.

Knudsen now had a car with a new engine, a main office with a new executive force and a company with declining sales. The hard question he asked was, For whom should the Pontiac be built? What kind of market for the Pontiac could be identified? To answer this question he took a market survey, one of the earliest in those days before Vance Packard's *The Hidden Persuaders*. The business of market surveys was new, and manufacturers were skeptical, often with good reason. In the early 1950's Chrysler took a survey to learn what kind of car the public wanted. The representative sample indicated that the public wanted a small car, so Chrysler built the abbreviated 1953-54 Dodge and Plymouth, and when those cars did not sell, the company lost a great deal of money. Pontiac's survey was valid, if unflattering; it revealed that Pontiac owners had no sense of product loyalty, and that the car, while free of negative image, actually lacked *any* image. To the people who bought and drove Pontiacs the car was, at best, nondescript!

The lack of product image was seen by Knudsen as a positive factor; the product could be changed without antagonizing anyone. Knudsen was free to build the all-new Pontiac. Where, he asked himself, could an expanding market be found? He answered his own question: with the young buyers, the members of the baby boom of World War II who were now coming of driving age.

In retrospect, the answer seems obvious, but it was not obvious then. Knudsen's plan to aim his product at the youth market can now be seen as astute, courageous and even visionary. A few years later, when the GTO was at the height of its popularity, the youth market began to get a lot of attention and was seen as an economic force to be reckoned with. Statistics revealed that there were eighteen million teenagers, and that the official median age of the country was 27.9 years and growing younger. Cars were synonymous with youth: twenty-six percent of all teenagers owned cars, and four percent of all new cars were purchased by teenagers. Cars were essential to what came to be called 'lifestyle.' University of California sociologist Edgar Z. Friedenberg said, "Kids . . . should have cars. It's the one basis of their social order. Cars are important. They are for all America. There's no other privacy."

In addition to owning a car, or wanting to own a car, teenagers influenced their parents' car-buying decisions. In 1962 Ford Motor Company took an owners' survey, and on the information supplied by that survey it moved away from four-door sedans and toward the building of sporty hardtops. In 1965 the Ford Division manager, Donald Frey, told a group of Chicago businessmen: "Seventy-eight million of our one hundred and ninety-six million citizens haven't yet reached their twentieth birthday. The sheer weight of numbers makes the youth of this country a faction that just cannot be ignored . . . Frankly, we are going all out."

That had been Knudsen's decision some eight years before! He had anticipated the growing army of youthful consumers, and recognized an important factor: Their buying habits were not fixed, they had not yet developed a sense of product loyalty. This would work in Pontiac's favor. Knudsen knew if he could build a car that would appeal to young people he had a market for that car.

And what kind of car would appeal to the young drivers? His statement summing up his automotive philosophy is well-known—"You can sell an old man a young man's car, but you can never sell a young man an old man's car." To get rid of the 'old man' image he got rid of the excess chrome, especially the strips on the hood and trunk. This might seem like a minor gesture, but it was an important one because it symbolized the break with the past. It had been his father, William S. Knudsen, who had put the chrome on the car some twenty years earlier, and that wide swath of chrome, the 'silver streak,' had become a styling motif as recognizable as the Packard grille outline or the Pierce-Arrow molded headlights. That story is part of the Pontiac/GTO legend.

Actually, the chrome had been removed two years earlier and, in a transitional stage, had been narrowed, doubled and moved from the center to the sides of the hood. One hears the story, but one never hears the *reason* for the change. The chrome swath had been necessary because the hood had been made in two halves and the chrome had concealed the seam where the halves joined. When Pontiac finally got a die large enough to handle the amount of metal required for a one-piece hood, the chrome swath became unnecessary. Therefore, in 1955, Pontiac moved the two narrow chrome strips to the sides of the hood. To Knudsen, that change was worse; they now looked like *suspenders*, and helped to reinforce the 'old man' image. He got rid of them completely, and after 1958, when all cars sported an excessive amount of chrome, Pontiac was characterized by the dechromed or 'blacked-out' look favored by customizers. From then on, Pontiac used chrome sparingly and effectively.

That cosmetic change on the hood was backed up by changes under the hood. Knudsen knew that young drivers in general were interested in performance—*speed!*—and he felt that this was a legitimate basis on which to sell cars. Hot rodders had immediately recognized the potential of the new Chevrolet V-8 engine, and had begun to swap it for their previous favorite engine, the Ford flathead; but by 1956 the Pontiac V-8 had begun to attract attention. It had the same general layout and ball-joint valve gear as the Chevrolet V-8, and its potential as the 'big Chevrolet' became even more apparent when, after stroking the crank, its displacement was upped to 317 ci.

Next, Knudsen did something really dramatic to change Pontiac's image: He gave the okay for the development of high-performance accessories. Pontiac soon became a cornucopia of speed equipment as its engineers designed racing cams, exhaust headers and new induction systems. A tri-power intake manifold mounting three two-barrel carburetors became available, and in 1958 it became an assembly-line-installed option. In 1957-58 the Rochester fuel-injection system was developed in conjunction with Chevrolet and became available in limited quantities.

The original V-8 had its bore and/or stroke increased each year through 1959, with displacements of 317, 347, 371 and 389 ci. In 1957 a customer had his choice of three engines: the 227-hp with the two-barrel carburetor, the 252-hp with the four-barrel carburetor or the 270-hp engine which featured an optional power pack consisting of a hotter cam, a compression ratio of 10.25:1 and two four-barrel carburetors.

The 1958 Bonneville with tri-power manifold was a real stormer. Rated "in excess" of 300 hp and weighing 4,400 pounds, it accelerated from 0-60 mph in 8.1 seconds, turned the quarter mile in 16.8 seconds and had an estimated top speed of 130 mph. In less than four years Pontiac had gone from a non-performance car to a real hard charger!

The 1959 Pontiac was the first model designed and developed by Knudsen and his engineers. In addition to the clean, dechromed look Knudsen had sought, it had power and, most of all, it had Wide-Track, which was part engineering feat, part promotional gimmick. John DeLorean explained in an early interview how the Wide Track concept came about. "We were building a show car with GM Styling. It had independent rear suspension. Styling wanted to make it a convertible, but there just wasn't clearance room at the back for the top motor and such because of the suspension. So we tried moving the rear wheels out a total of four inches. It worked then, but it looked funny. So we moved the front out four inches, too. *That* looked so good that they went ahead and put it on all the '59 Pontiacs."

The term Wide-Track caught on and was used as the central theme of that year's advertising campaign; in fact, it was so successful that it remained the dominant theme in all Pontiac advertising for the next dozen years. It had a positive effect on the car-buying public. It suggested stability, traction, safety, and it created the illusion of lowness. The car was, in other words, youthful—dechromed, lowered and very fast.

In 1960, Pontiac introduced a factory blueprinted engine, the Super Duty V-8. It had been available the previous year in kit form from dealers, but now it was readily available to the general public as a factory-installed option. Pontiac also had begun

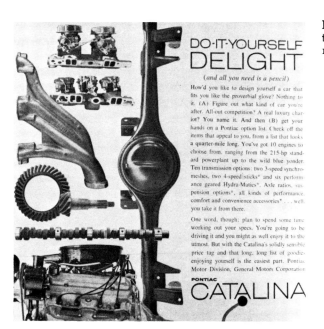

Key to Pontiac's popularity and success in competition was wide variety of performance equipment made available by factory.

a remarkable program whereby it made available through its dealers certain performance options; these were installed by the dealer, rather than by the factory. This avoided problems which would slow down the assembly line. Pontiac assured its dealers that it would stand behind the warranty, and encouraged dealers to sell performance equipment. The success of one dealership, Royal Pontiac in Royal Oak, Michigan, was based on this policy, although all Pontiac dealers had access to the high-performance parts. It was a policy which other car makers would emulate during the 1960's.

The Super Duty engine was a complete hot-engine package: forged pistons, special 10.75:1 heads with big ports and valves for better breathing, special four-barrel or tri-power aluminum manifolds and a choice of high-lift camshafts, the McKellar No. 7 or an Iskendarian E-2 grind which used solid lifters. Although no horsepower ratings were given to the engine in 1959, the factory wanted the car to compete in legal drag racing activities, and the National Hot Rod Association (NHRA) required that horsepower ratings be given. The factory rated the four-barrel-carbureted version of the Super Duty engine at 348 hp, and the tri-power version at 363 hp. It's important to note that Pontiac traditionally down-played the horsepower ratings of its engines, and it's safe to say that this engine approached the magic ratio of one horsepower per cubic inch.

The following year, a bigger engine, the Super Duty 421, was offered to a fortunate few. This was essentially a bored and stroked 389 V-8, with 11:1 compression ratio and a McKellar No. 10 high-lift camshaft. The Super Duty 389 and 421 were essentially the same except for displacement, and both used the same lower end with four-bolt main bearings. When the Super Duty 421 was given a horsepower rating for NHRA purposes it was rated at only 373 hp; this was later revised to 405 hp, but an independent engine tester put the engine on a dynamometer and got a reading of 465 hp at 5600 rpm!

In addition to blueprinted engines and performance parts, Pontiac was deeply committed to a full line of factory, dealer or owner-installed options: the new close-ratio four-speed transmission, cast-iron and even cast-aluminum headers, tachometer, bucket seats, Posi-traction differentials with a wide range of gear ratios, a very attractive eight-lug aluminum wheel and suspension and trim packages. The factory could even supply a number of optional aluminum body parts. In 1962 you could buy an aluminum hood, aluminum front fenders, there were even aluminum bumper brackets! The factory could not have sold many of these special body pieces, and it must have lost money on every piece sold; it says a great deal about Pontiac's new commitment to speed and competition. And the promotion of Pontiac as a performance car paid off in competition.

Pontiacs raced with great success on NASCAR (National Association for Stock Car Automobile Racing) circuits, first in the Southeast and later on tracks all over the country. In 1957 at Daytona, Pontiac triumphed over the car which had started the horsepower race, the favored Chrysler 300. On the beach course, a Bonneville averaged over 136 mph, and another Pontiac came in first in the Grand National race. This was an important event, and these wins cannot be overemphasized.

The following year Pontiac went 10 mph faster, and again won the Grand National race. In 1959 the race was held on the new 2.5-mile banked track, and it was won by Fireball Roberts driving a Pontiac. To show that this was not a fluke, Roberts won the race again the following year at a speed of over 150 mph. In the 1962 National 400, Fireball Roberts set a new qualifying record of 140.287, and took second in the race. The next three top speeds were set by David Pearson, Junior Johnson and Johnny Allen, all driving 1962 Pontiacs. Seven of the top ten cars were Pontiacs. In 1962, its best year of stock car racing, Pontiac won forty-three of the fifty-two top races.

Drag racing had moved from the semi-outlaw time trials held on abandoned air strips during the 1950's to an organized activity which attracted thousands of spectators. At the end of 1962 Wally Parks, president of the NHRA, said, "Organized drag racing has become one of the nation's leading spectator and participant sports." Attendance figures were up fourteen percent over the previous year, for a total of 2,142,161 spectators. There were 186,315 contestant entries at the 1,187 drag strips sanctioned by NHRA. An additional thirteen million people were exposed to drag racing through television sports programs.

Of the cars competing on the drag strip, seventy-three percent were dual-purpose cars which were also used for daily transportation, and Pontiac production cars were favorites because of the many factory performance options. In 1960 a Pontiac Catalina, built by Royal Pontiac and driven by Jim Wangers, won the new NHRA S/S (Super Stock) class and Top Stock Eliminator titles at the Nationals. He turned the quarter in 14.14 seconds with a speed of 102.04; he soundly beat everything else in his class, and the car which came in second was another Pontiac prepared by Royal.

Perhaps the most amazing feat to be written about in the Pontiac racing books was Mickey Thompson's one-day record-breaking assault on national and international records. On July 9, 1961, Thompson brought four Pontiac-engined cars to March Air Force Base in Riverside, California, and in the course of a single day set fourteen new records. Using Pontiac engines, Thompson broke records set years before by Bernard Rosemeyer in an Auto Union, Rex Mays in an E.R.A. and Rudolph Caracciola in a Grand Prix Mercedes-Benz!

Only a few years earlier no one could have considered Pontiac a competitive car, but by 1963 it was being raced everywhere. Ronnie Broadhead won the World Points Championship for stock cars at the drags when he got 315 out of a possible 320 points with his 1960 Pontiac Catalina. He broke the class record for C Stock three times during the racing year, and at the Grand Finale he set a new record of 105.72 mph with a time of 13.00 seconds. At the 1963 NHRA Nationals he performed equally well, winning the National Class Championship.

Without a doubt, the incredible success of Pontiac's racing program translated into an accelerated sales program. As John DeLorean said, "The car with an exciting image was now the talk of America's youth, the hottest product in the business. Pontiac's new image was firmly implanted in the minds of the car buyers."

By 1961, when Knudsen left Pontiac to become general manager at Chevrolet, Pontiac sales had risen to 373,000 units and the company was in third place, behind Ford and Chevrolet.

For Pontiac to move from sixth to third in sales in only five years had seemed an impossibility, and most who were in a position to know credited the success of Pontiac's racing program with the company's success.

Then, in the spring of 1963, the powers-that-be at General Motors issued an ultimatum: *no more racing.*

Many reasons were given for the General Motors ban on factory participation in racing. Some company personnel felt that Pontiac was now in a secure sales position, and that further competition in order to promote the car was unnecessary. Some felt, as they had all along, that horsepower ratings and racetrack victories did not sell cars anyway. Some did not want to see serious competition between the different GM cars, especially between Pontiac and Chevrolet. Some worried whether Pontiac could maintain its lead on the tracks, and feared that it would soon be eclipsed by Chevrolet, the new Chrysler Hemi or the Ford ohc 427 engine. It was no coincidence, some felt, that General Motors decided to pull out of racing just when Ford announced its intention to spend millions of dollars on a massive racing program which would involve Ford in European GT races as well as the Indy 500, NASCAR circuits and drag racing activities in this country.

Whatever the reason or reasons, the effect was clear. In 1957 the Automobile Manufacturers Association had passed a resolution which stated that no manufacturer would sanction or sponsor any racing activities, nor would it use racing results in its advertising. That resolution had been ignored by several car makers, most notably Pontiac. But now Pontiac was acknowledging the 1957 ban as updated by the current GM ban on racing activities.

George DeLorean, John's brother, who had been racing Pontiacs for several years, remembered the effect of the GM ban: ". . . the two people who were top-drawer at GM, I think it was Donner and someone else, they were president and chairman of the board, said they wanted no more performance activities to come out of GM, whatsoever. They called a total deadstop to any type of activity and told the general managers of all the various branches of GM—Olds, Chev, Pontiac, Buick—that if any performance parts were found in their places that they were in great trouble. I think that they had two weeks [to get rid of the parts]. Now, I don't know why two [guys] would do this but they said absolutely *no* high performance parts had better be found anywhere and they were coming down to look around.

"So Pontiac gave—I mean, you couldn't sell this stuff, in two weeks' time you couldn't search out a market, you could hardly transport the stuff out of your buildings, much less sell it—so Pontiac *gave* to Ray Nichels [Nichels's Engineering, Highland, Indiana] five forty-two-foot semi-trailer loads of performance parts; from body parts to engine parts to chassis parts, everything, all the heavy-duty stuff for oval tracks and drag racing, everything.

"Well, the middle of '63 we were running a [Pontiac] race car we couldn't get any parts for. . . ."

George DeLorean moved to a Mercury, and others found themselves in a similar situation without access to factory performance parts. At Daytona in February 1963 there were a dozen 1963 Pontiacs and five 1963 Chevrolets which had been acquired by racing teams before the GM ban had gone into effect. By September, when Darlington rolled around, there were only three 1963 Pontiacs and two 1963 Chevrolets entered. The NASCAR driver who had made the public conscious of Pontiac's performance capabilities, Fireball Roberts, moved to Ford.

Now Pontiac did not have to worry about how it would maintain its lead on the track, but it did have to worry about how to maintain its solid sales position. It had sold well because it was a performance machine and attracted young buyers. The question was: How could this image and energy be maintained without a racing program?

One person who was deeply concerned was Jim Wangers. He was the Pontiac account executive with MacManus, John and Adams, Pontiac's advertising agency, and he was faced with the problem of promoting the new Pontiacs. But he also *cared* about the product. When he wrote an ad for Pontiac it was the work of a creative artist who had integrity because he believed in the product he was promoting.

Wangers had not done all his work at a desk, either. He had been active in legal drag racing, and had won the 1960 NHRA Top Stock Eliminator championship. Wangers was faced with the job of developing an advertising campaign for the 1964 Pontiacs. He recognized the irony: Pontiac was almost back to the place it had been in 1955—it now had an image, but a performance car has to continue to' perform or the image quickly dissipates. He couldn't simply cite Pontiac's past record; and the new, big Pontiacs were getting too heavy to fit the concept of a true performance car. And then, he began to consider the Tempest, Pontiac's small car, and he began to wonder: *what if*?

The original Tempest, in production from 1960-63, was actually classified as an intermediate size, but there wasn't anything smaller in Pontiac's line. Semon Knudsen had been determined to get Pontiac into third place in sales and, while a dedicated racing program had helped to sell the big cars, there had been a need to develop an economy model. By 1960 there was a growing interest in compact

1960-63 Pontiac Tempest had revolutionary design with curved drive shaft and transaxle. Most had four-cylinder engine which was half a V-8; approximately one percent had optional V-8 engine.

and intermediate-size cars, notably American Motors's Rambler, Ford's Falcon and Chevrolet's Corvair. Knudsen had reasoned that if Pontiac had a small car it would balance the company's offerings without competing against the big Pontiacs.

What emerged was not just another small car, but a car which was truly revolutionary in design and engineering. Built on a 112-inch wheelbase, it featured a 195-ci four-cylinder engine which was actually the right bank of the 389-ci V-8. It had four-wheel independent suspension, and a transaxle which mounted the transmission next to the differential as a single unit. Connecting the front-mounted engine to the transaxle was a curved drive shaft. The car was a clear departure from conventional automotive design and, while the transaxle was developed from a Corvair assembly (the unit was reversed in the Tempest), the rest of the car was unique. Among other firsts, it was the first four-cylinder engine that General Motors had built since the 1928 Chevrolet, and it laid claim to being the "first front-engine, rear automatic-transmission car in the world." *Motor Trend* gave it the Car of the Year Award in 1961, two years after it had given Pontiac the award for its Wide-Track developments, and the magazine described the Tempest as "one of the most radical automobiles of the century."

The car was developed under Knudsen by Pete Estes, who was chief engineer at Pontiac, and the key person under him, John Z. DeLorean. Much of the difficult work was done by DeLorean, who was an outstanding executive and an automotive genius; he combined a love of machinery with a visionary's sense of theory. Tall (six feet, three inches), good-looking, sociable, he was also quietly aggressive, working with determination to see a problem through. Always curious about machines, he once confided to Bob Greene, then editor of *Hot Rod* and an avid motorcyclist, that he used to buy several motorcycles a year—but he didn't ride them, he disassembled and reassembled them, just to learn how they were made. In that same determined manner, during his first year as head of Pontiac, he made a point of meeting *every* Pontiac dealer in the United States. He was a magnet in the automotive world, pulling in young, bright engineers and executives. "You've got to love automobiles," he said in the mid-1960's. "We are looking for outstanding guys —guys who have gasoline in their blood."

Jim Wangers recently summed up his feelings about John DeLorean. "[He] is, in my opinion, perhaps one of the most sophisticated, well-rounded automotive men who ever came in and out of this town, and I still have nothing but absolute respect for him. I worked very closely with him. He is a rarity, in that he is an engineer, a manufacturing man, he's an automobile man, and perhaps most significantly he's a marketer. He took his knowledge of the automobile, the way in which an automobile goes together, the way in which it's manufactured, and applied that background to his knowledge of marketing—and in marketing I mean not only distribution but dealer relations, advertising, promotions, merchandising . . . The man's electric, he provides opportunities, he's exciting. . . ." DeLorean could have been the model for the auto executive in recent novels like Harold Robbins's *The Betsy* or Arthur Hailey's *Wheels*, battling entrenched autocrats to bring into being a revolutionary car.

But sometimes even visionaries come up with clunkers. DeLorean later considered the 1960-63 Tempest one of his failures. As he said in the book when he evaluated this revolutionary car, "The invention [of halving the V-8 engine into a four-cylinder] worked but never went well with the rear end transmission and axle combination on the car. There was no mechanical problem, but the car rattled so loudly that it sounded like it was carrying half-a-handful of rolling rocks."

The decision to terminate the unorthodox Tempest was based on the noise situation and alleged handling difficulties—Ralph Nader's book, *Unsafe at Any Speed* had just been published, and the Tempest shared with the Corvair a similar rear end assembly. The 1964 Tempest was completely changed—back to a conventional intermediate automobile, with a front engine/transmission, conventional drive shaft and a Hotchkiss rear end. Instead of the unitized body, the new Tempest used the traditional body and frame construction. It was a nice car, but, unlike its predecessor, not very remarkable and not very different from the Oldsmobile F-85 or the Buick Special.

That Tempest was the car Wangers had his eye on, and when he thought about the car, and the ad campaign that could be built around it, he wondered: What if they installed the 389-ci V-8 from the big Pontiac in the intermediate-size Tempest? And what if. . . .

Jim Wangers knew cars backward and forward, and he knew human nature; in his opinion few people bought cars simply to get from one place to another. A car was an extension of the owner's personality; you had to give a buyer a *reason* to buy a car, and you had to 'stroke the buyer's ego.' You had to make driving *fun*!

That was the kind of car that Pontiac was going to have to develop if it intended to remain third in sales. There were two clear reasons why an unusual car was necessary. The first came back to the old question: Why is there a Pontiac? How do you give the customer a car that represents a choice between Pontiac and the other GM cars it shares a body with?

As Wangers said years later, when discussing the origins of the GTO: "Let's face it, there is no real excuse for a medium-priced GM car like the Pontiac, Olds or Buick. A buyer can find any conceivable kind of car he needs in either a Chevrolet or Cadillac showroom. The Pontiac must be built on a strong image to obscure the fact that it is not what it really is: either a fancy Chevrolet or a low-line Caddy. We used the GTO image of youth to infuse the entire Pontiac line with a feeling of excitement. In that sense, the GTO was the key to the total Pontiac marketing scheme for half a decade."

There was another reason for developing an interesting car, and that was the insistent rumor that Ford had something up its sleeve, namely, an intermediate-size sports car with a healthy V-8 engine and sundry options. The rumor suggested the car would be named the Bronco or the Mustang or some such steed. Pontiac would have to compete with that pony car—but, with what? Again Wangers looked at the Tempest, and began to wonder: What if they used the big 389 V-8, and got a few of the tri-power setups back from Nichels, and a Hurst shifter, and . . . .

This was the car conceived "to meet a marketing need"—the GTO, brought into the world alive and kicking, a full-blown miracle. Wangers told me that he still has a copy of the memo he sent to DeLorean in the spring of 1963, suggesting that an intermediate-size body and chassis and an engine like the 389-ci V-8 would make an interesting machine. It was not an original idea, really, but something that hot rodders had been doing since the year one, or at least since the 1930's when kids began yanking the four-cylinder engine from Model A's and substituting Henry's flathead V-8. At the same time it was a real brainstorm, a stroke of genius —nothing like this had been done by a manufacturer.

The Tempest, in its earlier and present forms, was DeLorean's project, and he was interested in Wangers's ideas. DeLorean had thought that the 326-ci V-8 in the 1963 Tempest had performed well, and he had used one as his personal car. In fact, DeLorean had built two versions of a car similar to the car Wangers was proposing. He had installed 421 HO V-8's, engines optional on the full-size Pontiac, in early Tempest Safari station wagons.

George DeLorean remembers the experimental cars: "They put together a couple of them to see how they'd work. They felt they [the wagons] would have better weight distribution and get better traction. All types of stock [car] racing required a seven-inch tire and the car's weight-to-horsepower ratio demanded a bigger tire. They'd tried ballasting the cars and that seemed to help [traction] so they tried this little station wagon thing . . . but it didn't really pan out. But they did make two, I believe Arnie Besik had one and Royal Pontiac had one. Both wagons had a four-speed manual [coupled to the transaxle] and a 421 engine."

Jim Wangers said that he thought the cars had *two* transaxles, placed back to back to absorb the power. Even though the cars had seen only limited use, they had performed well—the big V-8 engine had fit in the small space, and there had been no handling problems to speak of.

Wangers and DeLorean took the idea to Pete Estes, who was also interested, and who became more interested as he listened to the ad man and the engineer elaborate on the basic plan. What if the car had bucket seats like some of the earlier LeMans, or like the Bonneville (which had been the first full-size car with bucket seats that had caused such a stir at Daytona in '58), hood scoops and a special trim package? Estes was interested, excited even, by Wangers's ideas and by his persuasive way of presenting them. He didn't want to dampen Wangers's enthusiasm, but they were getting excited by a concept which was, in the corporate sense, strictly illegal. The company had said no more racing!

Wangers countered by saying that this would not be a race car, per se, and that there would not be a racing program. This would be a hot road car, a 'sports car.' No one could object to the connotations of that term.

Thus the GTO was born, and instantly attained the status of myth; in fact, even its conception and birth have variant versions, and it would not be fair to all concerned if another version were not told. In a story about DeLorean, published in the mid-1960's, it was said that he had "put together a special car" for his "personal use" in early 1961, and that he "couldn't help thinking that there were probably a great many guys who would like to have a car much like the special car he had created for himself. And he told others at Pontiac of his view." Some ten years later in an article in *Special-Interest Autos*, he was adamant that credit for the GTO should be his. "The GTO was really a car that I built for myself originally, and I took a standard Tempest and sort of blacked it out, and put a bigger engine in it. And I just built it for my own personal use, and it was such a fun car to drive that we decided to go ahead and sell some. And that's what turned into the GTO."

In that same article another Pontiac executive, John Harwood, was quoted as saying that "DeLorean was, of course, the inspiration behind this unique car." This quote is somewhat ambiguous, and perhaps implies that credit should include others.

Later, in the book, DeLorean seemed to feel the same way, and he indicated that the successful birth of the GTO was due to the help given by several midwives. "The most memorable product coup while I was at Pontiac, however, was the birth of the muscle car craze. . . . I love to drive a good performing car, and so we put a 326 cubic-inch, V-8 engine in this lightweight Tempest, tested it and discovered that the car was surprisingly quick and exciting to drive. When we put a big 400 [sic] cubic-inch V-8 into the car, it was even more exciting. It was an electrifying car. It gave you the feeling and performance of an expensive foreign sports car."

This confusion regarding the GTO's parentage is understandable since the car was built in complete secrecy by a handful of dedicated people who quite simply *did not tell* Pontiac what they were doing! The tiny group met nights and weekends, working like monks in the dim recesses of the monastery, trying to construct an airship even as papal bulls circulated proclaiming that flight is both impossible and blasphemous. Estes should have informed his superiors about the GTO project, but he didn't; he had given the project his approval, and thus had laid his neck

John Z. DeLorean in 1965 with the ohc Sprint engine.

on the line. As DeLorean said much later, "The Engineering Policy Group technically should have been consulted about putting these bigger engines into the intermediate car, but we were afraid that they would turn us down or take so long to give their approval that we wouldn't get the car into production on time."

The development of the GTO shows what a small group of intelligent, imaginative people can do on its own, unhampered by corporate mandates or the committee mind. It fits DeLorean's dictum, expressed years later when he was building the limited production sports car that bears his name. "No great car was ever done by a group. Almost all the great cars in the world were individual efforts. The Bugatti was a man. Ferrari is a man. The car is an accurate expression of what he thinks it should be."

In this case the car required several men. The new car was built during the summer of 1963, and it was finished in the fall, just a few weeks after the introduction of the regular Pontiac lineup. That was a very short lead time, and meant that all the work—the paperwork, the tooling required for the trim package, the testing and so on—had to be accomplished quickly and with complete secrecy.

There was one more problem, a major problem, but one that was solved long before the car was finished. As if in anticipation of a move such as this clandestine group had made, General Motors had stated in its antiracing ban that no intermediate-size car could come equipped with an engine whose displacement exceeded 330 ci. The Tempest had been designed for the 326-ci V-8, but the sporty version would have the big 389-ci. Wangers had given this problem his consideration and—in the shower, or driving at a fast clip on Woodward Avenue, or waking in the night—had come up with a neat plan to circumvent the company's ruling. The big engine would be offered as an *option*—the Tempest would conform to the rules, with a smaller V-8, and the GTO package would be an option available to the buyer. At the bottom of the order form, in print so small the casual reader might miss it, was a box indicating the option. Put a checkmark there, and you bought the package.

The car was finished, but Pontiac Motor Division still did not know of its existence. The group had managed, in effect, to create a new model within the factory without the Engineering Policy Group of Pontiac—let alone the other GM divisions —knowing about the project. Then DeLorean did something astounding: To safeguard the new car he took it around to a number of Pontiac dealers and, after a ride and a brief sales pitch, asked them to put in an order for whatever number they felt they could sell. He emphasized that the car would be produced in limited quantities, and that whetted their appetites—as Wangers would say later in his famous GTO ads, the car is not for everyone, and when you tell someone they can't have a GTO they naturally want one.

It's difficult to know what degree of corporate resistance was due to the nature of the GTO itself, and what degree was due to the manner in which it had been developed; at any rate, there was a great deal of resistance. It was the classic struggle of youth versus age—the young auto makers, with young and fresh ideas, building an exciting car for young people, being opposed by the old guard who seemed determined to drag them all back to the chrome age of silver streaks and illuminated Indian-head hood ornaments. DeLorean has described the board meeting at which the GTO was announced. He said that the opposition to the car was so strong that a debate over the car very nearly became a fist fight. Several executives objected to a car, carrying the Pontiac name, built on the *image* of horsepower, spinning tires and roaring exhausts. They claimed that the car was not only a bad idea, it was *illegal*—in the corporate sense—two rulings had been broken: the antiracing edict and the forbidden use of an oversize engine in an intermediate-size car. The car, by God, smacked of anarchy!

There was a great deal of shouting and anger and the near-fist-fight. Then, as a conciliatory gesture, a middle ground was reached: Since Pontiac dealers were already sending in orders for the GTO, the factory would allow a limited production run of 5,000 units. Frank Bridges, Pontiac's general sales manager, who was unhappy about the GTO in just about every respect, shook his fist and challenged— dared, threatened—DeLorean to sell those 5,000 cars. They wouldn't sell, he was certain, and the company would be stuck with them—just you wait and see! Wangers told me that DeLorean slowly turned away from Bridges, whose fist was still waving in the air, and DeLorean turned to Wangers and, with a slow smile, said, "Okay, Jim, **Get Those Orders!**" And, at that moment, the initials of that imperative seemed to define the meaning of GTO.

The following is excerpted from Pontiac Motor Division data for 1964.
EXTERIOR
1. "GTO" replaces name "Pontiac" on radiator grille.
2. New simulated air intake castings are mounted in special depressions on each side of hood top panel.
3. Tricolored (red, white & blue) GTO triangular crest mounted on front fender.
4. GTO name in block lettering appears on rear quarters where the LeMans plaque would normally be located. Vertical ornaments forward of rear wheel opening deleted.
5. GTO name in block letters appears on rear deck lid where name LeMans would normally be located.
INTERIOR
1. GTO crest and name appear on RH side of instrument panel.
2. Special textured plate is applied to face of instrument panel.
CHASSIS
1. Coil spring - front and rear specifically designed for sports car ride and handling.
2. Shock absorbers - front and rear specifically valved for ride and handling.
3. 3.23 axle ratio will be used with 4-bbl. carburetor except air conditioning. 3.55 axle ratio will be used with tri-carburetors except air conditioning. 3.08 axle ratio will be used with synchromesh transmission and air conditioning. 2.93 axle ratio will be used with automatic transmission and air conditioning.
4. Engine to be premium fuel, 389 cu. in., 10.75:1 compression ratio. (H. O. cylinder head):
   (a) Horsepower 325 at 4800 RPM, torque 428 lb. ft. at 3200 RPM
   (b) 4-barrel carburetor
   (c) Special camshaft
   (d) Special valve lifters
   (e) Block and other internal parts same as standard 29 Series (Grand Prix) engine
   (f) External parts including left exhaust manifold basically same as V-326
   (g) Standard starter and battery will be 61 amps, same as released for 29 Series
5. The standard engine (less air conditioning) will use an engine fan clutch and 18" diameter seven blade fan.
6. Clutch is a 10.4" bent finger Belleville clutch with gray iron pressure plate having increased capacity to accommodate the V-389 engine.
7. 3-speed synchromesh with floor shift is standard. With optional automatic transmission, steering column mounted shift will be used.
8. Dual exhaust system is standard.
9. 14" x 6" JK wheels (same design as std. wheel except for rim width) specified for optimum handling. 7.50 x 14 red stripe GTO premium cord tire standard (7.50 x 14 white wall tire to be no cost option).
10. Radiator assembly is specific and basically the same as Catalina air conditioning radiator core with Tempest V-326 upper and lower tanks.
11. New and specific radiator lower support.
12. Balance of chassis generally same as 22 series with V-326 engine.
OPTIONAL EQUIPMENT
1. Changes in automatic transmission with GTO option are as follows:
   (a) Torque converter ratio is 2.2:1.
   (b) Six (6) plate reverse clutch pack with special backing plate.
   (c) Six (6) plate high clutch pack with special clutch apply piston and clutch hub.
   (d) Minor control changes to accommodate higher torque output (i.e., transfer plate, modulator, valve body springs, governor has 5200 RPM shift speed, etc.).
2. Changes in air conditioning with GTO option:
   (a) Specific radiator core is thicker (5/8") and has higher constant.
   (b) Front fender cross brace has specific piercing to accommodate new location of radiator upper bracket.
   (c) New refrigerant plumbing for new location of dehydrator.
3. Ride and Handling Package (available as factory installed item) only includes shock absorbers with modified valving to suit ride, and 20 to 1 steering gear ratio.
4. Consoles available (all with floor shift) (Vacuum Gauge and/or Tachometer as released for 21 & 22 Series are additional options).
   a. 3-Speed SM Transmission
   b. 4-Speed SM Transmission
   c. Automatic Transmission
5. Tri-carburetors are available as optional equipment.
6. All other option equipment released for LeMans series except as limited by the GTO Option will also be available.
389 GTO ENGINE
The GTO engine uses the basic 389 block but differs in the valve train and head assembly from the standard 389 engine. Although there are no specific service procedures written for the GTO engine, the 1963 Pontiac Chassis Shop Manual engine section covers the standard 389 engine. By using these procedures and the specifications and differences that follow, the 389 GTO engine may be serviced. The following is a comparison of the two engines and may be an aid in overhauling or a guide when ordering parts, while servicing the engine:
A) Hydraulic Valve Lifter Assembly
   Standard - Part No. 5231360 (Z)
   GTO - Part No. 5232265 (Z)
The valve lifter used in the standard engine has the same outside dimensions as the GTO lifter. The GTO lifter or "high ball" lifter differs in that it contains a small ball check valve spring and a rocker feed metering valve. The ball check valve spring applies pressure to seat the ball valve to prevent leak down of the lifter. The feed metering valve limits the flow of oil from the valve lifter to the rocker arm and serves as a check valve, to limit lifter pump up during high RPM operation.
B) Rocker Arm, Ball and Push Rod Package
   Standard - Part No. 540323 (Z)
   GTO - Part No. 9771045 (Z)
When comparing this area of the valve train, attention must be given to the oiling system in the heads. The standard engine has an oil gallery cast in the head which is fed from the block. Oil from this gallery is fed into the passages in the rocker studs. A small hole drilled in the stud provides an outlet for the oil, to the rocker arm ball area. Oil is also directed from the valve lifter up through the hollow push rod, to lubricate the push rod socket in the rocker arm.
The GTO rocker arm has a hole drilled in the push rod socket. The rocker arm ball area is lubricated from the valve lifter, up the push rod and out the small hole in the socket. Since the hole in the rocker arm socket is smaller than the hollow push rod, enough oil escapes to lubricate the socket.

C) Valve Springs
    Standard - inner Part No. 519112 (Z)
             outer Part No. 519113 (Z)
    GTO - inner Part No. 524598 (Z)
          outer Part No. 524593 (Z)

The GTO engine uses heavy duty valve springs, while the standard engine springs are lighter. The easiest method to identify the springs is to measure their wire diameter using a caliper. The wire diameter of the standard inner spring is .120", while the heavy duty is .141". The standard outer spring has a wire diameter of .162", while the heavy duty is .170". When the springs are new they may be distinguished by two yellow stripes on the heavy duty springs but none on the standard spring.

Early production GTO engines were equipped with the lighter springs but after 12-19-63 engine No. 190810, all GTO engines have the heavy duty springs.

D) Head Assemblies
    Standard - Part No. 9774766 (Z)
    GTO - Part No. 9770981 (M)

The standard 389 engine uses two different compression ratio heads depending on the type of transmission used with the engine. All standard 389 heads will have an oil gallery under the rocker studs. The GTO head is 10.75:1 compression ratio and is easily identified by the flat surface under the rocker studs. There is no oiling through the rocker studs, therefore, no gallery is necessary.

CHAPTER TWO

Into The Marketplace
1964

Get Those Orders! This should have been an exclamation rather than an imperative, because the car sold itself. There *was* a demand for a 'sports car' with room for five and all the options and power that the GTO offered. Wangers's marketing strategy paid off. Not only did the GTO compete successfully against the Oldsmobile F-85, the Buick Special and the Chevrolet Chevelle (cars which used the same basic A-type body and identical frames and suspension systems, cars which were so similar you'd have trouble telling them apart in a dark parking lot), the GTO also competed favorably against the new Ford Mustang, even though the latter was introduced with great fanfare and media attention while the GTO was, at first, almost ignored.

The GTO sold so well that the company lifted its limitation of 5,000 cars and allowed 32,450 GTO's to be built. Wangers believes dealers could have sold twice that number (which they did the next year) if they'd had the cars. Even with this limited number of GTO's, it became the fastest-selling first-year car in Pontiac history, and it helped to make 1964 the most successful year for Pontiac. Overall production was up twenty percent, and Tempest production was up eighty percent, for a total of 210,000 units. On June 8, 1964, E. M. Estes announced that a new production record had been set. A total of 590,072 Pontiacs and Tempests had been assembled during the 1964 model year, which was 117,000 more cars than had been built during the previous year. The car that broke the record was a cameo-ivory 1964 GTO that came off the assembly line at mid-morning at Pontiac's main plant. Estes told reporters that the GTO had been selected to be the record-breaker because it was the most successful first-year model ever introduced by Pontiac.

By the end of the model year even the critics of the GTO had to admit that the car was a success. General Sales Manager Frank Bridges said that the 76.4-percent increase in Tempest sales was the best increase in the industry by "a considerable margin." He added, "There's no doubt in our minds that the Tempest was the success car of the 1964 model year. Our dealers from Coast to Coast report that customer demand for the higher-priced GTO and LeMans models continues very strong." In retrospect, it's hard to believe that there were those within the Pontiac hierarchy who felt that the GTO would not sell. The success it experienced in its first year continued until 1970 when, for a number of reasons, GTO sales began to decline—the sales of other muscle cars fluctuated from year to year.

The 1964 GTO met with acceptance for a number of reasons. First, the car coincided with the trend toward smaller, more expensive cars; a trend that had been gaining momentum during the previous few years. A comparison between 1962 and 1963 sales showed that the increased sales were in hardtop and convertible bodies. Nearly the same number of two- and four-door sedans were sold both years; the additional 650,000 cars sold in 1963 had the more expensive bodies. Almost half the convertibles sold were in the compact or intermediate range. The sudden popularity of these cars amazed Detroit sales executives. According to an article in the January 1964 *Motor Trend*, "It's obvious that today's market considers compacts more as sports/luxury than economy cars. Many families are buying them as second cars, as they might buy a small foreign car. Many young people are buying them as their only car. Both these market segments demand performance and luxury more than economy and practical utility." This described the GTO exactly.

Second, the car from the very beginning had an image. Buyers liked the associations implied by the letters GTO, even if they had trouble pronouncing the name

GTO had clean lines, unfettered by chrome trim, the result of styling decisions made by Bunkie Knudsen eight years earlier. Mirror seemed too massive, but hood 'scoops,' even though nonfunctional, had appeal.

and had no idea what it meant. The name translated into performance, and the GTO was highly visible. Other cars were fast, but they seemed to almost hide that fact; you had to stand beside a 427 Ford or a 409 Chevrolet to identify it. The GTO, on the other hand, had image. It had instant recognition—those letters on the grille, trunk and rear fenders conveyed the message at the stoplight: Get The Others.

Third, the GTO was a neat-looking car, with a very basic appeal. Built on a 115-inch wheelbase, it had just the right stance, with limited overhang, front and rear. Unlike the earlier Tempests, which had 'sculpted' sides, the 1964 Tempest/GTO was essentially flat, with a single ridge along the side to stiffen the sheet metal. The front end was simple, using the split grille which had been a Pontiac theme since 1959, and the two horizontal halves separated by a strong vertical divider. The quad headlights were nicely integrated, and the air intakes were large, but unobtrusive, located in the bumper. Seen from the side, the car had a sporty look, due in part to the symmetrical wheel openings, front and rear. Except for a thin grille bar, the GTO identification plates and two nonfunctional hood 'scoops,' the car was bare of trim. The scoops were not unpleasant in appearance, but because they served no purpose except to imitate scoops found on true sports cars, they got a great deal of criticism. Unlike later scoops on the GTO, they could not be made functional. Some critics have blamed William Mitchell, head of GM Styling, for the scoops, because he had a penchant for them; but it seems unlikely that the conspirators who developed the GTO would have consulted with him.

Even the tires were elegantly plain. The GTO had special, fourteen-inch wheels with six-inch-wide rims which mounted red-stripe nylon cord low-profile tires. Three optional wheel covers were available: a deluxe wheel cover with the

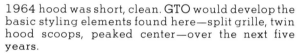

1964 hood was short, clean. GTO would develop the basic styling elements found here—split grille, twin hood scoops, peaked center—over the next five years.

appearance of ten spokes, an optional custom wheel disc with eight cooling slots and a three-prong spinner, and a wire wheel disc with a two-prong spinner.

The interior was very attractive, a nice compromise between a luxury car and a sports car. The dashboard especially developed this idea, being expensively appointed but with an element of the competition car. The four gauge areas were large, round and very readable. There were a speedometer, water temperature and fuel gauges, and warning lights for the ammeter and oil pressure. A matching tachometer was optional ($53.80); but because it was as much as ten percent fast, an aftermarket tachometer was often substituted. The tachometer was too far to the right to be read easily, and one test driver suggested switching the tachometer and speedometer so the former would be directly ahead of the steering wheel. A large, matching Rally clock was also optional.

With a full set of instruments, the dash looked very business-like; this attitude was complemented by the anodized strip backing them, which looked like it had been engine-turned. To carry through the competition theme there was a beautiful steering wheel, with a simulated wood ring ("Looks like wood but isn't.") and four stainless steel spokes.

Most people found the bucket seats comfortable, with sports car connotations. Others did not, desiring a wraparound bucket seat that would support the driver firmly. *Road Test*'s driver complained ". . . they are not buckets at all, but actually individual front seats with a modicum of lateral support." The seats were adjustable, but tall drivers had difficulty with the power-assisted seat because backward movement was limited. The seats were attractive, and over the years the Morrokide material has worn well; it's possible to find GTO's today with near-perfect original upholstery.

The sports car theme was carried out by the Hurst floor shift, standard with either the three-speed manual transmission or the optional four-speed manual or the two-speed automatic (a column-shift automatic was also available). The chrome shift lever was located beside the driver's thigh; the straight-line shift pattern allowed for faster shifting from gear to gear, and the throw was short, the movement

Front suspension of GTO featured heavy-duty shocks and springs, but light stabilizer bar and 9.5-inch brake drums.

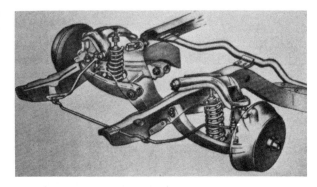

This 389-ci V-8 with optional tri-power was used from 1964-1966.

accurate. For a generation that had grown up driving cars equipped with Dynaflow there was something exciting about shifting for oneself—and to have a floorshift was even more exciting.

A beautiful, optional console was available; it mounted on the transmission hump and extended back between the bucket seats. It was a practical option too, with a locking storage compartment and built-in rear seat courtesy light. It also served as a location for the large optional vacuum gauge. Consoles were popular, and that was ironic because only four years earlier, with the Corvair and the transaxle Tempest, engineers had stressed the flat floor as a major selling point.

Fourth, while the basic car was attractive, a buyer could easily personalize his by checking the option list which was as long as a salesman's arm—no other manufacturer offered as many options. As the sales brochure put it, "Within the basic concept of the GTO, Pontiac feels that the buyer should be able to tailor-make his own car."

And, finally, the car, in any form, was affordable. The basic unit was within almost everyone's reach. The LeMans sport coupe sold for $2,491, the hardtop coupe sold for $2,556 and the convertible sold for $2,796. (The car came with a 215-ci six-cylinder engine rated at 140 hp, or with either of two optional 326-ci V-8 engines rated at 250 and 280 hp.) If one wanted the GTO option, one checked box #382, and for an additional $295 got the 389-ci V-8 rated at 325 hp (with the four-barrel carburetor), heavy-duty three-speed manual transmission with the Hurst floor shifter, twin hood scoops, dual exhaust system, a thermostatically controlled seven-blade fan, heavy-duty radiator core, heavy-duty shock absorbers and GTO identification plates.

Original upholstery, a material called Expanded Morrokide, has proven extremely durable. GTO was plain but not spartan; appointments included rear ashtray, courtesy light.

Dash featured large, readable instruments mounted in anodized metal-turned panel. Tachometer was an option. With Hurst floor shifter, bucket seats, optional console and locking glovebox, GTO had sports car flavor.

Actually, there were two option order forms: One for the GTO option package, and a second for other options, all very affordable. For example, one could order a four-speed transmission ($190), a simulated wooden steering wheel ($38), a handling package with heavier-duty shocks and springs ($3.82), another package which included a heavy-duty radiator, Safe-T-Track Posi-traction rear end and metallic brake linings ($75), and on and on. The list included the customary options such as power steering, power brakes, tilt wheel and so forth. The prices seem incredibly low today, and they were low then, too. As one tester said, "With every conceivable option on a GTO it would be difficult to spend more than $3,800. That's a *bargain*."

The optional engine was certainly a good buy: A 389-ci V-8 rated at 348 hp cost only $115 extra. This included a factory tri-power (three two-barrel carburetors) intake manifold with either vacuum or optional mechanical linkage to operate the two outer Rochester carburetors. The mechanical linkage was smoother and operated without hesitation, although some drivers preferred the vacuum linkage for improved gas mileage. Tri-power manifolds had been available earlier, for Pontiacs and other cars (the 1957 Oldsmobile J-2, for example), but never in quantity.

This new manifold was remarkable: While hot rodders usually set up multiple carburetion so that all carburetors worked in unison, Pontiac's tri-power would run on the central carburetor most of the time, even up to a hundred miles per hour. The center carb had 0.066-inch main jets; the two outer carbs had 0.073-inch main jets. Over a hundred, or at lower speeds when acceleration was required, the two outer carburetors would cut in for a total throttle bore of twelve square inches. You could hear the tri-power, those six thirsty throats sucking gasoline and air, and you could feel it cut in; it developed a strong power surge over 3300 rpm.

This engine featured the camshaft and the big port heads from the 421 HO; the result was an engine with good breathing characteristics. The McKellar-ground cam had a high lift (0.404 in.) with a conservative overlap (54 degrees); it developed horsepower and rpm—up to a point. Most critics of this engine focus on its use of quick-bleed hydraulic lifters as a limiting factor, and it's true that lifter pump-up occurred at around 5500-5800 rpm. While mechanical lifters would have allowed the engine to wind beyond this point, the results might have been disastrous. Malcolm McKeller felt that hydraulic lifters cushioned the valve train and limited the stress on mechanical parts; for the same reason the cam used a long ramp on the lobes. The result was a quieter engine which required far less maintenance.

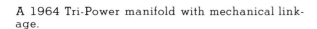
A 1964 Tri-Power manifold with mechanical linkage.

Both the 325-hp and the 348-hp engines featured chrome-plated rocker-arm covers, chrome air cleaner(s) and a chrome breather cap, which made an impressive sight when the hood was opened at the service station.

The GTO looked fast, and it was fast; that, finally, was the reason many people bought a GTO. It had power—muscle, macho, great gobs of tire-spinning power. In fact, as Jim Wangers told me, the GTO had so much power the car scared many prospective buyers, and after a fast trial spin they'd return to purchase a regular Tempest or a Catalina.

But there was that vast army waiting in the wings, the youth of America. *They* weren't afraid of power—they celebrated it! To sit at a light, stab the gas, clear the carbs, stick the Hurst shifter into low, stand on the gas when the light changed and hear the awesome sound of three two-throats sucking huge mouthfuls of air as the rear tires spun helplessly in clouds of smoke, and then a quick shift to second and the sound of roaring dual exhausts and the engine winding past 5500 rpm. The car was a bomb!

It weighed only 3,200 pounds, and with the 348-hp V-8 and the optional 3.90:1 rear end it could blast from 0-60 in 4.6 seconds, from 0-100 in 11.8 seconds and turn the quarter mile in fourteen seconds. It was the fastest production street sedan, and could even give the smaller, more expensive Corvette a run for its money. Such power from a car delivered off the dealer's showroom floor was unheard of; it was an automotive phenomenon and the only complaint drivers had was a lack of traction. They wrote letters to magazines that had tested the GTO and they expressed amazement at the speeds the test car had attained. They complained that ". . . at 4800 rpm I just sit and spin. . . ."

The GTO didn't drive like a big car; from the driver's seat there was no sense of bulk, high fenders or overhang, as was true of many American cars of that period. Although the GTO had a spacious trunk and a rear seat for two adults or three children, it responded as if it were a two-place machine. The danger was that one could overdrive the car: The rear end would break loose on dry pavement, let alone on gravel or rain-slick asphalt. The steering was slow (24:1), although a quicker

Here, Jim Wangers poses for a publicity photo in 1981.

If this 6.5-liter emblem, found on each side of the '64's, wasn't enough of a warning, the sales literature suggested "you could always fly the skull and crossbones."

manual steering (20:1) was available, as was power steering (17.5:1). The car had a heavy front end and a handling trait known as understeer, although this was partially neutralized by stiffer spring rates of 80/96 (as opposed to the stock Tempest rate of 66/96) and 90/110 for the heavy-duty package.

How did the GTO compare with the new Mustang? David E. Davis, then editor of *Car and Driver*, remembered years later a comparative test he had made of both cars in 1964: ". . . in purely visceral automotive terms, I remember only that the first Mustang I drove caused me to cut my finger on an exposed sheet metal edge in the trunk, while my first ride in a GTO left me with a feeling like losing my virginity, going into combat and tasting my first draft beer all in about seven seconds.

"I remember that the GTO slammed out of the hole like it was being fired from a catapult, that the tach needle slung itself across the dial like a windshield wiper, that the noise from the three two-throat carburetors on that heavy old 389-cubic-inch Pontiac V-8 sounded like some awful doomsday Hoover-God sucking up sinners. Conversely, I seem only to recall that the Mustang was red, or maybe orange . . . it's hard to say."

The GTO was not the first fast American production car, nor was Pontiac the first company to make performance parts available as optional equipment. In the 1930's Ford had offered Rocky Mountain brakes and Denver heads and Canadian aluminum heads and the Columbia overdrive. In the 1950's a number of manufacturers offered limited-production performance parts, primarily because of NASCAR competition. The 1956 Studebaker Golden Hawk combined its big 352-ci V-8 with the relatively light Hawk body and chassis. It weighed about the same as the GTO, and with 275 hp it had the best power/weight ratio of any car up to that time, and could accelerate from 0-60 in nine seconds and could claim a top speed of 120 mph.

But the GTO was the *first* example of a production car which used a manufacturer's big-car engine in a smaller-car body. This may be a slight distinction between various kinds of fast cars, but it is a very real one, and it was from this union that the entire muscle car craze of the 1960's emerged. George DeLorean, who saw it all happen, recalled how quickly the GTO caught on and the effect it had. "The GTO was developed to replace to some degree what Pontiac had been doing up to February 1963. It took hold and it got bigger and bigger and bigger. It just seemed to be the right package for more people than the real hot rods were in the early 1960's. It was a car that was accepted by mothers and fathers even, whereas prior to the discontinuation of the race cars at GM, only a few young guys here and there would buy a race car and pursue a racing situation. It [the GTO] was a real nice car, nice size, good performance; it had a warranty that went with it that the hot rods didn't have."

The automotive magazines liked the GTO as much as the public did; although, because it appeared a few weeks after the regular Pontiac line, it got off to a slow

Dennis Bornhorst's 1964 GTO is all original; it has optional custom wheel discs with stamped steel spinners, cooling slots.

start. Customers may have overlooked the GTO option box at the bottom of the form, but some of the problem was due to the factory's reticence to promote the car at first. An early ad made no mention of the GTO option. It pictured two convertibles with the caption, "A couple of terrible things just happened to our competitors." At the bottom was the source, "Both by the Builders of the Wide-Track Cars." The cars were a Catalina 2+2 and a LeMans. "Ask us what's new with LeMans (and every Tempest) for '64 and we'll pour you an earful." It listed standard and optional engines, but made *no* mention of the 325-hp or 348-hp engines (perhaps the factory hadn't been informed yet?). The only possible reference to the GTO was terribly noncommittal and vague: "Options? Tempest is a Pontiac, right?"

Hot Rod magazine's first article on the 1964 Pontiacs made no reference to the GTO, but it said of the Tempest: "Pontiac's compact is not so compact anymore. . . ." The 'big surprise' was that the old engine and transaxle had been done away with. When the magazine got wind of the GTO they came back for more. Defying deadlines and lead times only two months later it ran a lengthy, detailed report, beginning with the observation that ". . . this might be the '64 model dealers will sell faster than Pontiac can build."

Overall, the magazine's testers' view of the GTO was that it was an excellent car. They commented on the car's firm ride and excellent handling qualities. They found that "understeer is slight," a trait that later testers would describe as a defect. This was due in part to the 56/44 weight distribution, and the lack of a rear sway bar. The GTO did not have a rear sway bar until 1969 because, I was told, John DeLorean didn't believe in them!

Hot Rod found the brakes to be "ample" although later it described them as "seemingly adequate."

The test car had the 325-hp V-8 and a two-speed automatic transmission, which *Hot Rod* felt did not allow the GTO to perform to its maximum; the testers described standing-start acceleration as "mild," and would have preferred the optional four-speed or, if the floor pan had allowed sufficient room, a three-speed Hydra-matic. Otherwise, they had no complaints about the car and felt that its power would appeal to "performance enthusiasts" while its suspension should "make it a natural for sports car rallies."

Motor Trend tested two GTO's, one of which lacked the heavy-duty suspension (a lack that was sorely felt); but equipped with heavy-duty suspension, the car was just right. The testers noted that the car broke traction easily even when starting in second gear; that the Hurst shifter gave quick, precise shifts; that it handled well without excessive body lean or understeer; and that although the brakes faded after a dozen high-speed stops, they seemed adequate.

No one mentioned the low-restriction mufflers, which, even when new, were throaty, like a tiger's growl. *Motor Trend* mentioned that gas mileage was "reasonable," from 10 mpg in town to 16.6 mpg on the road, with an average of 12.9.

Both *Hot Rod* and *Motor Trend* noted that the Pontiac V-8, whether in the GTO or the larger cars, came equipped with hydraulic valve lifters. *Hot Rod* noted that "the GTO hydraulic camshaft is a good performance design."

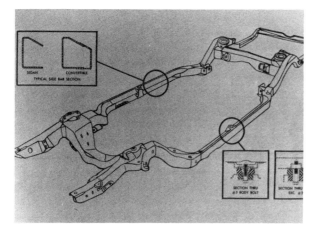

GTO frame was lightweight, low and incorporated four torque boxes behind front wheels and ahead of rear wheels to deaden road noise. This was all-new frame since 1960-63 Tempests had unitized construction; frame was beefed-up in 1965.

Motor Trend used cars supplied by Royal Pontiac—without mentioning whether the cars had had the 'Bobcat' treatment—and said that they kept the engines red-lined at 5500 rpm because the "engine flattened out considerably at 5800." Roger Huntington, who tested a good many GTO's over the years, later said that the use of hydraulic valve lifters was the engine's main shortcoming; it had plenty of torque but was unable to turn high rpm.

There were complaints, and some of these would continue to be heard for the ten years that the GTO was manufactured. The brakes were inadequate for the car's power. The car suffered from a chronic case of understeer because of all the weight up front. The new frame was too flexible. The steering, in any of the optional ratios, was too slow and the turning radius too wide. The rear axle would hop when the car was being subjected to hard acceleration or braking. There was a lack of traction when accelerating. And the list went on.

Some of these complaints were valid. They stemmed from the GTO's inherent design flaw: With the 389-ci V-8, the Tempest had a very favorable horsepower-to-weight ratio (9.65 pounds per horsepower); but the brakes, suspension and steering remained essentially Tempest. The brakes, for example, were simply too small for the car's tremendous power. In 1958, Pontiacs had twelve-inch drums, the largest in its class, but the 1960-63 Tempest had only nine-inch drums (which it shared with the Corvair) and a lining area of 115 square inches (fifteen square inches less than the Buick Special and Oldsmobile F-85). These were the brakes that the GTO inherited. The drum size on the GTO was increased by one-half inch, but the lining area was only 156 square inches. While these brakes were adequate at fifty or sixty, they weren't adequate at 120 mph. Fortunately, the optional metallic linings reduced brake fade.

Car and Driver, on the other hand, loved the car, and called the 1964 GTO ". . . the best American car we have ever driven, and probably one of the five or six best cars in the world for the enthusiast driver."

The reason for these variations had to do with whether a magazine considered the GTO a high-performance car or a sports car. Magazines whose editorial policy aimed at readers interested in acceleration and top end, loved the GTO; those with readers interested in a car's handling abilities tended to condemn or dismiss it. The sports-car-oriented magazines objected to the notion that the GTO could be a sports car—they even objected to it being called a GTO!

Pontiac spoke of the GTO—when it decided to acknowledge the identity of its child—as a sports car in order to disassociate it from any race car. Pete Estes said that the "GTO is a significant addition to Pontiac's list of individualized sports car developments." Those developments included bucket seats, a tachometer in the dash, "an engine-turned aluminum instrument panel appliqué," a floor-mounted gear shift, the "stylized air intake casting" on the hood and the suspension, which was "sprung similar to other sports cars."

Within five years Pontiac would describe the GTO as a muscle car, but at the onset the ads described it as a sports car—that was the point of the car's name. GTO did not stand for Get Those Orders! Nor did it stand for Great To Operate, Garbage Truck Option, Get Tickets Oftener, Go To Olds or Gas Tires Oil. It stood for *Gran Turismo Omologato*, and it's interesting how many ways that designation can be translated into the American idiom. Pontiac defined GTO as 'ready.' In later advertisements it elaborated on that definition: "In Italian that means about twenty thousand bucks. The way we say it is easier to pronounce and it costs less besides."

If it is true, as Wangers asserted, that three of every four GTO owners did not know the meaning of the car's name, then that meaning should be defined. Omologato is the past participle of 'omologare,' which means 'to ratify officially.' So Gran Turismo Omologato means 'Homologated Grand Touring' or 'Certified Grand Touring,' which is a classification determined by the Fédération Internationale de l'Automobile (FIA), the international governing body of automobile activities.

At the time this classification described a closed car, of which at least a hundred units had been built, available to any and all interested customers, with a catalog which clearly outlined the car's options. A car in the GTO class is a production car, not a racing car, but it is capable of higher-than-average speeds. Homologation refers to the formal process by which the car is accredited by the FIA. After that process, changes are permitted to the engine and drive train or to the chassis. Because of the Pontiac GTO, omologato became popular as a verb, 'to homologate,' meaning that a manufacturer had 'homologated' parts—special parts which were available to the public.

The use of the GTO designation by Pontiac created a stir among the sports car purists who felt that Pontiac had usurped a name which not only described a class of automobile but which already belonged to Ferrari; Enzo Ferrari's GTO model made its debut in 1962. A lot of ink was slung by writers who favored one car over the other. *Road Test* magazine was especially offended, by the car that Pontiac had described as a 'sports car,' and by the GTO designation. It ran a number of articles which were highly unfavorable to the GTO. "If Pontiac had any intention of producing a car which met these performance requirements, it failed miserably. Use of the Gran Turismo designation was proved to be only an advertising ploy...."

When the 1965 model came out, *Road Test* renewed its attack on the car and its name: "When is a GTO not a GTO? Answer: when it's a Pontiac." The writers were especially offended by the fact that Pontiac had not been serious enough about the name to follow through with the formalities involved. "... the Pontiac GTO is not and never has been homologated by the Federation Internationale Automobile [sic]. As far as we can determine, nobody at Pontiac even made an application for homolgation [sic]. This has nothing to do with the performance of the car but it strikes the observer as a bit chicken, leads him to wonder how honest the rest of the program can be and how many pickpockets are in the audience."

Most of this tempest was a matter of semantics; Pontiac never made formal application for FIA accreditation, but Ferrari never built a hundred units and therefore its GTO could not meet the FIA requirements, either. Nevertheless, Pontiac felt the sting of the charges, and responded by issuing a press release entitled: "How do you select car names? Pontiac tells." The point of naming a car was that, "As in the case of airplanes, cars take on more identity, distinction and glamour when they are given a name other than the name of the manufacturing company.... Pontiac spends considerable time and effort before selecting a natural sounding name guaranteed to please customers." The release explained the reason and etymology of the names Grand Prix, Bonneville, Catalina and Tempest, but only acknowledged that the name GTO did exist.

The nagging question was still there: How well could a Pontiac GTO stand up to a Ferrari GTO? At least that question was asked by Jim Wangers, who saw a publicity coup in the making. And so, in early 1964, he arranged a road test cum media event between the two cars with the staff of *Car and Driver* officiating. Because of bad weather, the event was held at Daytona, and, to the surprise of many, the Pontiac GTO proved to be an able competitor. The cover blurb of the March 1964 issue of *Car and Driver* exaggerated a bit but it told the story: "Tempest GTO: 0-to-100 in 11.8 sec."

The story proved such a success that Wangers, recognizing a good thing, arranged additional tests between the Pontiac GTO and the Ferrari GTO. At Bridgehampton, a GTO with a deformed piston lapped the track with a time only 4.5 seconds slower than the Ferrari. The Pontiac was actually faster on the straights but slower, of course, on the curves. All in all, it was a remarkable showing, and it was a comparison not only between two GTO's but between one costing three thousand dollars and one costing fourteen thousand dollars.

David E. Davis credited that GTO-versus-GTO road test with the 'making' of *Car and Driver*. He had been working to create a different automotive publication, and he described that one article as "... the turning point in my administration ... it accomplished just what we had been trying to do for months: to get the attention of the audience and clearly establish us as a contender in the automotive publishing biz. *Car and Driver* was finally on its way—and the GTO did it." From the very beginning the GTO established itself as a car that was more than a car—it was a media event, it made things happen, it changed lives—and how many cars can that be said about?

OWNERS' COMMENTS

I own a GTO because . . . it represents an era gone by, one which lives on in fond memories. This is the real reason I own one. Parts are a big problem . . . but the only fault I can find is its appetite for gas. I have *not* owned any other 'so-called' muscle car, because there is only *one* that is worth owning! DB of Minster, Ohio.

I bought mine in 1970 for $500 when it seemed that '64 GTO's and convertibles were going to become collectors' cars. It was original but had 90,000 miles. I now have 135,000 miles and have used the GTO for transportation but enjoy it mostly for pleasure driving. The car's best feature is power —screaming acceleration! It'll 'get rubber' in all four gears!! It rides and handles nicely—it handles better than most cars, but it won't corner like my Z-28 or my Jaguar XKE; but it wasn't designed for that. It's a good-looking car with clean lines. It also has been very reliable—very few mechanical problems. The front main bearing leaks a little oil and the transmission is a little noisy, but what can you expect after 135,000 miles? commented CP of Kingston, Tennessee.

It's like having two cars in one—a good-looking touring car and a muscle machine, a kind of Dr. Jekyll and Mr. Hyde combination. The car's best features are the comfortable bucket seats, the tri-power carburetion, great shifter (four-speed Hurst Competition Plus). It is also a dependable transportation automobile. The 1964 GTO, 389-ci tri-power is one of the fastest muscle cars ever made. Don't go by road tests either—remember, the '64 GTO came with little 7.50x14 bias ply tires—smoke city! said RB of Houghton Lake, Michigan.

It is a quiet, smooth-driving car, and I especially like the look of the car as it comes down the road—looking straight at the front. To me, it resembles a tiger on the prowl. CB of Houghton Lake, Michigan.

It was summer, 1967, and I was two years out of high school and my friend George bought a '64 GTO. When I got behind the wheel no one was as 'cool' as I was. Whatever teenage traumas you might be worrying about no longer mattered. Kids today need drugs to experience the elation that we felt on GTO takeoff. My '64 GTO does for me today what it did then. Whatever adult traumas (I'm a deputy sheriff) I might worry about disappear when I drive my GTO. JD from Granby, Colorado.

CHAPTER THREE

The Great One
1965

*E*very GTO aficionado has a favorite model year, but most agree that the years 1964-68 represent the Golden Time of Operation and that the 1965 was, in many ways, the best GTO. It was clean-looking, lean, unencumbered by antipollution equipment; and it was fast. It had become a bit bigger (3.1 inches longer) and heavier (by 340 pounds), but to compensate for this, the horsepower rating was increased by ten.

One person who thought it was great was LeRoi 'Tex' Smith, eternal hot rodder and now publisher of *Car Exchange*. In 1965 he said of the GTO, "Frankly, I've never been so thoroughly impressed by an American car. I'm a firm believer that the US produces the best automobiles in the world, and that virtually any factory could, upon necessity, build a special car to compete successfully with the best of any European racing builder. In this particular GTO, there is everything the most critical purist would demand—exceptional flexibility of engine, transmission and rear end, and a superior chassis/brakes combination. It's the most complete dual-purpose American car I've ever seen. Perfect for high-speed cruising or limited GT racing. Ideal for hill climbs and absolutely charming for around-town hops."

In 1965 the GTO won *Car and Driver*'s reader survey in the categories of Best All-Around Car and Best Sports Sedan. Of the latter, the editors said ". . . the GTO not only recorded the greatest percentage of the total vote of any car in any category, but it also scored the greatest margin of victory over its nearest competitor [48.3 percent as opposed to 9.3 percent for the Ford Galaxie 427]," and of the former they said ". . . the Pontiac GTO is a remarkably good all-around car. It combines acceleration, braking, handling, passenger space and convenience, and low cost in an undeniably honorable compromise that seems tailor-made for the one-car man with a five-car appetite."

Such praise was almost universal. The car was tested by every automotive magazine, and the reaction was generally positive; it was also being tested on the street and was found to be untouchable. The GTO was the car to be seen in—at the drive-in, the supermarket, the beach—while the radio played "My Mighty G.T.O." by Jan and Dean and "GTO" by Ronnie and the Daytonas. In the seemingly untroubled world of 1965, when cars were truly important, the GTO won the hearts and minds of a generation. It was a good car and a good year, the first full year of unfettered production, and a total of 75,352 GTO's were sold. This represented an increase of 132 percent over 1964. Of that total, 55,722 were hardtop coupes, 8,319 were sport coupes and 11,311 were convertibles. The price was right, too; $2,791, $2,727 and $3,026, respectively.

In 1965 *Motor Trend* gave its Car of the Year Award to Pontiac Motor Division ". . . for styling and engineering leadership in the development of personalized passenger cars." This was the third time in seven years that Pontiac had received the award. The editor, Charles Nerpel, said, "In styling, Pontiac shares body shells with other GM cars, but they've maintained, in our opinion, more model identification than their sister divisions. From the Grand Prix to the GTO, anyone can tell they're all Pontiacs." In praising Pontiacs in general, Nerpel singled out the GTO for special praise. "Pontiac for 1965 has everything and a few big plus items. Comfort with good handling, utility with beauty, performance with economy. This last combination was the subject of a lot of retesting, especially with the GTO. Here's a car with 389 cubic inches in the engine, acceleration that's almost unbelievable (delivering wheelspinning power to the rear wheels through a two-speed automatic transmission), yet is capable of over 18 mpg at 65-70 mph highway cruising speeds—this with a convertible model that weighs more than 300 pounds over the '64 car."

The additional weight was due to changes made in the frame. The 1963 Tempest used unitized construction, and therefore did not have a frame per se. A new

GTO emblems were inside car as well as on outside; on dash and door panels (6.5 liter).

Clean grille lacked horizontal chrome bar of 1964.

frame was designed for the 1964 Tempest/GTO, but there were complaints that it was too light, which allowed the frame to flex. There was almost no mention of the frame flexing in the road tests, the notable exception being the man at *Motor Sport Illustrated* who crawled under the car to assure himself that it did indeed *have* a frame!

Roger Huntington has probably tested more GTO's than anyone, and I recently asked him whether he felt that frame flexing had been a problem. He recalled the earlier Swiss Cheese frames built as an option by Pontiac, frames which had been drilled full of holes and which had had the lower edge removed in order to save weight. They were so fragile that sections of two-by-fours had to be temporarily inserted into the channel so that the frame assemblies could be moved around in the factory. Those were light! But of the GTO frame he said, "No, and I never heard any real criticism. Of course, the engine never developed enough horsepower to put any stress on the frame anyway." He suggested that if one were to put a 600-hp engine in the GTO, with wide tires on the rear, the GTO frame would be inadequate; but he felt that it was fine for the use it received.

Others must have felt that the 1964 frame was too light, because the 1965 frame was strengthened considerably. John DeLorean designed the new frame, and he considered it an achievement. It was called a swept-hip-perimeter design because of the sweep of the step at both front and rear kickups. From the cowl area forward and from the back seat rearward the frame was boxed. On the convertible the entire frame was boxed for strength and rigidity. The frame had three built-in cross-members, and a fourth cross-member bolted in behind the trans-

Styling changes in 1965 were stacked headlights, recessed grille, taillights which wrapped around fender, single hood scoop. With even less chrome, thin stripe along belt line created tasteful accent line.

35

mission. An X-member would have stiffened the frame, but it would have added weight, and this was an important consideration for many GTO buyers; so important, in fact, that Pontiac made GTO's available without undercoating or insulation. These cars were lighter, but tended to leak and rattle when used on the street.

Body changes were minor but distinctive. The grille was changed slightly; it was recessed, and the horizontal chrome strip removed, making the clean-looking front end even cleaner. The most notable change was that the quad headlights were now stacked vertically in pairs, with a slight hood at the peak of the fender over the top set of lights. The two nonfunctional hood scoops of 1964 became a single air scoop located in the center of the hood. The fuel tank filler neck was relocated behind the license plate. The taillights were concealed within a chrome strip which ran the width of the rear end and the lights wrapped around the sides of the rear fenders, following the bumper contour. Viewed from the rear, the 1965 GTO was clean and attractive, a perfect example of function dictating form. That could be said of the entire car; it was free of any chrome trim other than the GTO identification plates. An optional trim stripe ran the length of the body, from the front fender's upper peak to the taillight; this thin stripe accented the strong, almost unbroken fender and belt line.

Inside there was a new optional Rally cluster, with large dial gauges for the oil pressure, water temperature, a 250-degree sweep tachometer and 120-mph speedometer; 'idiot lights' served as fuel and ammeter indicators. The tachometer was available only with the Rally cluster. Hidden from view was the new two-step doorstop which kept the door from flying fully open. There was the new airfoil

1965 optional Rally I wheel.

Bottom transmission is three-speed fully synchronized model made by Ford for Pontiac GTO; top is Muncie four-speed.

radio antenna, and the new Rally wheels. The latter were made of steel, with a wider base, slightly offset, to accept the larger tire size and, while they resembled the popular magnesium wheel, they sold for only $35.00 *a set*! Changes in the exhaust system (introduced in mid-1964) made it more resistant to corrosion. The cold (right) side muffler was changed from aluminized steel to stainless steel for the shell and heads.

There were changes in the engine department. The 389-ci V-8 with the four-barrel had its horsepower increased by ten, from 325 to 335 hp, with 431 pounds-feet of torque at 3200 rpm. The 389 V-8 with tri-power had its horsepower increased by twelve, from 348 to 360, with 424 pounds-feet of torque at 3600 rpm. As was usually the case with Pontiac, the horsepower ratings were conservative, even as regards the big 421-ci V-8 (unavailable as GTO factory-installed engine) which, with tri-power, was rated at 376 hp, the highest rating of any American production engine up to that time.

Additional horsepower was the result of improved breathing characteristics, lightened reciprocating parts, camshaft timing and carburetion changes. The engine used the heads and camshaft from the 421 V-8 in altered form. The cylinder heads were reworked to change the combustion chamber profile to remove restrictions and abrupt changes. Both the 389-ci and 421-ci engines used big valves,

Dash had standard wheel, standard column-mounted shift for automatic. Aluminum machine-turned appliqué on panel has given way to imitation walnut grain material.

This 1965 GTO has custom interior installed by Pontiac. To emphasize tiger theme, decor included furry carpets, tiger skin panels and tiger paws for seat belts.

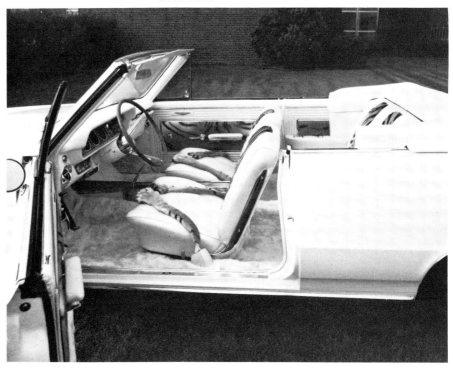

the intake valve size being 1.92 inches and the exhaust, 1.66 inches. Changes were made in the heads so that the valve train received its oil from the valve lifters up through hollow pushrods to the new rocker arms through a hole in the rocker arm, and then to the rocker-arm ball. The valve stem was lubricated with oil spillage from the rocker arm. Another feature of these heads was that the valve guides were an integral part of the head, and they extended a good distance down the length of the valve stem, thereby cutting down on excessive valve sideplay.

The five-bearing camshaft, in spite of being from the 421 V-8, had a McKellar grind not available in any other 1965 Pontiac engine. The lobes were ground at an angle so that the hydraulic lifters could rotate, and the lift was set at .395 to .417 inch. The cam in the 335-hp engine had valve timings of 273-degrees intake and 289-degrees exhaust with fifty-four-degrees overlap. The 360-hp engine had a timing of 288-degrees intake and 302-degrees exhaust with sixty-three-degrees overlap. The result was a cam that gave strong acceleration and yet allowed the engine to run in traffic without excessive lope; it also contributed to the throaty tiger-growl exhaust sound.

Metal had been removed from static parts like the intake manifold and re-ciprocating parts like the crankshaft. Surrounding the crank was a newly designed oil pan and oil-pan baffle which allowed a six-quart oil capacity without getting excessive churning of the oil at high speeds. There was also a new self-cleaning crankcase ventilator valve.

Running gear and suspension were essentially unchanged. One change, however, was the new differential which incorporated a casing of peralitic malleable iron for greater strength. It used new ring, differential and side gears, ten-tooth pinions for maximum stress balance and strength and a larger pinion cross-shaft for reduced stress. The 1964 GTO had experienced pinion gear trouble when the rear end was subjected to severe stress, which was often. The semifloating rear axle was strong enough to survive this rough treatment without undue breakage.

Eight rear axle ratios were listed, ranging from 2.56:1 to 4.33:1. A ninth, a 4.11:1, like the 4.33:1, was an option which had to be dealer-installed. But there were numerous combinations of rear axles, including the standard rear end, the standard rear end with metallic brake lining, the Safe-T-Track rear end and the Safe-T-Track rear end with metallic brake lining.

The standard rear end ratio with the 335-hp engine was 3.21:1, and with the 360-hp engine the ratio was 3.55:1. These were the standard ratios regardless of

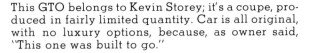

This GTO belongs to Kevin Storey; it's a coupe, produced in fairly limited quantity. Car is all original, with no luxury options, because, as owner said, "This one was built to go."

the type of transmission, but a buyer could do some dealing if he preferred a different gear ratio. Dick Jesse of Royal Pontiac recommended the 3.90:1 rear end, which was an optional ratio but which was supplied without additional charge at the time of purchase. He felt that this was the best compromise between low-speed acceleration and high-speed cruising, and was a more suitable ratio for driving in city traffic, especially if the car had the four-speed transmission.

There were decisions to be made regarding transmissions too; in addition to the two-speed automatic, the three-speed and four-speed manual, there were close-ratio and wide-ratio gear combinations. The GTO four-speed Muncie transmission came with wide-ratio gears, low gear being 2.56. An optional close-ratio gear change was available at no extra charge, with low gear being 2.20, second 1.64 and third 1.28. This transmission, combined with the 3.90:1 rear end, worked out well at all speeds.

Correct gear choices were essential, not only for speed but also for economy. John Ethridge, testing a 335-hp GTO for *Motor Trend*, got 19 mpg on a two-hundred-mile trip cruising at a steady 65-70 mph; on a secondary road where speeds

John DeFelice's GTO is Montero Red, has optional wire wheel covers.

Mike Rainey's GTO has four-barrel, four-speed wide-ratio transmission, Safe-T-Track with 3.23:1 gears.

fluctuated he got 17.6 mpg; a combination of town and country driving gave an average of 13.2 mpg. That's incredible mileage from a car which was also capable of such high speeds. Eric Dahlquist tested a similar GTO for *Hot Rod* and drove it on a dry lake "with the needle swinging past 125." He reported that the car "cruised phenomenally well, easily in excess of 90 mph," and at a steady 75 mph it got 15.5 mpg.

Almost everyone had only praise for the GTO. John Ethridge felt that the car had exactly the right combination of good looks, power and options. He also praised its metal work and finish, and cited the quality of the sheet metal, even though body parts for Oldsmobiles and Buicks were made at the same plant. "The test car had the usual ripple-free body panels that help make Pontiac the wonder of the industry. For that matter, the whole car had a standard of fit and finish that would've been unimaginable in a mass-produced car a few years ago."

Minor complaints ranged from the instrumentation, which some felt was difficult to read, to the chrome-plated pedals, which could cause the driver's foot to slip off the pedal. *Road Test* again said that the bucket seats were not real bucket seats because they didn't cradle the driver and passenger properly. The new hood scoop was different from the twin scoops on the 1964 GTO; it was an air inlet blocked on the underside. A few people suggested that the factory should have unbolted the sheet metal so the hood scoop would be functional, and late in the 1965 model year Pontiac did offer a Fresh Air package as an option on the GTO.

Some older, more serious complaints persisted. There was the problem of rear wheel hop under extreme acceleration, but that could be cured by replacing the rear axle stabilizer rubber bushings with metal bushings. The lack of traction in fast standing starts could be at least partially corrected by using wider rear tires. GTO brakes, which a number of test drivers found barely adequate, had not been enlarged in size but they had been improved by the optional heavy-duty brake package, which included aluminum front drums and organic linings, or the metallic linings and the vacuum booster. *Car Life* found that this was a very good combination: "And the metallic brakes are great. Pedal pressure with the vacuum booster is reasonable . . . and there is no noticeable fade under very rough braking conditions."

1965 GTO having front sheet metal attached on assembly line.

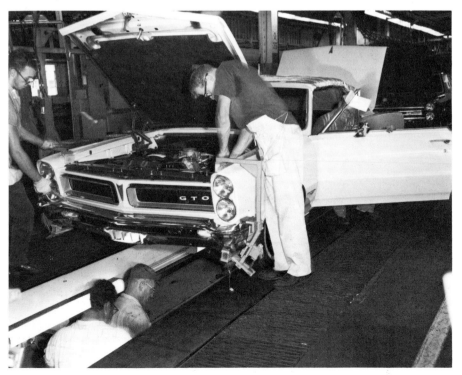

Even those drivers who were in love with the GTO complained about the slow steering, whether their cars were equipped with manual or power, regular or fast ratios. The car was fine doing what it did best but was difficult to handle on a winding road where its power constantly drove it ahead of its steering. Part of the problem stemmed from the fact that the GTO and Tempest LeMans used the same basic foundation—same frame, steering, brakes, suspension—but the Tempest LeMans had 140 hp and the GTO was pushing 360 hp.

Then, there was the problem of weight distribution. The 389-ci engine weighed 675 pounds, seventy-five pounds more than the 326 V-8 and 210 pounds more than the six-cylinder engine. All this weight was located right over the front wheels. It created an imbalance, with fifty-six percent of the weight on the front wheels and forty-four percent on the rear wheels. This imbalance had two effects: one, because the rear end was lighter, there was a loss of traction to the rear wheels when the car was accelerating; and, two, because of the heavy front end, the car suffered from a strong case of understeer. The latter problem was not as severe as it was in the Tempest Sprint, but it was very real.

The GTO had a front stabilizer bar slightly larger than that found on the Tempest, but lacked any bar at the rear because, as mentioned, John DeLorean didn't believe in them. The GTO and the Oldsmobile 4-4-2 used the same frame and suspension but the 4-4-2 handled much better when thrown into a hard curve; this seemed to be due to the 4-4-2's large rear stabilizer bar.

Those problems diminished in importance when the owner of a GTO was doing what he had paid money to do: go fast in a straight line. *Car Life* ran a stone-stock, non-Royalized GTO with the big engine and four-speed and got these times: 0-40 mph in 3.6 seconds, 0-60 in 5.8 seconds, 0-90 in 11.4 seconds, a speed of 100 mph in the quarter from a standing start and top speed of 114 mph. *Car Craft* took its strictly stock GTO to the drag strip and turned 101 mph in 14.65 seconds—feeling that the car wasn't running to its potential abilities, a set of aftermarket headers and a pair of big slicks were added to the rear. With the headers uncapped the car turned 102 mph in 13.77 seconds.

Even those times could be improved upon. *Car Life* asked Roger Huntington to test a 360-hp GTO with the four-speed. Huntington, in turn, had Milt Schornak of Royal Pontiac tune it up a bit—this was not a Bobcat kit, it was a mild example of speed tuning. Schornak unhooked the exhaust pipes, installed Champion J-12-Y plugs, took off the air cleaners and the underhood padding and moved the spark advance to sixteen degrees BTC. He also installed a pair of M & H Super Stock 9.00x14 tires on the rear. Although the driver, Dick Jesse, couldn't get the engine to rev past 5200 rpm, the car turned 0-30 in 2.6 seconds, a little more than a blink, and it turned 0-60 in 5.4 seconds.

It was clear to all that with a little work the Great One could become even greater.

OWNERS' COMMENTS

A solid, well-built automobile, with an abundance of torque, ample horsepower and overall good reliability. However, the GTO's suspension is no match for its motor, and it has poor handling characteristics. RF of Manchester, Iowa.

After I saw a '64 GTO blow the doors off a supercharged Avanti and the town's fastest 283-ci Chevy back to back, I had to have one. I purchased my 1965 GTO new and in two years had only one problem with it—the pin fell out of the shift linkage going into reverse. My '65 had clean lines, unlimited performance, beautiful interior, super instrument panel, great suspension and charisma! It was also the fastest factory hot rod to hit the streets—brutal! ER of St. Ignace, Michigan.

It had a lot of nip and was very comfortable to ride in. I always thought the rear end was too low and it would sometimes drag on steeper driveways, said MER from St. Ignace, Michigan.

My GTO has one basic fault that led to the destruction of many of the early models. This fault is that the driver gets such a thrill at 3000 to 5000 rpm that he simply cannot let off before he reaches the 6000-rpm red-line area. Many people got carried away, went too many rpm, and blew the engine or wrecked. Under full acceleration, some GTO's are difficult to hold on the road . . . Shortly after I purchased my GTO, I was riding through town with the top down, when a young boy called, 'Hey, you old goat!' It took me a few minutes to realize that the reference was not to me, since 'goat' was a common title given to GTO's. BG of Waddy, Kentucky.

I acquired my GTO from the original owner. The day I picked it up I used the license plate from another car and on the way home I got stopped by a cop. I asked, grinning, "What's wrong?' He said, 'Well you're going eighty in a thirty-five and you've got the wrong plates on the car.' I explained the situation to the officer, who was around thirty-five years old, and he shot back, 'Yeah, I know, I used to have one. Can I look under the hood?' He was tickled to see one like his old one. I asked him if he wanted to drive it but he said no, not while on duty. I asked for his phone number and said I'd get a hold of him, off duty of course, so he could. I did, he did, and he's looking for one again. KS from Cleveland, Ohio.

On The Line—Michelle Peters

I worked there [Pontiac] from June 1963 to 1976. When I started they were just finishing up the '63's and starting the GTO's. I hired in at the engine plant, and worked as a rod grinder—my dad got me the job. He was an executive at Pontiac. He worked there thirty-nine years; he was in charge of back end repair in Plant Eight, and then he was the assistant superintendent in the Refinish Department. I was making $3.01 an hour and lots and lots of overtime. That was good money. From there I went to the foundry; then to the differential plant from 1965 till 1975; from 1975 till 1976 I worked at the assembly plant.

The differential plant is where I got the most experience because I worked as a gear cutter. Ring gears, pinions, side gears, side pinions—I worked as a blanker, during the different blanking stages, I worked in the gear lapping section, assembly section, front end assembly, rear end assembly, I worked in ring gear tryout, all of them.

The Pontiac rear end was one of the best rear ends in the industry. We'd rate them: Class A, B, C according to the noise factor. The rear ends that weren't that good, say, B noise factor, we'd sell those to Oldsmobile and Buick. We'd give them all the junk. We'd take the good stuff and put it in our cars.

I've seen the power locks twist in two because of the torque, but the power locks were made someplace else. The carriers, the tubes, the axles, the gears, all that was made right there in the Pontiac plant and they were all perfect. Back in those days, people working on cars [did careful work]. I can remember if they [the parts] were just a *little* bit off they'd throw them out, make them do it all over again. I knew most of the people who worked on those cars and if we knew they went into a GTO they'd get extra-special care. Everybody had pride in their workmanship in those days. You see, a lot of the people on the assembly line were kids, and they had those kinds of cars, too. We always said we wouldn't let nobody else get that kind of stuff.

I had a '64 and a '65 [GTO], and both were built in the Pontiac plant. My '64 was one of the first two hundred built—it was Yorktown blue, white interior, dark blue carpet, 389-ci engine, deluxe push-button radio, reverb console. It was 348-horse, tri-power, four-speed, and it was a coupe. The '64 coupe was the lightest one—they had 200-pound-lighter frames than the hardtops or the convertibles. It was really shocking because of the low gear ratio; standard gear ratio was 3.42:1, and mine was built with a 3.55:1 gear. That was the lowest you could get out of the factory. Those other gear ratios you'd have to put in yourself; they were not dealer installations, unless you went to a dealer who'd cooperate with you. It had little bitty hubcaps and whitewalls, so it looked like a LeMans—it was really a sleeper. I remember when I first got it we used to go out on Woodward Avenue and race people, and it really surprised people who were used to seeing old LeMans around.

I paid $2,700 for my '64 and I paid $2,750 for my '65—that was with the factory discount. I told my dad what I wanted and he went in the office and ordered it. When an executive orders a car they put a sticker in the window and then the employees are supposed to take better care of it.

That '65 was a coupe, the lightest one. The coupes weighed 3,040 [pounds] in '64 and 3,030 in '65; where that ten pounds [difference] came in at they changed the front end a little bit. But they built some GTO's without undercoating, without headliners, without carpets, without weatherstripping to get more weight off them. My '65 didn't have the console because I wanted to cut more weight. I put my own tachometer in it, I had a Sun transistor. That car was Capri gold with a black interior, small hubcaps and red-line tires. The red-lines were supposed to get a little bit better traction, but anybody who was serious took them off and put on slicks anyway, put headers and stuff on their car and went that route.

The '65's had stripes on them, and the early ones were put on by hand. They had these guys over in Plant Seventeen that used to stripe these cars—boss went around on the production line and asked has anybody used to be a striper? They had some real old guys who went over and they hand-striped those cars. Later on they had a thingamajigger to stripe them.

I had one of the fastest cars around. Lots of times I'd get off work, there was a little hump in the factory parking lot and we always tried to hit that little hump when we hit second gear so we could get the [front] wheels off the ground. Everybody did that. There were lots of kids who used to work in the factory, and we used to drag race.

Or we'd take it to the drag strip. Back in those days you could take a car and go out to the drag strip, drive it down, and just do a little tuning and you could race and you could be competitive. There were so many GTO's out there it was pathetic. I had one of the fastest ones around—I could pick the front wheels off the ground in first and second gear; there wasn't very many that could do that. I turned a 12.98 [e.t.] with it. That was fast. It was running close to a national record.

It was faster than others because I was changing the suspension, changing the gear ratio, there was a lot of tuning tricks. And I was pushing a lot of horsepower out of mine. It was run on Joy Fair's dyno and it was far more than what they said it was—it was supposed to be 360 [hp] and I remember it was over 400 horses. The guy said, 'Is this a 421?' and I said no. He said, 'Boy, this is an awful powerful 389.'

I never had trouble with wheel hop but there was no way to get traction. You'd have to take off at maybe a fifteen or twenty [mph] roll in order to do any good, but even then you'd break the tires loose. If I was coming out of the hole I'd come out in second gear. You would get wheel hop and traction loss if you left the factory suspension with the factory tires on it. I had mine changed. I changed my front and rear wheels. I had narrow wheels on the front and I had my front end jacked up a little bit. I changed my shocks too; I put 90-10's on the front and 50-50 action on the rear. I changed the bushings on the back, I put solid aluminum bushing in the back [upper differential control arms] and changed the gear ratio to a 4.43. I changed the axles, put heavier axles in it. The engine had a little work done on it too, but it was mostly [a matter of] tuning. All the hood underliner was stripped out, and we put aluminum foil around the fuel line which kept it running cooler. There were a couple other tricks too.

It was a fast car—I mean, let's face it, there weren't many cars in '64 that would come out of the factory [which were that fast]—a lot of these kids would get four-barrels and wide-ratio four-speeds, they didn't know the difference between a close-ratio four-speed and a wide-ratio. They didn't know what kind of gears they were getting either. They'd just get the standard rear end—Posi-traction—which was like the 3.40 rear end. They didn't know what they were getting. You have to be right on top of that stuff. When you're working in the factory like I was, you work on that stuff all the time. My dad worked there thirty-nine years. So we knew basically what kinds of combinations worked the best. We tried different experiments ourselves. That was probably the difference between my car and a lot of the other cars.

You could get any kind of gear ratio you'd want. We put a little dab of paint on them so we'd know, and so others could distinguish them by the colors. Gray was 41.16; red was 39.14; orange was 41.14; yellow was 40.13; blue was 39.11; black was 41.11; green was 39.10. People changed them, 'cause mine changed mine. Mine was built with a 3.90 gear, this was my '65, with a four-speed and with a 2.20 first, and tri-power, that was a 360-hp 389-ci. The only difference between that and the '64 engine was the cams were changed, the heads were a bit different, and they [the tri-power] had progressive linkage. That's where the extra horsepower came from. But the heads weren't that good, they had lots of problems with the valve guides. They used to have to take those heads off and remachine them, knurl the valve guides and put bigger valve stems in, some of them out of the 421's. I had some trouble with axles, too. With an eight-inch rim and slicks I was getting so much traction I was twisting axles. Then in '66 they went to a different type axle and they magna-fluxed all the axles. Before that they weren't magnafluxed. They brought in a special machine and a guy, just for the job of magnafluxing axles.

Back in those days they were still covered under warranty. Unless they could prove you were doing some kind of drag racing, they'd replace it [the broken part]. But they knew you were racing them—it's the only reason people were buying those cars. I blew up an engine and Pontiac replaced it. Why not, they knew what those cars were for. I threw a rod, it sucked a valve. That was my '64. By the time I got my '65 I knew some of the things I did wrong with my '64.

I had trouble with the '65 too, mainly with the heads—valve guides. I had my engine rebuilt a few times. You can't take those cars and run a 4.33 rear end on the street and expect it to hold up for 50,000 miles. I had 65,000 miles on my GTO. But I went to different kinds of camshafts—Engle, Isky, I used different factory camshafts, a McKellar No. 7 and 8. I drove it from here up to Grayling once on the expressway and it overheated a little. With the 4.33:1 rear end in it. You got to expect that driving 80-90 mph for over 150 miles straight with the 4.33 rear end. You got to expect them to overheat. That's the way I used to drive those cars. Drive them, drive the heck out of them! Every time I got a chance I'd be on that car. I had fun with it. Really hot rod it.

We used to go out on Woodward all the time, but mostly on weekends. We didn't have nothing to do—you'd go water-skiing all day and at night you'd go out and race on Woodward. We'd get out there and drag race and carry on, meet other kids, stay out until three or four o'clock in the morning, then come home.

Everybody drove fast on Woodward. In fact, they had a terrible time on Woodward—sometimes traffic would be backed up because people would slow down to drag race. They had so many people racing that they [the police] couldn't stop it. They could be pulling somebody else over and the drag racing would be going on right in front of them. I had my license taken away for racing—you get six points for drag racing. Once I got a ticket for drag racing and obstructing traffic. That's because we had to slow down to get a roll. I didn't see the cops until we got up to about 100. He said, 'I didn't think we were going to catch you.' See, that's the thing: they couldn't catch us. The cop cars wouldn't go that fast.

We could still get that Sunoco 110 octane gas. We used to take the clips off the tanks—it would run up to 120, Sunoco 120, but you could take the clips off and get up to 130—and that way you could get pure octane. That was in the gas station down there next to Ted's. Ted's was kind of the place where the kids used to congregate, a drive-in on Long Lake and Woodward. There was a lot of fast cars down there in those days—supercharged cars and everything. I had a really fast car, but I got beat once. That was a guy in an older Chevy and he worked for General Motors. He beat me. But that car was running around 550 horses. But I raced a Cobra one time and beat him, beat him bad! I was running slicks too. They didn't care back in those days, but they didn't want you uncorking your headers. They didn't like you doing that—the cops would write you a ticket.

That was a neat little car. I had a lot of fun with it. I had a nice sound system, had a reverb in it. It was fun, it was fast. I remember once I was on the highway and I just pulled off in first and second gear kind of slow—to me it was slow, but this guy was next to me in a Catalina and he must have been on it or something because we went up to about 90 or 100 mph, and I really had a 90-mph tick to mine. I'd get up to about 90 mph and I'd be getting my peak power then, it'd be up to 120 in no time. That was about top end in my car, but mine was pretty much in top end when it was going through the quarter mile—it'd be doing about 110-115. That was pretty fast!

Those were real good engines, and they were carefully built. Plant Nine made all the engines—they made engines for everybody. But where the assembly plant was they only made thirty-eight percent of all the Pontiacs there. That leaves the other sixty-two percent made elsewhere. B-O-P plants they were called—Buick-Olds-Pontiac. Now, how well they assembled their cars, who knows? But I know one thing: that all the repairs were made off the assembly line at the Pontiac plant, and they were not at the other plants. So that means that if any major repairs had to be done the dealers would have to do them, and whether they would do them who knows? Whereas if a dealer got a car from the Pontiac plant they were happy. They knew that car would probably be perfect because anything that needed to be done was done there. They didn't let those cars out of their sight unless they knew they were good. Back in those days, people did careful work.

I remember when we had to do something for an engine, like a NASCAR engine, we made sure it was perfect. They had guys come down and say this is for a certain car, a special job, and they'd take those parts and give them to

Michelle Peters's second GTO, a quick 1965 built late November 1964. It was gold with black interior and had a four-speed transmission, Posi-traction and 3.90 gears. The car weighed 3,030 pounds and had tri-power on the 360-hp engine.

us and we'd have to machine them and make sure they were just right. Some of those engines were disassembled off the assembly line to make sure they were okay.

Pontiac was doing lots of interesting things in those days. Like they built some LeMans in 1963 with 421's for police departments and stuff like that, because my dad was in charge of that. Production-wise they were 326's, but they were really the 421's, they were 405 horse. I think that was the Super-Duty engine, because they had some bigger engines, they had a 425-horse, too. They built stripped GTO's for racing. Like Royal Pontiac ordered a bunch of stripped cars, there were some police departments that ordered some [special] cars, and some of those cars I know had dual quads on them—not built that way, but they'd take them over to the engineering department, and I saw some with dual quads. I remember a guy [who] lived down the street from us, Dykma, and he was an engineer, he worked over at the engineering department, and he was always trying out something like that. They had a ram induction system in '65 too, but I don't think it was released to the public, and I saw a couple [GTO's] with fiberglass hoods, stuff like that. Pontiac was pretty hot to trot, they were doing all kinds of stuff like that. They figured it like this: if they could build a good racing car and it'd hold up good, then it'd be good for the average person.

CHAPTER FOUR

GTO Hype

A car doesn't exist in a vacuum, but insists itself into our lives. Henry Ford intended his Model T to be a prim, black utilitarian vehicle. But it soon became much more than a means of transportation: a corn shucker, a power unit for a buzz saw, a means of bringing people together, a vehicle for courting, the subject of songs, jokes and tall tales. The GTO had a similar effect: It was a car, but also a catalyst, a shaper of behavior, and it, too, was the subject of songs, jokes and automotive legend.

The GTO divided time into before its arrival and after. Enthusiast Ed Reavie found that his GTO changed his life, and he remembers March 22, 1965, the day it came, with great clarity: "After the dealer called, I had almost two days to think about the arrival of 'the car.' I got so hyped-up I got a severe headache, which quickly developed into the flu.

"I spent most of Friday in the bathroom, trying to get healthy. We woke Saturday to a March blizzard, and my condition had not improved, either. So my wife, Mary Ellen, and her friend Brenda Blair agreed to drive our 1961 Impala sport coupe to the dealer's to pick up the GTO. For the next four hours I paced between the bathroom and the front window, peering into the blizzard which was getting worse by the minute. On one trip to the bathroom I stepped on the scales and realized that I had lost eight pounds during the past two days!

"Finally, I heard it! I put a parka over my hooded robe, put on gloves and boots and shuffled across the parking lot à la Tim Conway, looking very much like the Grim Reaper.

"The Nightwatch blue GTO looked great against the pure white snow, the dual pipes puffing exhaust evenly into the cold air, the 'gurgle' of the mufflers, music to my ears. We drove around the rest of the afternoon—gas was cheap, great music by the Beatles came from the back-seat speaker, and we didn't even notice the weather—and I was healed, almost like a miracle!"

Ed might have also heard a popular song entitled "GTO" coming over that back-seat speaker; other drivers all over the country did. And as they thumped their fingers in time to the music against the steering wheel of whatever they were driving, they realized the softness, the oldness, the *plainness* of their car. No one knows how many GTO's were sold because of that song, but it's safe to say that it was responsible for a good number of young people exchanging their money for an ignition key.

The song, "GTO," like many other things connected with the car by the same name, was developed by Jim Wangers. He's been credited in print with producing the record, and credited elsewhere with writing the song, although his name does not appear on the record label. To separate myth from reality I'll pass along what he told me.

One day two kids knocked on his door and said that they'd written a song about the GTO. They'd brought it to Wangers because he was in charge of the Pontiac advertising account and they thought he'd be interested. He wasn't. His company wasn't in the recording business, and Pontiac wasn't either, but they persisted and so he said, "Send me a tape." When the tape arrived a week later he played it and found the lyrics simply incomprehensible. But there was something catchy about the tune, and something appealing about a song celebrating the car he had been writing ad copy to promote. He began to rewrite the lyrics, trying to capture the *essence* of what the GTO meant. "Come on, turn it on, wind it up, blow it out. . . ."

After he had exercised his musical abilities to his satisfaction, he used his considerable influence to have the record produced. He wanted the Beach Boys to do the song because their West Coast 'surfing sound' was extremely popular and it fit Wangers's idea of the car's image: youth, California, drag strips, sunshine, surf boards. The Beach Boys wanted a bundle up front, however, and he began to work his way down the ladder until he found an obscure group called Ronnie and the Daytonas who recorded "GTO" with "Hot Rod Baby" on the flip side.

> Little GTO, you're really lookin' fine,
> Three deuces and a four-speed, and a 389,
> Listen to her tachin' up now, listen to her wii-iind,
> Come on, turn it on, wind it up, blow it out, GTO.

"G.T.O." by Ronny and The Daytonas.

46

The lyrics are simple and repetitious, the lead guitar sounds a little anemic by today's standards, yet "GTO" is pleasing. It's light, has a breezy refrain, an insistent beat, captures the 'surfing sound' of the 1960's with its chorus of "Whoooooo yeah yeah yeah." The final line of each stanza suggests action through a series of compressed phrases: "C'mon, get it on, line it up, blow it out, GTO."

It's a song every youthful driver can identify with even today, and it's *optimistic*: If you have a GTO you can do anything! There are no blown transmissions, broken axles, bumpy roads; and certainly no conflicts, anxieties, protests, police actions, wars—all complications of the later 1960's which were to take over the music as they did the headlines. The bouncy music and optimistic content mirrored the times; the GTO represented the culmination of the American Dream which had really got started in the 1950's and was, for many, soon to end. In this song the only problem that is posed is buying the car—"Gonna save all my money, and buy a GTO"—which is not really an obstacle but merely a matter of time.

"GTO" was an immediate hit; it made the charts, was number four on the Billboard survey in September 1964, eventually sold a total of 1,250,000 copies and was played on the radio an estimated seven million times! The success of the song also helped the car. "It did more than anything else to build up the GTO's image," Wangers said later. "It was a protest car, though we weren't calling it that, then." Because of a clause in his contract, Wangers received no money for the song or his efforts to promote it.

Meanwhile, out in Califonia, a popular duo called Jan and Dean sensed a good thing and quickly released in June 1964 a single called "My Mighty GTO." It was on the Liberty label (number 55704), and on the flip side was their popular song "The Little Old Lady from Pasadena," later included in their album "Dead Man's Curve." This song also sold well, and increased Jan and Dean's popularity as well as that of the GTO.

Pontiac had hoped to sell 5,000 GTO's the first year just to test the public's reaction; that it eventually sold over 32,000 was due in part to the two songs which celebrated the car. The whole scenario was a promoter's dream: The airwaves filled with songs promoting the product, and all for free! Because of the success of the songs, in 1965 Pontiac made, promoted and distributed its own record. It was called "GeeTO Tiger" and the musicians, who have not been credited with any other record, were called, aptly, The Tigers.

A GTO owner could be identified at business and social gatherings by these GTO cuff links. Also available was matching GTO tie bar.

GTO cologne by the leading manufacturer, Max Factor. Only GTO owners had special cologne for Saturday night cruising.

Front cover of sales brochure for the 1965 GTO was also used on a record jacket for promotional record produced by Pontiac.

Inside view of brochure/jacket. The record was in the center, photo layout informed potential buyer of GTO's key features; note big photo of smoking tire! Captions were from song "GeeTO Tiger!"

On back cover were The Tigers, noted for this one record. "GeeTO Tiger!" was a hit, but flip side was interesting for its realism. 250,000 copies were sold by factory for 50 cents each.

"GeeTO Tiger" opens with the sound of throaty mufflers, a revving engine and a car, obviously a GTO, accelerating quickly through all four gears and, as the exhaust noise grows distant, there is the heavy, insistent sound of an electronic guitar:

> There's a Tiger on the market and I got the very first in town!
> GeeTO Tiger! GeeTO Tiger!
> She's got a Hurst floor shifter and the wildest screamin' mill around!
> GeeTO Tiger! GeeTO Tiger!

Most of the song reads like an options list or the window sticker put to music—well, it *was* produced by Pontiac as a promotion item, and the real profit in muscle cars was in the options—but there's the promise of action as the GTO searches for a Ford or a Chevrolet, Pontiac's closest competitors: "We're goin' huntin' for a Mustang or a dual-quad four-oh-nine!"

The song has a bouncy beat and the 'surfing sound.' It uses long lines and has a tune which *forces* you to sing them as long lines, and there is the contrapuntal "Tiger Tiger" and "GeeTO Tiger! Go Go!" It's the kind of tune and lyrics that you find yourself humming throughout the day. And if the song itself didn't get you into the showroom, the record's final seconds would: There is the sound of a revving engine, wildly spinning tires, a quick shift to second, burning rubber and so on through all four gears. It's incredible to imagine a company promoting and selling a car on the basis of its ability to spin its tires, and it's even more incredible to imagine this record being played on the radio. One can picture a kid stuck at home on a Saturday night hearing that song, or a Walter Mitty poking through traffic in his six-cylinder turkey. It captured the kinetic sense of motion; one did more than listen, one participated!

"GeeTO Tiger" was recorded on the Colpix label (number 773) to be sold in stores, but Pontiac marketed a special version of the record through the mail. On the record cover was a 1965 GTO convertible and on the car's hood was a tiger skin, the head with its odd, blank look hanging over the grille. The back of the jacket showed a photo of the musical group The Tigers. On an adjoining panel were the words to "GeeTO Tiger" and at the bottom was the credit "Printed in USA by Tiger Lovers." Enclosed inside were a series of photos showing a smoking tire, a tri-power setup, a Hurst shifter and some copy which began, "A musical tribute to America's most popular performance car . . . the GTO!"

On the flip side of the record was a sound collage called "Big Sounds of the GeeTO Tiger" and subtitled "At the GM Proving Grounds." This was a kind of documentary which picked up on the idea presented at the opening and closing of "GeeTO Tiger"; that it was possible on a record to give a person a sense of what it was like to drive the GTO.

"Little GTO," recently released by Rodney and the Brunettes, indicated high level of interest in the car, the song, the sixties. Rodney used royalties to buy his own GTO.

49

The record opens with the sound of voices and revving engines in the background, and then a voice addresses you, the listener, apologizes for the delay and invites you to take a test ride in a GTO. "Ah, there it is, that special gold hardtop over there, next to the blue Bonneville . . . the GeeTO Tiger. . . ." Then he runs through a checklist: "Yeah, we got the big engine, 360 horses, 3.90:1 Safe-T-Track rear end, close-ratio four-speed 2.20:1 first gear and a Hurst floor shifter. Say, how do you like this wood steering wheel—really feels like wood. . . ."

The record combines a folksy, conversational style with technical terminology. At times the test drive sounds like a space shot, and the driver who is in contact with Pontiac Central Control sounds like an astronaut talking with Mission Control: "Roger . . . Control, this is 36."

The car is cleared by Control, and we get the point of the record: the sounds of speed. "We've just reached blacktop, speed fifty, very little tire noise, up to sixty, handling perfect, gonna take her up to seventy. We're coming to the torsion bumps and washboard now . . ." There is a terrific awareness of rising exhaust sounds as he accelerates to each 10-mph increase, and then his voice takes on an urgency, as if he is poised for reentry to our atmosphere. "I'm getting a little vertical sheet metal shake. . . ."

Then, there is the high-speed test, with Control warning the driver that he's "only cleared for a hundred and ten miles per hour." Car 36 revs its engine, there is a roar as a Grand Prix goes past and leaves the track, then the driver of 36 stands on the gas and there is the incredible sound of exhausts and spinning, spinning tires. "There's a hundred," the driver reports. "Point-oh-five. Point-oh-seven. One-ten. Moving at one-ten, no sway, no sheet metal flutter."

After completing ten laps at 110 mph, there are the brake tests, when the driver slams on the brakes at a hundred miles an hour. "Mark! Brake line pressure was at 1,850 psi." He does this twenty times and then moves on to the acceleration tests. The driver winds it out through the gears and remarks on his time: "102.5 mph."

Control says, "That was a good run, 36. You turned the quarter in 14.4."

At the end, after ten minutes of spinning tires, there is a nod toward the idea of safety, and the question: "Well, that's the GeeTO Tiger, what do you think of it?"

Hurst shifters first appeared on production line in the GTO, but even after they became an option on other makes Hurst used GTO's in advertisements. Indirectly, a Hurst ad was a GTO ad

If you can take your eyes off the girl for a minute and get past the message on the car, you'll see **Hurst's revolutionary new custom wheel.**

This was a promotional gimmick, and it must have been extremely effective. There was the sense of immediacy, the sensations, the noise and the feeling that you, too, could participate if you had a GTO. It captured the authenticity of the GM Proving Grounds even though, as Jim Wangers told me, "It was all done in the studio—out in California."

The record cost only fifty cents, and Pontiac sold 250,000 of them. Few have survived the years, however, and whenever a copy surfaces it is grabbed up by a GTO fan. That's true of the other records also. "GTO" by Ronnie and the Daytonas, "My Mighty GTO" by Jan and Dean and "GeeTO Tiger" by The Tigers are currently listed in record collector catalogs at prices ranging from two to four dollars, but they actually sell for many times that amount at swap meets. "GTO" has recently been rerecorded (as "Little GTO") by a Los Angeles group called Rodney and the Brunettes, backed up by Blondie and American Spring. This version follows the original, but the tempo has been stepped up, since these are faster times. Rodney is Rodney Bingenheimer, a disc-jockey, and he has used the profits from the record to buy his dream car, a 1967 GTO.

These records were early examples of the media blitz used to sell the car, and an example of GTO spin-offs. The songs were successful as songs, but every time one was played it reinforced the name of the car in the public mind.

But the hype didn't stop there. On the back of the "GeeTO Tiger" album sold in stores was a contest announcement: "Win a Tiger!" To enter, one sent in a piece of paper listing the number of times the word 'tiger' had been mentioned in the song, and wrote an essay in twenty-five words or less on the subject "Why I'd like to win the *original* GeeTO Tiger" which was the first prize (won by Alex Lampone of West Allis, Wisconsin). There were also full-page advertisements in leading automobile magazines for the contest: "Win the original GeeTO Tiger—a wild '65 GTO with special Hurst-gold paint and unique tiger-appointed interior." The sponsor of the contest was Hurst Performance Products. So, there was a commercially produced record which was really a promotional piece for Pontiac, sponsored by an after-market accessory manufacturer!

Even if you were walking you could own a GTO—shoe, that is. Italian styling is apparent. Contest to promote 1966 GTO involved tie-in with Pontiac, Hurst and Thom McAn.

George Hurst gained fame and fortune in the 1960's because of his floor shifter which allowed people to convert their manual or automatic column shift to a floor shift. He sold a substantial number of shifters to individuals, but what he really wanted to do was to interest a manufacturer in his product so that it could be installed on an assembly-line basis. As Wangers told me, "George Hurst was knocking on doors all over Detroit with no success until I got Pontiac interested in his product." Pontiac was the first manufacturer, and for a while the *only* manufacturer, to use the Hurst shifter. Before the end of the 1960's, however, several companies, including such unlikely ones as American Motors, would send their cars out equipped with George Hurst's device.

The beauty of this arrangement was that every time Hurst advertised his shifter he was also advertising the GTO. For several years Hurst used only GTO's in his eye-catching full-page ads, with captions such as this: "Wouldn't you know that Hurst would introduce its new automatic control wrapped in a '67 GTO?" This continued when he began to make special mag-type wheels. And when he began to build headers, the first two sets were installed on a pair of GTO's about to be tested by a magazine.

These double-duty ads were highly beneficial to both products, giving the GTO two or three times the exposure Pontiac's advertising budget would allow. As a result Jim Wangers sought to develop this kind of cross-advertising, and he began to tie the GTO campaign into a number of seemingly unrelated products. For example, there was the Thom McAn GTO Shoe which, as the ads put it, was "Made to fit the Tiger." It had "the slot car track" which meant that "The heel and sole on the GTO [shoe] were made to grip the accelerator . . . You can see where the bottom is raised and grooved for extra traction." It was a narrow, somewhat unattractive shoe in the Italian style which, frankly, *looked* uncomfortable. But

Television's Monkeemobile built by Dean Jeffries.

MPC's touring drag strip was a familiar sight at car shows. It used dual GTO bucket seats, dashboards, Hurst shifters. Budd Anderson standing beside the Mystery Tiger.

the ads said that it was "The first shoe for dragging that looks and feels great off the strip."

Another shoe, designed for younger kids, was called The Wide-Tracker. It was described as having "a split grille, stacked headlights, fastback styling and an accelerator-pedal heel . . . unique sole tread for better brake and clutch action, which means better traction on the street." Radio ads for the shoe said wearing them was ". . . like taking a trip right through the hills, on fast-turning wheels. . . ." Once again there was a contest, sponsored by the shoe company, and the first prize was a black-and-gold 1966 GTO.

The spin-offs accelerated: Wangers got Max Factor to market a GTO cologne, and there were GTO cuff links, a GTO tie clasp and GTO socks. This was years before the T-shirt craze, yet the well-dressed GTO owner could reveal his product identification in style. Ed Reavie remembers driving his '65 GTO dressed in all of the above items plus a GTO sports jacket, and on his hands he wore Hurst shifting gloves.

The GTO was seen everywhere. *My Three Sons*, a popular TV show starring Fred MacMurray, always used cars supplied by Pontiac. One episode revolved around Robby's desire to own a new car; he got one and, of course, it was a GTO.

Another popular TV show was *The Monkees*, which featured a quartet of rock musicians who were more comic than the Beatles. The show appealed to youth; Pontiac appealed to youth. What could be more right than that the two should come together. Pontiac had Dean Jeffries build an outlandish GTO 'touring car' with an ungainly top, and this revamped GTO, called the Monkeemobile, was often the star of key action scenes. In addition, each of the four Monkees was given a new GTO for his personal use. One Monkee, Mike Nesmith, generated a lot of publicity for the group and for the GTO when he was stopped on the Hollywood Freeway one night after having been clocked at 125 mph! Then Jim Wangers got the idea for a contest where the winner would get a 1968 GTO convertible—customized by Barris, but more tastefully done than The Monkeemobile—and the next fifteen winners would get stock 1968 GTO hardtops.

To promote this contest, Wangers involved the Kellogg Company by advertising the contest on the back of several kinds of Kellogg breakfast foods. Kellogg's promotional material sent to its dealers emphasized the youth market and product

Two 1965 GTO's and Monogram kit.

Very rare 1964 GTO model kit by AMT.

tie-ins: "What a natural! 3 teenage favorites [Kellogg's, the Monkees and the GTO] packed into One Promotion to keep the sales of Rice Krispies and Raisin Bran soaring!" It's hard to imagine the amount of exposure a product seen in that space can have. Of that contest, Wangers once said, "So we're on forty-two million boxes. They tell me that an average box of cereal comes out of the package shelf and onto the breakfast table six times before it gets thrown out." Forty-two million boxes times six equals a lot of exposure.

Kids who consume breakfast food while watching *The Monkees* also build model cars. So it was no surprise to learn that the "all-time best-seller in terms of model automobiles" was the Monkeemobile GTO. The model-car business boomed during the 1960's, primarily because of developments in the intrusive plastics process, and a number of companies brought out GTO models. The first one was Model Products Corporation's 1965 GTO designed by Budd Anderson. It was promoted at twenty custom car shows around the United States.

MPC also designed an electronic racetrack which gave young people the chance to race their model cars from a cockpit which had the verisimilitude of a real GTO. The track was a scale-model drag strip which required the drivers to make a shift at certain rpm. If the shift was off, that driver would lose the race. Two young racers would get into racing position by sitting in genuine GTO bucket seats which were bolted to the floor. At their sides were genuine Hurst four-speed shift consoles, and before them were GTO instrument panels.

MPC capped the custom car show circuit by giving away two real GTO's to the high-point winners of the International and Grand National Championship classes for show cars. Other companies brought out models of the GTO, including American Model Toys which marketed a 1964 and a 1965 GTO which could be built in one of three different styles. Most of the models are now unavailable, ex-

From the film, *Two-Lane Blacktop*, starring Warren Oates (left), singer James Taylor (right) and ex-Beach Boy Dennis Wilson (center). Another star was the 1970 GTO Judge they're sitting on.

cept for those which are found from time to time on the dusty shelves of an old hobby shop, but at least one has been reissued. The original MPC Monkeemobile GTO was brought out again a decade later, called The Fonz Dream Rod.

Part of the GTO's appeal was that it was *more* than a car; it was, as Pontiac said, "A device for shrinking time and distance," which was a poetic way of saying it was fast. It was also a machine that made the journey as important as the destination; a machine in which you could, as Ed Reavie said, drive around all afternoon and feel "healed." The GTO, like the road, was a metaphor for the times.

The journey theme has been around at least since Homer, but it has become unmistakably important since the automobile came into prominence. The Okies in *Grapes of Wrath* were able to make their exodus to the Promised Land because they had automobiles. In a more optimistic vein, the footloose youth of post World War II America, as seen in Jack Kerouac's *On the Road*, turned cross-country drives into a religious experience. The literature and films of the 1960's are loaded with examples of the journey theme. One, *Easy Rider*, a film in which two characters set out to discover America, was seen as a metaphor for disenchanted youth.

Since the so-called energy crisis, such films have become passé, which says something about the way we live. The last notable road film was *Two Lane Black-top*, released in 1970, which starred James Taylor, Dennis Wilson of The Beach Boys, and Warren Oates as drifters who race across the country. For most viewers the real stars were a 1955 Chevrolet (the same car that was used in *American Graffiti*) and a 1970 Judge (with The Judge logos replaced with GTO decals). It was published as a script in *Esquire*, which called it "the first movie worth reading," and it was later made into what has become a cult film for GTO devotees.

It's not hard to see why. Much of the film has to do with racing. And when the cars aren't racing, they're driving cross-country, flat-out, as if movement has a meaning in itself, or as if to stop moving would bring an end to the world as they know it. Cars are the center of this film, and the dialogue is remarkably real for Hollywood, where cars are usually treated as props.

The Mechanic, who rides in the '55 Chev, suggests to the character called GTO, who drives the car of the same name, that he put a Chevrolet V-8 in the Pontiac: "Look, what you need is a big Chevy Rat Motor that cranks in the mid-elevens. Get yourself a '68 427 Chevy and stroke it out to a 454. Get some L-88 heads, a Sig Erson cam, Crane roller-bearing rocker arms and Crower lifters, Thompson rods. Put on a three-barrel Holley with a 1050 rating . . . There's a lot more. Hell, you could really honk."

That kind of dialogue attracts genuine muscle car freaks to this film. They're also attracted by almost two hours of burning rubber and the sounds of two cars barreling along secondary roads at a cruising speed of 120 mph. And they see the film because it's a celebration of the muscle car, and the GTO, in particular. GTO sees the metaphorical extensions of the film. Regarding his own car, he says: "It's more than just a factory car. It's an institution."

The film focuses on the cross-country grudge-race between the two cars. In the '55 Chev are the Driver and the Mechanic, who, like gunfighters of the old west, ride into town and challenge the fastest car. They always win, and because they bet on themselves this is a form of employment. Somewhere in Arizona they meet up with GTO, and the drivers engage in a cross-country race for pink slips—whoever gets to Washington, D.C., first, wins; and to prepare for that event they mail their titles to Washington.

That's the plot, but the film is structured around contrasts: life on the road as opposed to the stasis of daily life, the factual attitude of the Chev's occupants as opposed to the fantasies of the character called GTO, serious racing as opposed to fast driving and so on.

The film itself has the stark quality of 1950's type *cinéma vérite*, meaning that it is very realistic, which, in a sense, it is. But overall, it is a fantasy, and has a surrealistic quality, as if the action were taking place in a dream. Speed, speed, speed: the car cruising at 120 mph across the flat Midwest, the sun poised on the horizon as fields of golden wheat flash past on either side.

During a brief stop the Chev's Mechanic tells GTO how he could go faster. GTO says: "I go plenty fast enough."

The Chev's Driver says: "You can never go fast enough."

GTO is a veteran who has just returned from Vietnam—or so it seems, because he is given to lying; he also suffers from paranoia, loneliness and hostility. The problems become acute, and speed, whether literal or metaphorical, can't solve them. "Everything is going too fast and not fast enough. This car doesn't even go fast enough. Everything fell apart on me, my job, my family. Everything." That confession might be the truest thing he says.

At some point the race falls apart, with GTO apparently heading for New York City. In the published version, the Chev sits on a remote air field about to drag a chopped and channeled '32 coupe, just as it might have done fifteen years earlier —the traditional early-model hot rod and the traditional late-model hot rod, caught as if in a time warp.

At this point the film disintegrates in flame, as if to indicate that the era of drag racing, cross-country racing and muscle cars is dead. Washington, which holds the titles to these cars, has sounded the death knell.

CHAPTER FIVE

The Tiger Scores Again
1966

GTO fever spread because of the car and the media hype, and in 1966 a total of 96,946 GTO's were sold—almost a hundred thousand cars. Only two years earlier some people had doubted that there were 5,000 buyers for a car like the GTO. And this was during a bad year, with car sales down by approximately one million units. Pontiac was the only manufacturer to gain in total production, but of the dozen models that showed increased sales, seven were what could be called 'performance' cars; the market was there and growing, thanks to the GTO.

In 1966, the GTO was still the number-one muscle car. It won for the third time the *Car and Driver* Readers' Choice award, and the editor had this to say about the car: ". . . the GTO is one of those rare automobiles that has managed to gain acceptance within all of the little specialized realms of automotive enthusiasts. A great favorite among the drag racing and teen-time drive-in set, the GTO is also respected among mature high-performance buffs because of its dazzling power and above-average handling."

With that kind of praise, and with expectations of high sales, Pontiac allowed the GTO to become a series rather than simply an option to the Tempest and LeMans series. As Pinocchio had become a 'real boy' through a series of trials which developed his character, so too had the GTO become a 'real car.'

In 1966 the GTO, along with the entire Pontiac line, was extensively restyled. The new body was more rounded, with a venturi shape. The front and rear fender lines merged with the belt line which dropped where the door and quarter panel met, like the configuration of a bow tie. This styling motif was repeated at the rear where the fender tips were emphasized by the chrome trim.

Earlier model GTO's had side sheet metal which was fairly flat, a flatness made even more emphatic on the 1965 model because of the stacked quad headlights. The flatness was broken by the horizontal rub strip and the strong ridge which ran along the body from the front bumper to the rear bumper. The new model was only an inch longer but the expanses of sheet metal, unbroken by any interruption, made the car seem much larger. The venturi shape was emphasized by the stripe which followed the belt line and the full-length rocker panel chrome molding with its extensions on the front and rear fenders. Unchanged were the symmetrical front and rear wheel cutouts, which gave aesthetic balance to the car's design and the desired sports car look.

The roof on the hardtop was new, and was set inward from the fenders and dropped sharply. It created a 'faster' profile, with the appearance of a fastback but with good rearward visibility, and the roofline worked well with the kicked-up back fenders. There was more vertical rear window area and, because the roof didn't come down to the trunk lid, there was more trunk space. The roof was impressive from the rear, too, because the large window was flanked by sharp-edged roof supports which tapered into the area on each side of the trunk lid.

The front end again used the quad headlights placed vertically, with the fender extending at the top in a slight hood over the light. The new grille had the bow-tie

Large air intake was built into front bumper. Parking light bolted to grille mesh.

New styling emphasized venturi shape, retained stacked headlights, traditional split grille. Engine and running gear were essentially unchanged.

motif, and the split design gave the car the appearance of being wider. The wire-mesh-pattern grille was recessed, framed by a chrome molding, and painted black. Each grille side had a parking light bolted to it. Because the lights were not integrated into the sheet metal this touch seemed almost an afterthought, but the lights were not unattractive. In the center of the hood was a functional scoop, and in the bumper, set somewhat lower than before and less conspicuously, were the large air intakes.

Interior of a '66 with standard shift, wood-grained dash, console with locking storage compartment.

A 1966 389-ci with tri-power, chrome rocker covers, oil breather cap and stock header-type exhaust manifolds.

At the rear the bow-tie motif was picked up again; that design treatment, repeated front, side and rear, seemed so conscious, yet the back end of the 1966 GTO appeared somehow unplanned. The quarter panels were flat, then turned inward at a right angle, then downward at the same angle to meet the trunk lid; these angles were compounded because the metal also bent downward toward the rear. The trunk lid avoided being smooth and flat because of a final downward angle near the lip. This complex of planes was gathered together and held in place by the bow-tie chrome molding which seemed to have been put there for that purpose. There were so many angles and no way that they could have been rounded off, so the rear end was truncated abruptly and tied together by the chrome molding.

The flat panel which resolved this confusion also held the taillights, which were interestingly different. They were behind six narrow, horizontal louvers, three on each side, and each louver was capped with a thin chrome strip. This treatment was consistent with Pontiac's blacked-out or Frenched-in look. The taillights were the first examples of the narrow, horizontal light that Pontiac would later use on the GTO and the 1968 Firebird.

The suspension, transmission and rear end offerings were unchanged from 1965, the complaints from some quarters regarding the car's lack of handling notwithstanding. One change had been made regarding the brakes: The front drums now featured cooling fins (a feature that had appeared on the Studebaker Hawk ten years before).

The engine and performance options were unchanged, with the exception of an optional induction system. The tri-power setup now had three carburetors of identical size, the Rochester 2GC with $1^{11}/_{16}$-inch throttle bores, rather than the setup with two different sizes; and it was offered with the optional Fresh Air Package. This option, which had become available late in the 1965 model year, directed air into the carburetors. The prototype was designed, built and tested by Royal Pontiac on its 1965 GTO drag car. Royal built a crude sheet metal box around the tri-power unit, and air entered at the cowl, was directed through three flexible hoses into the box where it entered the carburetors. A good example of the factory paying attention to the hot rodders, the idea was picked up by Pontiac and offered as an option. The GTO system used air from the hood scoop, which entered the

New styling emphasized hooded headlights, grille.

From left to right are: optional rally wheel with functional cooling slots revealing red brake drums; optional cast-iron brake drum with integral hub; optional custom wheel disc, anticipating mag-style

Rally II wheels, with functional brake-cooling slots; deluxe wheel disc. Red-line nylon tires were standard; rayon cord whitewalls optional.

Robert McKenzie still owns this 1966 GTO hardtop he bought new. Car has 335-hp engine, four-speed, optional rear window defogger, tinted windows, power steering. McKenzie's GTO is all-original with exception of wheels and tires, which were lost when the car was stolen.

Interior has original upholstery, optional custom sport steering wheel, optional console with locking glovebox, optional rally gauge cluster, optional factory Verba-Phonic speakers. Note GTO emblem, grab bar above glovebox.

Paul Zazarine's 1966 GTO is original to striping on belt line. It has tri-power, two-speed automatic, 3.55:1 Safe-T-Track rear end, AM-FM radio with Verba-Phonic speaker.

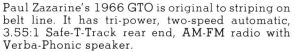

tub surrounding the carburetors. It was not a ram-jet system; it depended upon the temperature, rather than the force, of the entering air to improve performance. Because the incoming air was cooler than the air under the hood by thirty to eighty degrees, it was more dense, and therefore contained more oxygen. Tests showed that the air temperature at the center carburetor after a quarter-mile run was fifty-five degrees cooler than the air around the engine.

The option, which cost only $40.00, consisted of the cover plate that fit over the carburetors, a foam-rubber gasket which sealed the air box (and which allowed the use of the three stock air cleaners within the box) and a special duct to the hood scoop which became functional when a section of the hood was cut away to open the air passage. The complete package included a different camshaft, heavier valve springs and larger carburetor jets. The factory didn't release any horsepower figures to document the need for this package, but one road tester estimated that the Fresh Air Package, alone, was good for ten horsepower, or 2 mph and 0.2 second on a quarter-mile run. It did improve performance greatly and, because it was essentially a bolt-on item, it caught on and was later copied by other manufacturers.

These changes, although modest, allowed the GTO to maintain its superiority on both street and strip. With the larger carburetors and the Fresh Air Package the engine's horsepower had obviously been increased but the factory rating of 360 hp was unchanged. This gave the GTO a distinct advantage when running at sanctioned drag strips which required an official horsepower rating, since most manufacturers gave an inflated figure.

Not all of the nearly 100,000 people who bought the new GTO were interested in drag racing. That may have been true in the beginning, but now many people were purchasing it for many different reasons—racing, cruising, touring or simply for everyday transportation. An advertisement for that year emphasized that the GTO was a dual- or multipurpose vehicle: "The genius of the GTO is that it's the world's greatest compromise." And it was, because it was quick, beautiful and well-optioned. It even got fairly good gas mileage when driven with care. The tri-power setup used only the center carburetor most of the time, and the car would attain speeds up to 100 mph on the single carburetor. For quick acceleration, or speeds over 100 mph, when the gas pedal went past the two-thirds mark, the two auxiliary carburetors cut in with the help of a vacuum servo unit.

The car was a tiger, but it could be a docile one in traffic, and had a great deal of flexibility. There would eventually be faster muscle cars, and while they would beat the GTO on the track it was often difficult to keep them running in traffic. Therefore, the GTO had wide appeal, not just for the youth market at which it was aimed but for businessmen, young marrieds, working women, people in all age groups and from all segments of society.

To make the GTO adaptable to such a diverse group there had to be compromises; and to make it new, there had to be changes, not always for the better.

Jeff Stewart is second owner, car has only 39,000 miles. It has been repainted with lacquer, has aftermarket wheels. Rear end emphasizes 'bow-tie' styling motif.

As a portent of this, John DeLorean had said in 1965: "Our philosophy at Pontiac is this: Each year, our cars have to be significantly better in all important respects —smoothness, quietness, convenience, durability, fuel economy, performance and braking." In 1966 he continued with that traditional theme: "Our new models are a true reflection of Pontiac's policy of continuous and evolutionary progress in automotive design. . . ."

For some reason, whether it had to do with compromise or image, the GM order to ban performance equipment or 'evolutionary progress' in the performance area halfway through the model year came down the line: no more tri-power units. Multicarb setups were okay on the Corvette, but from now on only a single two- or four-barrel carburetor would be allowed on GM cars. Whatever the reason, the ruling was a blow to the people who felt that Pontiac was synonymous with power.

The car was still competitive, even though it was an inch longer and 300 pounds heavier. It could be ordered without insulation or sound deadener, which made it a little noisier in terms of road rumble, and it weighed an honest 3,475 pounds. It was possible to rework the four-barrel carburetor so that it was almost as effective as the tri-power unit, and you could take the car to the drag strip and be competitive.

But with so many people now buying GTO's, it seems likely that many owners were less interested in valve float and advance curves, and more interested in trim options and the GTO image. Pontiac took away the tri-power but expanded the option list. The Rally I wheels were very attractive, a black center surrounded by a stainless steel cap and full trim ring, with exposed chrome acorn lug nuts. This wheel had six cooling slots, and if you bought this optional wheel, the finned front brake drums were painted red so that they could be seen through the wheel's cooling slots. It was a unique touch; personalized, and, to a degree, functional. It looked especially nice with the new red plastic fender liners, which could be cleaned with a garden hose, and the red-line tires. Also available were the new optional head restraints, the optional walnut shift knob, the restyled dash with full instrumentation, the bold body striping and the reclining bucket seat, to mention a few. It's possible that many of the people who bought their GTO's during the second half of the model year didn't even notice that the tri-power option was unavailable.

Was Pontiac already resting on its laurels? Did the public want a car which rested on the reputation earned by the 1964-66½ GTO? Such assertions seemed

New for 1966 were optional red plastic fender liners; very showy with red brake drums, red-line nylon tires.

At Pontiac's home production facilities in Pontiac, Michigan, a 1966 GTO grille is bolted in place while simultaneously another worker puts on the mufflers from the pit below.

to be borne out by two rumors floating around Detroit in late 1966, rumors which at first glance seem to be contradictory. One rumor insisted that Pontiac intended to standardize its V-8 engines by using a 400-ci engine for all Pontiacs—the Bonneville and Grand Prix as well as the Tempest and GTO. The other rumor insisted that Pontiac would bring out an *economy* GTO which would have a low-compression engine, a two-barrel carburetor and a 326-ci V-8 with no more than 250 hp. In a car like that, one could have the status of owning a GTO but with lower payments, lower insurance costs and, no doubt, fewer tickets.

With such rumors given currency by the factory's ban on the tri-power, it looked as though the tiger would soon be overweight, sleepy and toothless.

OWNERS' COMMENTS

My father owned a 1966 GTO. He bought it new and I always loved it. Unfortunately, he sold it and the boy he sold it to totaled it. When I turned sixteen I started looking for one . . . Car's only fault when you really get down on it hard in lower gears, first, second, third, the car fishtails pretty bad, said JS of Sutton, West Virginia.

I bought mine used in August 1978 for $3,000 from the original owner, a sixty-five-year-old man who was retiring from his job . . . I flew out to get the GTO, which was in immaculate condition, and the owner was reluctant to see it go. We took the Goat out to a side road for one last full-throttle blast. 'You know, it sounds just like a tiger when you stomp it to the floor,' he said, as the GTO effortlessly roared up to some 120 mph, much to his delight. TB of Billings, Montana.

The one fault that all GTO's commonly share are the fiber timing chain gears, which are easily replaced with steel gears. Only other problem is finding parts, especially rare options, and the fact that I can't come up with the money to buy every GTO I see! JT, Anna, Ohio.

Faults are brakes, brakes, brakes!!! That and the rust around the rear window! Have you ever seen a '66 that didn't have some rust around there? PZ from Temple Hills, Maryland.

CHAPTER SIX

Royal Pontiac
And The Bobcat

*T*he GTO was conceived in Bloomfield Hills, born in Pontiac and raised in Royal Oak.

What connects these three towns is Woodward Avenue, a natural metaphor, and since the early 1950's the favorite drag strip for Detroit-area street racers. They gathered at Ted's Drive-in, harumped through the parking lot, the big stick loping, stabbing the throttle to clear the carbs. And then, after picking an opponent, the cars hit the lights on Woodward, which had been marked off in quarter-mile sections. Nearby was Willow Run Highway, built during World War II to speed workers from Detroit to the war industries located in Willow Run; and for years that highway lacked a legal speed limit.

The whole layout was a street racer's dream, and in Royal Oak, the middle ground between Bloomfield Hills, where Jim Wangers's ad agency was located, and Pontiac, where the factory was located, was Royal Pontiac, one of the hottest, if not *the* hottest, dealerships in the United States. "In the 1960's," Jim Wangers told me, "you couldn't come to Detroit without stopping at Royal. People traveled from all over the country just to *see* the place—like it was a shrine!"

Royal Pontiac was a flourishing dealership owned by Asa 'Ace' Wilson, Jr. Perhaps it was helpful to have a dealership in close proximity to the Pontiac factory; perhaps it was also helpful to have it in an upper-class area where young people had the money to spend on performance equipment—but it would have been possible to have had a mediocre dealership even with all those advantages. Royal Pontiac flourished because of its emphasis on speed and performance. In addition to selling new Pontiacs it also sold performance parts, and it marketed a Bobcat kit which made Pontiacs into real stormers. Royal took the assembly-line hot car concept, which Pontiac had pioneered, one step further, and during the mid-1960's sold a thousand Bobcat conversions a year.

Royal Pontiac was a new agency in 1959, the transitional year when Pontiac went from pussy-footing to Wide-Tracking. Pontiac was deeply involved in various racing programs, including Daytona Speed Week and NASCAR events, and as sales figures rose it became apparent that there was a correlation between competitive events and the sale of cars. The agency was unexceptional until it got into the performance business, and then it became clearly exceptional.

Some say that Royal Pontiac was the brainchild of Jim Wangers, that he was responsible for its success and perhaps its very existence. Others give credit to Ace Wilson, who, it is said, approached Pontiac with the idea of establishing an agency which would stock and sell over-the-counter a complete line of factory high-performance parts. Pontiac threw the ball back in his court, suggesting that *he* try out his own idea, and thus Royal's racing program was born.

In some ways the success of the agency was due to the aggressive actions of both men, whose vision caused them to see more than profit in the sale of fast cars. It was due also to men like Milt Schornak, Royal's performance service manager, who created the snorting, wheel-spinning machines which were also docile enough to be driven on the street. And there were others involved in the program; men like Dick Jesse and Pete Seaton, who later built their own outstanding drag-racing funny cars.

Ace Wilson realized that the best way to advertise his line of factory speed equipment would be to build a competition car; and so, taking a new 1959 Catalina

Dave Warren of Royal Pontiac installing a Bobcat distributor curve kit.

Status symbols on the street were Royal Pontiac license holders, Royal Bobcat window decals.

hardtop from the showroom floor, he created the first of three Hot Chiefs from Royal. These cars competed successfully throughout the Midwest and in February 1960 they raced at the Winternationals at Daytona Beach. Later that year, at the NHRA Nationals held in Detroit, Hot Chief No. 1, driven by Jim Wangers, won the national S/S class in the Stock Eliminator category.

This win brought national recognition to Royal, and the word spread among Pontiac aficionados that this dealer had a direct pipeline to the factory performance options. The sale of over-the-counter performance parts rose sharply, as did the sale of new Pontiacs. During 1961-62, optional equipment accounted for fifteen percent of the company's total sales.

Royal's next step was to build a performance machine that could be sold to the public on a quasi-assembly-line basis. There were three cars, the brainchildren of Jim Wangers, and they ranged from mild to wild: the Royal GP kit, the Tempest Tiger kit and, the most famous, the Royal Bobcat kit.

The Royal GP was a Grand Prix with a Paxton supercharger and custom trim kit; only one was built. The Tiger kit was adapted to the four-cylinder Tempest; it also involved engine modifications and a trim package. The price was only $75; a small number of Tempest Tigers were built.

400-ci engine with the Bobcat rev kit.

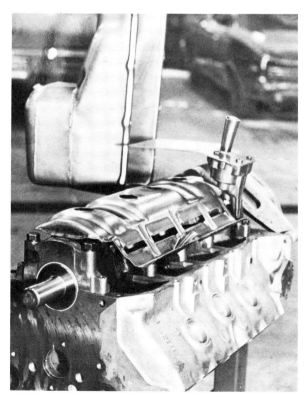

The lower end of a Pontiac 400-ci four-bolt engine showing Royal Pontiac's experimental deepened oil pan, oil baffle and special pickup on the pan and pump.

The big news was the Bobcat kit, which was very popular and anticipated the GTO Bobcat kit. The earlier one, however, included a trim package as well as an engine modification package. In the area below the trunk the word Bobcat appeared. That name was decided upon, Jim Wangers told me, when he went through the trim drawers at Royal and took the letter 'O' from the word Pontiac, took two 'B's' from the word Bonneville and 'CAT' from Catalina. The name gave the Pontiac a special identity; this recognition factor was important, and it would be exploited with the development of the GTO.

Ace Wilson claimed that the options he sold were available to other Pontiac dealers, but that ninety-nine percent of the dealers didn't realize that they were available. He said, "We do give the performance-minded person three things which he had difficulty getting elsewhere—our absolute willingness to stand back of a car, our ability to service a car so that it will run on a drag strip, and our know-how. The important thing is that we know that these Pontiacs are built to run, and we know how to get that performance out of them. By experimenting with these cars, we feel we've learned more about their acceleration abilities than anyone else. We've learned things the factory people don't even know about them."

The purpose of reworking a Pontiac, said Wilson, was to have a good dual-purpose machine. "My theory is that the average individual can buy a stock Pontiac from me, make a few minor modifications, be a consistent winner at the drags and still drive the car to work five days a week."

To 'stand back of a car' implied a warranty, and Royal was willing to give its own warranty on a car which was, no doubt, going to be driven hard.

Jim Wangers said that the success of the Royal racing cars was due primarily to experience and gearing. "I believe that what pays off is our experience in getting just the right combination of engine, transmission, axle, tires and other equipment to fit the situation. Our biggest secret is the wide choice of rear axles that are available. . . ."

It's unclear how Pontiac Motor Division felt about Royal Pontiac. Wilson claimed that he received no factory assistance other than the performance parts which were available to any dealer. Some policy-makers felt that Royal was doing a great job of promoting Pontiacs, and they knew that many people bought a Grand Prix or a Bonneville because of the racing abilities of the Catalinas. Royal Pontiac was a good example of this theory: In 1965 Royal sold 2,507 Pontiacs—that's almost seven cars a day—of which 834 were GTO's.

With the advent of the GTO, Royal Pontiac developed a new Bobcat kit; an outgrowth of the old one, it was the work of Dick Jesse and John Martin. In addition to installing the Bobcat kit in the Royal shop, they began a mail-order business which accelerated faster than a hot GTO. By the late 1960's Royal was receiving over three hundred pieces of mail *a day* regarding this kit and other performance equipment. The mail-order Bobcat kit consisted of:

1) Performance centrifugal advance curve kits
2) Super-thin (0.022) head gaskets
3) Blocked heat-riser gaskets
4) High-performance Champion (J-10) spark plugs
5) Special carburetor jets
6) Hydraulic lifter restrictor kit
7) Gaskets
8) Complete instructions

Bobcat kit for the 400-ci engine.

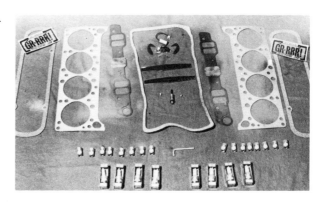

The kit could be installed in only eight hours, and could be done with simple hand tools by anyone with some mechanical ability. The price was around $70; or, if you could get your car to Royal they would, on an appointment basis, make the conversion in their shop for $200. This price included equalizing the combustion chambers and milling the heads. This was really a super tune-up rather than an extensive blueprinting job, and the changes were all legal within the NHRA classifications. The modifications made a difference of about 3-5 mph in the quarter mile.

A comparison was made by *Car Craft* between a stock GTO and one which had the Bobcat kit. These were 1967 models, which meant that they had the 400-ci V-8's with the Quadrajet. In stock form the GTO turned speeds of 98-100 mph, with an elapsed time in the 'low 14's'; the best run was 100.00 mph with a time of 14.11. With the addition of M & H Super Stock tires on the rear the speed was increased to 100.78 mph with a time of 13.72 seconds. The GTO had lots of torque but was not a high-revver, due primarily to the use of hydraulic lifters. In this test, quarter-mile speeds were limited by a lack of rpm due to hydraulic lifter pump-up, which meant that shifts had to be made at approximately 5000 rpm, well below peak horsepower levels. The Bobcat kit was a package with everything contributing to the engine's efficiency. Perhaps most crucial was the valve train work; maximum rpm could be increased by almost a thousand by checking valve lash.

The GTO with the Bobcat kit, running street tires and closed exhausts, turned 105.14 mph with a time of 13.86. With M & H Super Stock tires on the rear it turned 105.63 in 13.32. The removal of the mufflers made a big difference: The speed increased to 107.01 mph and the time dropped to 13.08. Moreover, the engine was now able to rev to almost 6000 rpm, with shifts made at 5800 rpm, an increase of 800 rpm.

The Bobcat kit not only upped the GTO's performance, it was considered a prestige item on the street. Royal included Bobcat decals in the package. A black and white Bobcat decal on your quarter window indicated that you were someone to be reckoned with at the stoplight. The Bobcat kit was so successful, and there was so much demand for Pontiac performance parts, that Royal formed a club, the

George DeLorean, circa 1964.

George DeLorean's $20,000 supercharged GTO "funny car."

Royal Racing Team, in early 1965. For a membership fee of $3.00 one received a membership card, a newsletter, window decals, a jacket patch, the Royal Pontiac catalog and a Royal license-plate frame. One also got less tangible things, like the sense of belonging to a group who felt strongly about the GTO.

In addition to supplying members with access to parts and information, a major aim of the group, reported *Car Craft*, was "to keep the GTO's from being raced on the street. Drive 'em on the street, sure, but only race 'em on the strip, is the idea." It's doubtful that belonging to the club kept anyone from racing on the street, but it did help those who raced to win. Pontiac refused to become involved in competitive events, but Royal served as a surrogate father figure.

The GTO got an incredible amount of magazine coverage, thanks primarily to Jim Wangers, who never missed an opportunity to promote the car. It was tested repeatedly by all the automotive magazines, and almost every car tested had been prepared by Royal Pontiac, including some that had been given the Bobcat treatment.

Roger Huntington recalls Jim Wangers and the road tests they did together: "He [Wangers] promoted it [the GTO]; he used to get magazines to come in and do these tests. I did lots of them, and others did them. And he'd doctor these cars up, and take them—we'd take them—anywhere. There was one drag strip up in Mount Clemens, or we'd take them down to Milan sometimes, or sometimes down to Detroit Dragway. I remember a 421 we tested at Detroit Dragway in the middle of winter—it was touch-and-go whether it'd be snowing that day. He'd get them tested early in the [model] year so that the test would be coming out about February, March or April.

"Yeah, he was a great promoter. He had a gift of gab a mile long. He could make you think the moon was made of green cheese. I tell you, he was good.

"And he didn't miss a trick. This was all off-hours stuff. I can remember being over there on Sundays with him and normally a guy'd do something else, and he's over there at Royal Pontiac and we were talking all day and testing all day, on a Sunday. He loved the car, and this was all stuff that he did on his own.

"They were all doctored. But I never saw a car that wouldn't do what he said it would do. You couldn't buy a GTO that'd do the same thing. The ones that were tested were doctored so that they'd run faster than the ones you could buy."

Perhaps, but Wangers pointed out to me the reason for using 'prepared' cars for testing. He recalled that *Hot Rod* magazine did one of the first road tests, and

Hyman Pontiac's dragging GTO.

Royal Pontiac's drag-racing GTO's.

that GTO's were so rare in those first months that the Los Angeles dealer contacted by *Hot Rod* didn't have a car to lend for a test, but the dealer's wife had just received hers and that was offered. The magazine crew borrowed the car for two days, and in their test report they described the GTO as 'mediocre.'

When Wangers read that test he was furious! He threw the magazine on John DeLorean's desk, saying that he had worked like hell to promote the GTO and because the magazine had used an unprepared car the result was a lousy opinion of an outstanding car. Without a word DeLorean opened his desk drawer and pulled out two forms, which, when presented to the front office, would release two GTO's to Wangers for as long as he might need them. Wangers took the two GTO's to Royal Pontiac and said, "Tune them." When Royal finished 'tuning them' the GTO's would turn the quarter mile at 106 mph, which was a sizable increase over the 92 mph that *Hot Rod* had wrung from its unprepared GTO.

Wangers used those two cars for the next fifteen road tests, then turned them back in to the factory when the 1965 models came out. He then got two new GTO's, which he had Royal 'tune,' and these cars were the ones used for the next series of tests. Each year after that, Wangers added cars to the test fleet until, by 1969, he had nine prepared GTO's.

But, Wangers is quick to point out, he always indicated to those who were testing the cars that these cars had the Royal Bobcat kit, and that that information was always included in the text. There was no attempt to deceive anyone, but rather every effort was made to bring out the GTO's full potential. Besides, anyone who desired a GTO which could perform like the one that had been tested had simply to shell out an extra seventy dollars for the Bobcat kit.

Plenty of people did want that kind of performance and were willing to pay for it. During the mid- and late-1960's Royal Pontiac was a hotbed of activity. Everyone, it seemed, was thirsty for information and the performance equipment that would make a hot GTO even hotter. Membership in the Royal Racing Team increased until, during the years 1967-69, the club could claim over 75,000 members. Orders for Bobcat kits and speed parts grew until Royal had to hire two people to fill and ship orders.

George DeLorean (1981).

A pair of GeeTO Tigers taking off on a quarter-mile run at Motor City Dragway in Detroit. The Royal Pontiac Mystery Tiger is at the wheel of the closest GTO.

71

Royal continued to grow and expand its offerings. It developed a Ram Air kit for the GTO. When the Firebird was put into production Royal aimed its Bobcat kit at that market also. In 1968 Pontiac still had a ruling against the factory installation of engines larger than 400 ci in the intermediate or A-type bodies; but Royal was bound by no such rule and so it began installing the big Pontiac 428-ci V-8 in GTO's. The cost for this engine swap was only $650, exchange, and that *included* a Ram Air package and Bobcat kit for the big engine. A GTO with the 428-ci engine traveled the quarter mile in 13.8 seconds at a speed of 104 mph and this was with all the street equipment.

Pontiac was out of the racing picture, but Royal was actively engaged in competition. It campaigned two GTO drag cars on strips all over the East and Midwest. This was serious racing, but as a promotional gimmick Royal had a driver dressed in a tiger mask and billed as the Mystery Tiger. Wherever the Royal cars appeared other drivers flocked for a chance to compete against the mystery driver.

Royal Pontiac had become synonymous with performance, and to celebrate its role it began to hold an annual open house. This was a gala event, and it attracted hundreds of people. Royal had on display its complete line of mail-order performance parts, and Milt Schornack and the entire Royal crew were on hand to answer questions. There were also amusements, as well as refreshments; and there was no charge!

The GTO was doing extremely well; the entire muscle car phenomenon had grown to become an industry as well as a sport. And business at Royal Pontiac was booming when, in early 1969, the performance side shut down. This is the way that George DeLorean, owner of Leader Automotive in Troy, Michigan, remembers the situation: ". . . it got bigger and bigger and bigger; pretty soon it got to the point where Royal Pontiac was having too much trouble in their service department with the kids, and so in early 1969 Ace called us and he said, 'I want this whole performance thing out, I don't want it anymore . . . so I'm selling it, do you want to buy it?' I says, 'How much?' He says, 'Twenty grand.' I says, 'I'll buy it.' So we bought the whole shop. Originally we got all the guys who were associated with it, like Milt Schornack, Dave and Sid Warren, Brian Dowlish, and, oh, a number of other guys—they all came over. We ran the thing out of our shop. . . . We still do it on a small scale—we primarily build performance engines, but we still do Bobcat kits, too."

Royal Pontiac continued as a dealership for three years until early 1974 when Ace Wilson sold it to devote himself to a long-term land development project north of Detroit. Perhaps Jim Wangers didn't actually create the *reason* for Royal's existence, but it seems too much of a coincidence that the performance side of Royal should have folded at the same time Wangers quit his position at MacManus, John and Adams.

The following is excerpted from a Royal Bobcat catalog.

1. ROYAL BOBCAT ENGINE PACKAGE
   Includes everything necessary to convert your car into a genuine Royal Bobcat. All 4 bbl. or Tri-Power V-8 Engines.
   Includes:
   2-Super Thin Head Gaskets.
   2-Blocked Heat Riser Gaskets.
   Carburetor Jetting Pkg. Distributor Curve Kit including H. D. Mallory Points and Condenser.
   Special Hydraulic Lifter Rev Kit.
   8-Special Range Champion Spark Plugs.
   2-Rocker Cover Gaskets.
   1-Valley Cover Gasket.
   2-Royal Bobcat Emblems.
   Complete and simple installation and service instructions. $65.00, Standard Ignition; $55.00, Transistor Ignition

2. LET US CONVERT YOUR CAR
   into a Royal Bobcat in our special high performance department. Here's your chance to duplicate the street machines described in the magazines. Our experienced and trained mechanics, the same men who conceived the Royal Bobcat, will personally set up your car. In addition to installing all the parts included in the above package, we will *c.c.* and *mill your cylinder heads* and fine-tune the car for ultimate Bobcat performance for both street and strip. Bobcat tune up and installation by appointment only. Allow two full days. Call or write Milt Schornack or Dave Warren at 313-547-6100 for more details. $200.00

3. ROYAL BOBCAT ENGINE PACKAGE FOR OHC-6
   Includes everything needed to convert your car to a genuine Royal Bobcat. 4-bbl. Engines only.
   Includes:
   Special Distributor Advance Curve Kit.
   Carburetor Jetting Package.
   Special Range Spark Plugs.
   Complete and simple installation and service instructions. $34.95 Standard Ignition; $26.95 Transistor Ignition

4. LET US CONVERT YOUR OHC-6
   into a Royal Bobcat in our special high performance department. We will *c.c.* and *mill your cylinder heads* in addition to installing the above mentioned parts and fine-tune the car for ultimate Bobcat performance for both street and strip. Bobcat tune up and installation by appointment only. Allow one full day. Call or write 313-547-6100 for more details. $120.00

5. ROYAL'S "BABY" BOBCAT
   The same as the full Bobcat treatment, except cylinder heads are not removed. Distributor is reworked, carburetors rejetted, heat risers blocked and hydraulic lifter restrictors installed parts and Labor. $120.00

6. SPECIAL PERFORMANCE KIT FOR GTO 400 HO (ALL), TEMPEST 350 HO, FIREBIRD 400 (ALL), FIREBIRD 350 HO
   Designed to eliminate that lazy sound. Includes low restriction chrome air cleaner, distributor advance Curve Kit, rocker arm lock nuts and valve spring shims. $44.95

7. CONVERT YOUR '67 OR '68 FIREBIRD OR GTO TO A '68½ RAM-AIR
   Kit Includes:
   2-Cylinder Head Assemblies
   1-Camshaft
   16-Rocker Arm and Push Rod Packages
   1-Set of Doug 4-Port Headers.
   $525.00

8. RAM-AIR SCOOP (4-bbl.)
   '67 Firebird $100.00
   '67 GTO $85.00
   '68 Firebird and GTO $55.00
   Guaranteed increase in quarter mile times. Use with special jetting package for best performance.

9. AIR SCOOP (Tri-Power)
   N.H.R.A., A.H.R.A. approved. Fits '65 or '66 Tri-Power GTO's only. Specify year. $46.15

10. DOUG'S TUNED 4 PORT HEADERS
    Specially fabricated for All GTO, Tempest and Firebird V-8s. Ideal set-up for street and strip. $135.00
    1968½ Ram-Air . . . . (All) $150.00

11. ROYAL'S SUPER DUTY THIN HEAD GASKETS
    Legal for N.H.R.A. and A.H.R.A. Per Set $9.40

12. SPECIAL BLOCKED HEAT RISER GASKETS
    Keeps heat away from intake manifold. Provides a cooler mixture of fuel and air in cylinders. Per Set $5.90

13. THRUSH STRAIGHT THRU MUFFLERS
    Healthy deep tone—Legal for street in most states. Each. $12.95

14. SPECIALLY FITTED '66 GTO TAIL-PIPES
    Get rid of that ugly hanging resonator. Perfectly cut in straight line, complete with chrome extension. Easy to install. Improve performance and recapture that "healthy" GTO sound. '66 GTO only. $8.95

15. SPECIAL PERFORMANCE CENTRIFUGAL ADVANCE CURVE KITS FOR ALL PONTIAC V-8 DISTRIBUTORS
    Includes points and condenser, distributor weights and springs, and advance stop designed for your particular car. Complete with instructions. $12.00

16. SEND US YOUR DISTRIBUTOR
    Let us tailor the exact curve for your performance needs. Specify type of engine, transmission, rear end ratio and how you use your car. Parts & Labor included. $24.50

17. DISTRIBUTOR KIT FOR TRANSISTORIZED IGNITION SYSTEM
    Weights, springs and advance stop. $5.00

18. MALLORY DOUBLE LIFE DISTRIBUTOR
    Comes with the correct advance curve for your car. Complete with H. D. dual points, condenser and cap. State year & engine. $49.95

19. THE FINEST IGNITION PARTS MADE BY MALLORY
    H. D. Points . . . . Per Set $5.50
    H. D. Condenser $1.50
    H. D. Coil $17.00

20. HI-PERFORMANCE IGNITION WIRE SETS
    A do-it-yourself kit includes 20 ft. of stainless steel silicone wire (orange color) that will withstand engine heat and deliver high voltage.
    8-Rajah Clips 8-Spark Plug Boots $25.00

21. CHAMPION SPARK PLUGS
    UJ-10-Y (V-8 only)
    UJ-12-Y (V-8 only)
    UN-10-Y (6 Cyl. only)
    UN-12-Y (6 Cyl. only) $1.00
    Special Racing Plugs:
    J-63-Y J-61-Y $1.75

22. ENGINE SAFETY CONTROL
    Shuts off engine at a pre-determined RPM. Prevent dangerous overwinding. $35.00

23. HYDRAULIC LIFTER REV KIT
    Allows you to rev your engine to maximum RPM. Kit includes special lock nuts and instructions. $14.95

24. 4 BBL. CARBURETOR ENGINE JET KIT
    Needle and seats, metering rods and jets. Reworked accelerator pump. Specially calibrated for Q-Jet or AFB. State year and carburetor make. $12.50

25. CARBURETOR JET KIT (Tri-Power)
    Includes special needle and seat assembly. Specially calibrated jets for normal air intake or for engines using air scoops. State cubic inch of engine. $12.50

26. ELECTRIC FUEL PUMP
    A real must for the strip. We recommend using two in series. Prevent vapor lock. If you use your car on the strip, whether it's an all out race car or a Sunday C-Stocker this is an absolute must to stop the fuel from boiling in the gas line. $38.95

27. HIGH OUTPUT OIL PUMP KIT
    Increases pressure and engine life (80 LB. P.S.I.) $8.75

28. HURST LINE/LOC
    A new development by the famous performance leaders. An absolute necessity for drag racing. Automatic finger tip controlled brake lock, prevents rolling into the lights while holding maximum engine RPM's on the starting line. Mounts on shift lever for easy use. $34.95

29. ROYAL'S SPECIAL WEIGHT TRANSFER PACKAGE
    Here's the tried and true formula that will let you "come out of the hole" at 5000 RPM's with M & H tires. Includes 90/10 front shocks, special ball joint spacers for front coil

springs and rear Air Lifts and hoses. Also included are detailed instructions for complete disassembly of front suspension and installation and set-up procedures for above items. Legal for the strip. $100.00

30. M & H "RIPPLE WALL" DRAG STRIP TIRES
8:00-8:50 x 14 or 9:00-9:50 x 14. Specially developed by the M & H Tire Company for Royal Pontiac. Absolute increase in traction GUARANTEED. Specify engine, transmission and rear axle ratio when ordering. Pair $90.00 (8:00-8:50x14); $95.00 (9:00-9:50x14)

31. AIR LIFTS FOR DRAG RACING
Fits inside of rear coil springs. Helps stabilize rear end. A must for transferring weight. Specify make and year. Not available for Firebird. $34.95

32. CURE RIDE SHOCKS
Especially calibrated to our specifications. Each $18.95; Pair $38.95

33. LAKEWOOD TRACTION BARS
The ideal set-up for traction on Firebirds only. No welding necessary. Easy to install. Per Set $69.95

34. HURST K. P. O. SHIFTER KITS
'64-'66 GTO, '67-'68 GTO $18.50
'67 Firebird Competition Plus shifter assembly. $69.95

35. SCHIEFER CLUTCH PARTS
Improve acceleration on both street and strip.
Aluminum Flywheel $79.95
Rev-Lok Pressure Plate $74.95
Clutch Disc $28.00

36. LAKEWOOD CLUTCH HOUSING
When it comes to safety you need the very best. Stronger precision machined and lighter. Approved by all safety Associations. $99.95

37. GEARS—GTO-TEMPEST-FIREBIRD (All)
Ring and pinion. 3:08-4:33 $70.00

38. GEARS—PONTIAC (1965-69)
Ring and pinion. 3:08-4:33 $70.00

39. GEARS—PONTIAC (1958-64)
Ring and pinion. 3:08-4:10 $70.00

40. TURBO HYDRAMATIC "BEEF-UP" KIT
Firmer and higher positive shifts, automatic or manual control. Includes all parts and gaskets necessary with complete instructions. $39.95

41. OFFSET CAM KEY
Advance or retard cam timing. Retarding must for '64 GTO's. Advancing a must for '68½ Ram-Air's, for best performance. Includes all necessary gaskets and installation instructions. 4° $4.50; 6° $6.50

42. CAMSHAFTS
A complete line of factory cams including the old Super Duty McKellar solid lifter to the great new '68½ Hydraulic Ram-Air. For advice on the best cam for your particular use, send a self-addressed, stamped envelope giving full specs on your car and how you intend to use it. Prices Vary

43. RAM-AIR VALVE SPRINGS
'65-'66 and Early '67's $40.00
'67½-'68½ $38.00

44. FLEX FAN BLADES
Draw less horsepower at high RPM. Fits all models. $24.95

45. REVERSE SUPER-DUTY STARTER HOUSING $24.95

46. SUPER-DUTY STEEL RODS
Here is the answer for reliability for blueprinted engines where RPM's are in excess of 6000. approx. $12.00 each

47. ROCKER COVER GASKETS Each $1.45

48. VALLEY COVER GASKETS Each $.70

49. ADDITIONAL ROYAL RACING TEAM DECALS $.50

50. GTO CUFF LINKS
6.5 litre GTO emblem set smartly in plain silver background. A must for every GTO owner. $3.95

51. GTO TIE BAR
6.5 litre GTO emblem neatly and smartly adorning your tie. $2.95

52. SET OF GTO CUFF LINKS AND TIE BAR $6.00

CHAPTER SEVEN

An Idea On Wheels
1967

*T*he GTO was presented as The Great One and The Ultimate Tiger, and the supercar image that the GTO had pioneered remained as strong as ever for 1967. *Car Life* raved: "King of the Supercars! Pontiac's Ram Air GTO can lay claim to this title on several counts. If this accolade infers this is the first car to be produced among currently popular Supercars, GTO qualifies. If it means the most performance per dollar, GTO it is. If it signifies the quickest through the quarter, as purchased, the GTO is certainly among the front-runners. If styling, both interior and exterior, is an important criterion, GTO is a winner. By anyone's Supercar yardstick, the GTO is the standard of the U.S."

That stance of pure muscle was still struck in the factory advertisements, but it was more subdued. Early GTO advertisements had emphasized performance; speed sold cars, and so the factory brochure said, quite honestly, that the GTO could break traction in all gears. As if traction loss were a virtue, GTO ads often showed a color photograph of a spinning rear tire, close-up, clouds of billowing blue-white smoke buffeting against the fender well. This was a remarkable basis on which to sell a car, and it worked! In three short years, however, times had changed.

The 1967 GTO would burn rubber like crazy, even when equipped with Firestone F70x14 Wide Oval tires, but the factory, perhaps anticipating, perhaps even fearing, federal legislation, wanted to emphasize safety. The Idea on Wheels, the *concept* that was the GTO, had taken a different turn. One indication of this change was the factory's ban on the tri-power manifold mid-way through the previous year. Another indication was John DeLorean's announcement that the new GTO would be a safer car: "By extensively following Pontiac's continuous policy of making safety our major objective in the design, manufacture and testing of our cars, Pontiac again this year meets the highest standards in the automotive industry."

New safety features included an energy-absorbing steering column, a dual braking system (standard on all 1967 cars), a four-way warning flasher, a lane-changer signal and "an inside rear-view non-glare tilting mirror" (similar to the one Pontiac had offered in the early 1950's). Optional safety equipment included front seat shoulder straps, seat belt retractors, a safeguard speedometer which set off a buzzer when the speed limit was exceeded, cornering lights and a fire extinguisher.

A desirable safety feature was the new optional power-assisted front-wheel disc brake system. Finally the car with go had been given sufficient stopping power; the brakes worked smoothly and without fade. Power assist was increased by enlarging the diaphragm diameter from eight inches to nine-and-a-half inches. This unit worked in conjunction with a single-unit master cylinder that contained two master cylinder pistons in tandem; one cylinder piston operated the front brakes, the other the rear brakes. *Car Life* said ". . . front-to-rear proportioning of this system was nearly perfect. Deceleration rates of 29 ft./sec^2 were obtained time after time, with rear wheel lockup easily avoided without extreme care in brake application. The small amount of lockup that was encountered caused no loss of directional control, and occurred only at low speeds. Pontiac is to be commended for an exceptionally fine braking system. Perhaps Pontiac and the remainder of Detroit manufacturers will see fit to match such performance in other models." With the introduction of optional front disc brakes, Pontiac canceled metallic brake linings and aluminum front brake drums as production options. A new fourteen-inch wheel, specifically designed for use with disc brakes, was introduced.

Roof 'fins' extended back to trunk lid.

1967 GTO hardtop with optional wire wheel covers and vinyl top. GTO emblem has been lowered, bolted to wide rocker panel chrome.

Exterior styling changes were limited. The bow-tie look had been retained, but was deemphasized at the rear by the removal of the chrome trim. The outline now was essentially rectangular, with eight narrow taillights, four on each side. Without the trim, and with the various planes made smoother, the rear end was less truncated and better integrated. At the front the waffle-grille insert which had been painted black was now a polished aluminum wire mesh. The narrow rocker molding of the previous year had become a seven-inch-wide swath of stainless steel which ran the full length of the car with chrome extensions on the lower edges of front and rear fenders. This wide molding covered the lower part of the door, serving as a rock shield and kept the paint in that area from becoming pitted. Nineteen sixty-seven was the only year that this much bright trim was used on a GTO. Also new were the optional Rally II wheels.

Perhaps the most remarkable thing the casual observer noticed about the new GTO was the tachometer which was mounted on the hood! This was a new

Main styling change was to rear end where bow-tie shape was eliminated, eight taillights 'Frenched' into flat area. Roofline offered low profile, large rear glass for excellent visibility.

In this side view Gordy Cowan's GTO shows hood-mounted tach.

dealer-installed option, and while most 1967 GTO's had the tachometer mounted in the dash, enough examples appeared with the hood-mounted tach to start a trend. The hood-mounted tach was a functional instrument as well as an effective sales ploy. It indicated engine speed and shifting points, had a fairly large face for readability and, because it was mounted directly in front of the driver, he did not need to take his eyes from the road.

There were a couple of problems with the tach, although no one mentioned them then: Moisture would condense on the inside of the glass, making it impossible for the driver to read the calibrations. Second, a tachometer is a delicate instrument, and a hood-mounted tachometer is subjected to sharp blows when the hood is closed. Practical considerations aside, the hood-mounted tach, although slow to sell as an option at first, soon caught on and became a status symbol for the Woodward-Avenue-type cruiser.

Turning up that tachometer was a bigger engine. The 389-ci V-8 had been bored to 400 ci (which gave substance to the rumor of the previous year that Pontiac would standardize its engines, but now the 421-ci had also been enlarged, to 428 ci). The standard engine was the 335-hp 400-ci V-8 with Quadrajet carburetor; optional engines were the 255-hp 400-ci V-8, the 360-hp 400-ci V-8 and the 360-hp HO 400-ci V-8. The variations had to do with carburetion, camshaft grinds and compression ratios. The 255-hp engine was equipped with a two-barrel carburetor, low-compression ratio and a 269/277-degree camshaft. The 335-hp engine came

Custom wheel disc was optional, gave appearance of mag wheel. Had chrome-plated stainless steel; three-prong spinner had black inset with red PMD.

Rally I wheel with cooling slots. Rally II wheel was stamped steel, had mag-wheel look.

Sleek new 1967 GTO convertible.

with the four-barrel carburetor, and used a 273/283-degree cam with the automatic transmission and the 273/289-degree cam with the manual transmission.

The 360-hp HO engine used the old tri-power cam, which was 288/302-degree grind. The new 360-hp Ram Air engine used a 288/302-degree cam with the automatic transmission combination it was designed for. Another example of differentiation in the interest of performance was the HO engine; it came with a special air cleaner and special low-restriction exhaust manifolds having individual streamlined runners. All the GTO engines had a new oil pump assembly with a three-quarter-inch oil inlet pipe (to replace the five-eighth-inch tube). This change helped to reduce the partial vacuum that occurred when aerated oil expanded; and it assured a solid flow of oil to the engine at high speeds.

If there was a movement within the factory toward standardization of engines and parts, there was still concern that those engines perform correctly, as evidenced by the number of different cam grinds available. Malcolm McKellar was busy! While none of these grinds can be considered wild, each was suited to the engine and transmission combination for which it was designed.

The heads on the 1967 engines had been greatly changed. The new heads had larger ports, screw-in rocker-arm studs and stamped steel pushrod guides. Because of this arrangement, the valve spacing and valve angle had been altered. The valve spacing was changed from 1.82 inches to 1.98 inches, and the angle moved from a twenty-degree inclination to a fourteen-degree inclination. This

Dashboard of Gordie Rognrud's 1967 GTO with automatic transmission console.

Hood was flat; low air scoop was functional on Ram-Air engines. And the mesh in 1967 grille differed from that used the previous year.

moved the centerline of the valves to a position directly over the center of the combustion chamber.

The 1967 GTO came equipped with a new four-barrel carburetor called the Quadrajet. This was a big Rochester carb with an airflow capacity of 700 cfm (the old Carter four-barrel had an airflow capacity of 500 cfm), and while some mourned the factory ban on the tri-power, others felt that the Quadrajet could be reworked until it would be as effective as the tri-power. For those who were willing to switch parts, the 1967 heads would fit the earlier 389-ci engines and the pre-1967 tri-power units would fit the 1967 engines.

What had been called the Fresh Air Package was now called the Ram Air option, to be known later on the street as Ram Air I. The Ram Air engine had a longer-duration camshaft with stronger valve springs, and was assembled at the factory, while the tub around the carburetor and the hood scoop were bolted on by the dealer. The Ram Air engine also came with heavy-duty axles and axle housings (something which could be special-ordered with other engines).

Although the new engine had more cubic inches, a high compression (10.75: 1), different heads and cam, the factory rated it, as before, at 360 hp. Knowledgeable people estimated that the Ram Air option gave a ten-horsepower increase, but the factory continued to underrate the engine's horsepower which gave the GTO a decided advantage in competition.

New optional front disc brakes, available with power assist.

Pontiac 400-ci V-8 crankshaft was forged steel, had three-inch mains.

Pontiac 400-ci engine with valve covers, intake manifold removed.

And the new GTO did run! *Car Life* tested a GTO with the Ram Air engine and ran it through the quarter mile at a speed of 102.8 mph with a time of 13.9 seconds, even though the driver experienced "audible valve float" at 5600 rpm. The test car was equipped with the new Turbo Hydra-matic three-speed transmission, which was seen as a big improvement over the two-speed, a transmission which dated from the early Tempest. Actually, DeLorean and Estes had wanted the three-speed transmission for the 1964 GTO; but their efforts were thwarted by company officials who felt that the A-bodied compact 'image' called for a two-speed automatic. With this new transmission the test driver described the acceleration run this way: "The Ram Air GTO provided a level of acceleration beyond belief to anyone not accustomed to Supercars."

Having the new transmission was like finding the missing link. For some reason many of the GTO's previously tested had the two-speed automatic, and although there had not been complaints about the transmission itself it's clear that the four-speed manual transmission allowed the GTO to perform to capacity while the two-speed automatic did not. With the three-speed automatic the GTO had more flexibility. *Motor Trend* tested two 1967 GTO's to compare transmissions.

J. L. Whitehurst's '67 convertible.

Pontiac 400-ci V-8 engine.

Both cars had 400-ci 360-hp engines; both had the Bobcat treatment (and were equipped with the first two sets of Hurst headers); both ran 8.50x14 M & H Super Stock tires on the rear. The two GTO's were identical in every respect except that one had a four-speed manual transmission and the other had a three-speed Turbo Hydra-matic.

The writer praised the automatic and the new dual-gate shift quadrant. "In its conventional pattern, each gear can be held as long as desired and then the stick can be moved forward or backward without anything happening until the governor says OK. This is the way it's always been on many cars, but the Hurst version has a second slot with built-in detents that allow the shifter to move only one gear at a time. Slight pressure on the stick while moving it forward locks it into the next higher gear. There's no chance of skipping a gear or going all the way into neutral at full rpm—which can be a costly mistake."

When *Motor Trend* compared the two cars, the four-speed-equipped machine ran 0-60 mph in 4.9 seconds—"one of the fastest 0-60 mph times we've ever seen. . . ."—and it ran the quarter mile in 13.10 seconds with a speed of 106 mph. The car with the automatic ran the quarter mile in 13.40 seconds with a speed of 105 mph, and made one run with an elapsed time of 13.36 and a speed of 106-mph-flat. While top-end speeds were similar in both cars, the manual transmission offered a definite advantage at the start. The four-speed could jump off the line because the driver could rev the engine to 5200 rpm and pop the clutch; the driver of the three-speed automatic had to hold his engine speed down to 1200 rpm to avoid stalling.

Car Life brought up an interesting point not mentioned elsewhere: "With regard to [valve] float speed, it should be reported that the Ram Air GTO is somewhat unusual among domestic automobiles in that top speed in high gear must be approached with great caution. The 107 mph top speed, grossly illegal in almost every state, is not only potentially dangerous to occupants, but severe damage to the engine is likely to result. The Ram Air GTO carries a 4.33:1 axle ratio as standard equipment. This ratio enables the engine to easily exceed valve float speed in high gear—in a very brief elapsed time. Most passenger cars are geared in such a way that they cannot exceed float speed in high gear without a very long sus-

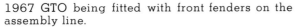
1967 GTO being fitted with front fenders on the assembly line.

tained speed run, if at all. Not so with the Ram Air GTO. Exceeding 5600 rpm in high gear was not difficult and, with the high gear acceleration potential of this automobile, drivers were able to run up to this speed without being conscious of having reached such velocity. A close watch on the tachometer definitely was in order to prevent engine damage."

Car Life loved the GTO, but decided that it was not really a family car: it "surged, loped, and generally ran miserably at part throttle up to 60 mph [3000 rpm]," it overheated in traffic and with the 4.33:1 rear end there was an undue amount of engine noise at 70 mph (3500 rpm).

The writer mentioned that he did *not* experience that old bugaboo, wheel hop, but the author of a test published in *Car and Driver* did. "Our only complaint in the suspension department arose from severe wheel hop encountered during hard braking from over 80 mph. The car stops in a hurry, but the shaking and sudden noise scared the hell out of us. We were particularly surprised in view of the seemingly adequate number and strength of the links locating the coil-sprung rear axle; the severity of the judder caused us to check under the car to assure ourselves that Pontiac hadn't gone back to leaf springs on the GTO. . . ." This same problem was encountered on the new Firebird, which *did* have leaf springs; the following year the Firebird's rear axle assembly was redesigned with staggered shock absorbers, which helped greatly, although this arrangement was never used on the GTO.

In general, *Car and Driver* was enthusiastic about the 1967 GTO. "Other manufacturers have built Super Cars with more brute acceleration, but when it comes to building a fully integrated package that combines ride, comfort, handling, style and performance—all at a bearable price—the GTO is very tough to beat. . . ."

David Noto's clean GTO is all-original, has Rally II wheels.

Compare the GTO rear end with this of a 1967 LeMans.

OWNERS' COMMENTS

I like the size of the car. Not too big and not too small. It has plenty of room inside. And it has a large trunk. Underhood serviceability is good, also. My car has factory air in it and it really isn't that hard to work on. If I were to complain about a GTO, I would have to say that brakes are the only thing that aren't up to par. . . . I also owned a '69 GTO with drum brakes and no power assist. It didn't stop very good from high speeds. GC from Sharon, Pennsylvania.

I feel the GTO has two qualities I find attractive: one is speed, and the second is that it's a nice heavy-handling car. The only fault . . . is it's too much of a gas hog to really enjoy. I've had my car five years and the last two years have been very rough on the pocket book, said DN, Glendale Heights, Illinois.

I can't seem to pin-point any particular option that could be called the GTO's best single feature. I believe it is a combination of many things, and the feeling you get when you sit behind the wheel of a Goat. You just can't get that feeling out of the plastic cars they are building today. JB, Jr., of Elyria, Ohio.

Jeff Denison drove his 1967 GTO convertible from Michigan to massive gathering of muscle cars at 1980 Street Machine Nationals. Car has only 29,000 miles; changes include 1972 exhaust splitters, Cragar SS mag wheels.

Engine in Denison's GTO has 1966 tri-power setup with rare Ram Air tub.

CHAPTER EIGHT

GTO Advertising

*T*he GTO was, without a doubt, one of the best-promoted cars of all time. Its image was established immediately, and this basic image of the GTO as a tire-spinning performance car, a tiger on the street, was developed year by year. The GTO songs, shoes, socks, contests and sundry spin-offs helped to reinforce the car's image and to sell the product, but conventional advertising in the popular automotive magazines was the most effective means of telling the world about the GTO. Or perhaps it should be called unconventional advertising, because the ad campaign was the responsibility of Jim Wangers—and his approach to promoting the car on the printed page was, as elsewhere, arrestingly unconventional.

In 1970, Pontiac's advertising agency, MacManus, John and Adams, released the results of a survey that it had taken five years before to show the profile of the 'typical' GTO owner. The agency found that the person who bought a GTO differed from the average car buyer in many ways: The typical GTO owner was young, often single, often lived with his or her parents, had more education, had a better income and probably owned another car. Here are the results of the survey:

	1965 GTO Buyers	All 1965 New-Car Buyers
Median age	25.6 years	43.0 years
Not married	43%	(NA)
Living with parents	30%	6%
Attended college	60%	46%
Median household income	$11,100	$10,450
Multiple-car households	74%	49%

Like many surveys, this one, taken in retrospect, told the advertising agency what it probably already knew. The agency's Pontiac ads had aimed at the younger car buyers, had emphasized speed and performance and through literate copy had made an appeal to educated people. To reach the audience described in the survey, for the past eight years Pontiac had advertised in the youth market publications, which included magazines like *Hot Rod* and *Car Craft* as well as general-market automotive publications like *Motor Trend* and *Car and Driver*. This survey report claimed that Pontiac was "the first new car advertiser to make consistent use of the medium [magazines] with a planned campaign and ads tailored specifically to the audiences of these magazines."

The advertising situation, and Pontiac's image, were quite different in 1959. Although Pontiac had been working for three years to build a car which would appeal to young people, it had advertised the car in a way that John DeLorean described as "at best, nondescript." He had developed the new Pontiac and had named its stance the Wide Track, a term which he felt would be a good basis around which to center an advertising campaign. The advertising agency opposed the idea, and DeLorean won out only because Bunkie Knudsen insisted that the term be used as the central theme of that year's campaign. To use a quotable phrase which summed up the new Pontiac, it was extremely successful; and the term Wide-Track was used in Pontiac advertising for the next dozen years.

About this time Jim Wangers entered the picture. As the executive in charge of the Pontiac account at MacManus, John and Adams, Wangers fit in beautifully with Estes, DeLorean and the new Pontiac: He was young, creative and so interested in product performance that on weekends he was drag racing one of the Royal Pontiac Catalinas. Moreover, he was an artist, independent, somewhat arrogant, able to put ideas into words, eager to anticipate rather than to play follow-the-leader. Pontiac in the early 1960's was the perfect place for a person like Jim Wangers.

His ability to write captivating ads for Pontiac developed with the evolution of the car. All of the early Tempest ads were done in black and white. In some the emphasis was on hip language and obscure literary allusions, with the car in the background, often used as simply a prop. Those ads have an odd quality, and certainly lack the dynamic selling power of later ads. More interesting are the ads that emphasize performance. In one a Tempest drives through standing water; the caption reads: "Nothing like a quiet Sunday drive to soothe the nerves." This ad placed less emphasis on speed, and more on the *fun* of driving, a theme that Pontiac would pick up again in 1970.

A third type of ad is remarkable because it doesn't show the car; a friend calls this advertising approach "selling the sizzle without showing the steak." Perhaps the most amazing ad of this type is a black-and-white photo of a speeding 421 emblem. No car is shown, but the streaks on the emblem suggest speed, as does the caption: "Hands off the grab bar, Charlie, you're tearing out the dash!" The text, which is pure poetry, reveals how that situation could arise.

Those Tempest ads seem like a warmup for the GTO ads, and, indeed, the technique of not showing the car foreshadows the famous GTO ads where neither the names GTO nor Pontiac is mentioned.

Two of the earliest GTO ads struck another new note. The space was divided so that a sequence of uncaptioned photographs could reveal details of the new car. A December 1963 ad showed photos of the Hurst floor shifter, the exhaust

Illustration from a U.S. Royal Tiger Paw tire ad. Caption read "What happened when we popped the clutch at 2400 rpm's." Car was a GTO.

splitters, the carburetor, the GTO identification plate and so on. Another was divided into four equal frames and captured a sense of movement through the details: the car being shifted, the rear wheel spinning, the steering wheel being turned and the GTO rounding a corner at high speed. This kind of advertisement was straightforward, effective, objective and gave the reader a great deal of information about a car which he had probably not seen.

At that time, the factory wanted to limit GTO production to 5,000 units, and if those who wanted to push the car hoped to up that number they had to **G**et **T**hose **O**rders! These ads informed the public about the car, and they did it without being cute or resorting to hucksterism. The second ad not only informed the reader but involved him in a kinetic response to the copy. It managed to create the illusion of motion, and the longer one studies that ad the more that sense of motion is reinforced.

Another interesting angle seen in the early GTO ads and the sales literature involves reverse psychology; in a 1964 ad, the reader is told that he probably doesn't want a GTO and probably wouldn't be able to handle one anyway. "To be perfectly honest, the GTO is not everyone's cup of tea. . . . Its dual exhausts won't win any prizes for whispering. And, unless you order it with our lazy 3.08 low-ratio rear axle, its gas economy won't be anything to write home about."

Jim Wangers wrote those ads, and I asked him whether he really believed that a negative approach worked. "I wouldn't call it negative," he said. "Perhaps arrogant. If I take your cup of coffee away, tell you you can't have it, you want it all the more. That's what I was doing in those ads. And of course what I said was true—the GTO wasn't for everybody. I saw people who were *intimidated* by the GTO. Too fast. They were fearful of it—and they'd buy a Catalina, or a plain Tempest. *That* was the car for them."

One of my favorite GTO ads, which doesn't fit into any of the above categories, shows a 1964 GTO headed down the road at the camera, with the caption: "I wouldn't stand in the middle of the page if I were you . . . It's a Pontiac GTO!" The text picks up that idea: "If you insist on reading at a time like this—that's a 6.5 litre Gran Turismo Omologato aimed right at you." After the description of the car's equipment and options, the text ends: "Quick, get off the page!"

During the strike at General Motors at the beginning of 1965 all advertising was curtailed because the companies had no cars to sell, but when that strike ended there was an abundance of money to be spent on advertising. Wangers needed a central theme to build the campaign around, and he decided to develop the tiger image that had been used somewhat during the previous two years. During a five-week period after the strike had ended, Pontiac advertised extensively in newspapers all over the United States; the ads centered on the GTO and its tigerish qualities. In March Wangers began a new phase of the campaign by placing four-color full-page advertisements in many of the popular automotive magazines. These were eye-catching and colorful ads, especially in contrast to the black-and-

Postcard announcing the 1965 GTO emphasized the tiger motif.

white ads used by many other companies (compare them with, say, the ads promoting Oldsmobiles of the same year); other manufacturers didn't really catch up with the Pontiac full-color ads until around 1967-68.

There was, for example, the two-page layout with twelve panels on each page showing in color such details as the front disc brake, the various transmissions, the Ram Air option and so on. Or there was the full-color ad showing a Tempest hardtop and a GTO convertible parked in the desert; a beautiful woman is between them, a hand on each car's hood, and at her feet is a *live* tiger.

In addition to the use of color, the ads use copy which is close to poetry. A 1964 ad shows an empty garage and has the caption: "There's a tiger loose in the streets," indicating that the garage is empty because the car is presently being driven. To *not* show the car in a car ad is pretty remarkable; to substitute poetry for technical information is even more remarkable, and that copy is worth quoting at length:

"It's late and your bedroom window is open. It's so quiet you can hear the frogs croaking out by the crossroads a good quarter mile away.

"After a while a big-engined Something rumbles by in the night. It checks for a moment at the lights, then swings out onto the highway.

"Suddenly, a rising moan overrides the rumble as a bunch of extra throats get kicked wide open and start vacuuming air by the cubic acre. The moan gets drowned out in its turn by a booming exhaust note that someone ought to bottle and sell as pure essence of Car.

"Three times the sound peaks, falls back, peaks again. The last shift into fourth, a throttling back to cruising speed, a dwindling grumble of thunder, and . . . gone. The frogs take up again where they left off."

Another ad of the same time, for a Pontiac 2+2 actually, is extremely clever and uses language effectively: "A flying machine for people who can't stand heights . . . It's what you might call a sudden automobile. Meaning that if you had started accelerating when this sentence began, you would now be feeling enormous pressure on your abdomen."

In addition to the color advertisements in magazines, in 1966 Pontiac marketed a set of five full-color action photographs, 26" x 12", which sold for twenty-five cents. The factory received over 100,000 requests for the photographs before the offer was terminated, which indicated the popularity of the car and the effectiveness of the advertisements.

Ad for 1969 GTO confronted FTC ruling against ads which relied on speed. Car was static, but low-angle photography emphasized sleek lines, and text cited GTO's achievements without mentioning speed or racing.

Others have caught on.
But they haven't caught up.

The Great One by Pontiac

In 1967 the Federal Trade Commission advised the automobile manufacturers and their advertising agencies that magazine and newspaper ads emphasizing high-performance abilities were taboo. This hurt Pontiac because high-performance was what it had been emphasizing for the past ten years—its performance image had got Pontiac into third place in sales and kept it there. Now Pontiac could only advertise Wide-Tracking.

But Wangers, always thinking, figured out ways to confront or circumvent the ruling: He simply showed the GTO at rest—no more spinning tires! And he advertised on radio; or had a spin-off product do the advertising; or, finally, he simply *did not name* the car being advertised!

A good example of the first kind of ad was one in 1969 which bore the caption: "We'd like to put in a good word for hoods." The photo shows five young men standing in the shadows, and although they are well-dressed the suggestion is that they are 'hoods.' The light falls full on three Pontiacs, and this clarity emphasizes the menacing quality of the young men. The text does not mention speed or performance, but uses 'toughness' as a metaphor. "Why not? We've got the toughest looking hood in the business. Take that sweep of metal on the '69 Pontiac Grand Prix. You won't find a longer stretch from Sing Sing to Alcatraz.

"The two bulges on the Firebird 400 and GTO are pretty unsubtle, too. . . . Now, you can order a tach for each of these hoods. And they'll look tougher. But let's face it. No hood's complete without a persuader."

Wangers advertised on the radio through such spin-off products as the Thom McAn shoe, and in those ads he could discuss speed and handling, even though the copy seemed a parody of the GTO copy. This is, after all, an ad for a pair of shoes! "It's like taking a trip right through the hills on fast turning wheels that give your blood chills. And as long as you both got to stay on earth, there's nothing like Wide-Tracking!"

And finally, Wangers created ads which did not name the car. To not name the product in an expensive ad seems even more remarkable than to not show the product, but Pontiac's image was clearly established, and this was especially true of the GTO. All Wangers had to do was to cite The Great One.

An example of this was a beautiful two-page, full-color ad which showed four GTO's, from 1964 to 1967, in the background, and a 1968 GTO in the foreground. The caption read: "There's only one Great One. We've been proving it for five years." The name Pontiac was mentioned in miniscule type, but everyone *knew* that those were GTO's!

The most notable ad of this kind—perhaps the most notable of all GTO ads, because of the way it silently summed up the GTO—showed, in a two-page full-color layout, a GTO up close at a median crossing. No other cars were in sight, and the GTO was not moving. Nowhere on the page was the name Pontiac or GTO mentioned; the only copy on the entire two pages were, at the bottom of one page, "The Great One." Higher up on the same page one noticed a road sign: "Woodward Avenue." The ad was like a poem; the reader had to assemble the pieces, and to understand the implications and allusions. It assumed that people all over knew about Woodward Avenue, the street where the GTO proved its mettle in innumerable races. Performance was *not* mentioned, but the allusion to Woodward Avenue conjured up more street racing imagery than a page of text could describe—if it were legal for an ad writer to describe such things.

The tiger theme, which Pontiac used in its massive advertising campaign of 1965, is the most recognizable theme ever used to sell a car, ranking with lines like "Somewhere West of Laramie" and "Ask the man who owns one." It's outstanding because it was developed over a short period of time and because it not only focused on the GTO—capturing those 'tigerish' qualities of the car—but extended to numerous other automotive products. And again there was a transference; the very mention of a tiger in conjunction with spark plugs or tires referred back to the GTO.

Jim Wangers didn't originate the tiger idea, but he was primarily responsible for its wide popularity during the 1960's. The tiger image was first used by Enco gasoline when it urged motorists to "Put a Tiger in your tank." For a while the ads were seen only on the East Coast, but after Pontiac had picked up the tiger theme to promote the GTO, Enco began a nationwide advertising campaign. Enco used a friendly-looking cartoon tiger resembling Tony the Tiger of Kellogg's cereal fame, and most of the ads were related to auto racing.

The slogan "Put a tiger in your tank" enjoyed great popularity, and—with variations which suggested combinations of speed, power and sexual abilities—was a common catch-phrase. There was even a tiger joke: The tigress said to the tiger, "Where have you been? You smell like gasoline!"

The tiger image became associated with Pontiac in early 1962 when Jim Wangers and Royal Pontiac teamed up to build some special Pontiacs, one of which was the Tempest Tiger. Few of the conversions were made, but the Tiger name remained.

The first Pontiac advertisement using the tiger theme was written by Roger Proux in 1963, and used the caption "One Tiger—Two Tiger—Three Tiger" to show the different stages of engines available. Another ad from this period developed a similar idea. It showed a Tempest from the front and another from the rear, and asked, "Can you tell which Tempest is the tiger?" The text gave the answer: "Easy. The LeMans on the right gets its power from our four—that's the big four that stalks around acting like a V-8. So you have to call it a tiger. The other LeMans Sport Coupe has our new 326 cu. in. V-8 tucked away under the hood—all 260 bhp of it. That's good for *two* tigers."

The tiger theme predated the Mustang or other animal names associated with the muscle cars of the 1960's (the Sunbeam Tiger, with the Ford V-8 engine, emerged in 1964). The 'tigerish qualities' the ad conveyed were speed and handling, agility and grace, toughness and independence and, of course, the throaty 'growl' of the dual exhausts. The name was also intended to intimidate people who did not drive Pontiacs!

The ad campaign which used the tiger as its central theme began in earnest in early 1965; for five weeks ads appeared in all the major newspapers, urging people to check out the new GTO tigers. By March similar ads in full color appeared in magazines. Suddenly, tigers were everywhere, as if a cage at the zoo had been left open and the exotic beasts were roaming the streets. Pontiac dealers were supplied with large window banners and posters depicting larger-than-life tigers. Imitation tiger tails were given away to be tied to gas caps and radio antennas, much like the raccoon tails of earlier years.

Then Pontiac released the record, "GeeTO Tiger," which was played endlessly on pop radio stations. Two-page advertisements in automotive magazines promoted the car and the record: "You don't know what a real tiger is until you hear this GeeTO Tiger growl."

There were also tiger contests. "Unmask the Tiger!" was a contest sponsored by Royal Pontiac, whose "Mystery Tiger" driver competed in a full-length tiger suit. Hurst sponsored a contest which was tied-in with the new record; a co-sponsor was Petersen Publications, and the event, offering as first prize the "Original 'GeeTO Tiger'" GTO, received a great deal of publicity in Petersen-owned magazines. The tiger concept was on everyone's mind!

By now the tiger image had become synonymous with Pontiac, and the company further exploited this image by using a real tiger in its ads. Pontiac first used

The Judge was introduced to bolster sagging sales.
Text compares The Judge with the competition;
dramatic photograph makes the point.

this tiger in a magazine ad, along with a LeMans sport coupe, a GTO convertible and an exotic-looking woman. The live tiger in that photograph helped Pontiac make the transition to television, and it was used in a series of TV commercials which predated Mercury's cougar by several years.

The tiger image was so powerful and so successful that numerous other products used that same image with the hope of benefiting from the momentum that Pontiac had generated. What Pontiac had started now caught on like wildfire and, of course, every ad which included a tiger referred back to Pontiac and, especially, the GTO.

M & H Tire Company, which specialized in racing tires and slicks, built its ads around a tiger roaring from within a tire. "Stop pussy-footing around. Put an M & H tiger on your wheels and go-man-go!" M & H offered a full-color tiger-in-the-tire decal for twenty-five cents. Columbus shock absorbers used the tiger image, which it referred to as the 'streaking cat,' in part because of its participation in the East African Safari. There was also the GT Tiger Hi-Performance muffler. Wolf's Head Motor Oil perhaps mixed the metaphor when it showed a can of oil with a straw sticking from it and the caption: "Tiger's Milk."

A contest sponsored by DuPont car care products was entitled "Win a Pet" and offered as prizes a series of live animals whose names were by now also affixed to cars. You could win "a car of the same name" or "Animal lovers may choose a real beast instead of a car."

AC modified its tiger image to a kitten with the caption, "Self-cleaning AC Spark Plugs for cool cats. . . ." It's not surprising that AC should use the tiger image because it's a division of General Motors but, again, the identification of the product with the animal was no accident. "Cars that act like turtles—Turn into Tigers with AC Fire-Ring Spark Plugs." Nor was it an accident that the AC ad should often appear on the facing page from the "Can you tell which Tempest is the Tiger?" ad.

There were many variations on this theme. Holley said that "Holley Hi-Performance Carburetors and Pep Tuneup kits are 'best of breed . . . Makes even *Tigers* turn tail!'" The company also offered membership in the "Tiger-Taming Club." Bridgestone photographed its new motorcycle with a lion and the caption claimed, "Caution! This is no Pussycat!" Kelsey-Hayes said that its new Mag Star I wheel was "The new Grrrowl in sports car wheels." There were custom headers by Cheetah which used a cheetah as logo. Fat Cats tires, which were black with a red stripe,

(We take the fun of driving seriously.)

The quick way out of the little leagues.

The Humbler.

1970 GTO ad emphasizes seriousness and fun; puts serious car in fun context. Photograph of that wide hood is awesome.

gave away reflective Fat Cats Eyes. Then there were Scat Cat competition mufflers "for Car Cats," and the Cal Custom Panther hood scoop, similar to the GTO scoop, which was, the ad said, "a beast."

At times the tiger image bordered on the silly. Honest Charley offered "the growling tiger horn . . . Let a tiger growl from your car." Auto accessory shops sold tiger tails which were hung from antennas and gas filler caps and "Tiger Decals" including tiger-track decals which could be transferred to the car's surface. The suggestion would seem to be that a tiger had walked all over your car, but the ads said that this was a way to "Show 'em where the action is!" The JEM Company advertised a "Console Cushion Go-Go" in a tiger-skin pattern which felt "like real fur." And at the height of Pontiac's tiger advertising campaign a company called Safari Decals advertised: "Hotrodders! Put a Tiger ON your car. Looks like real TIGER SKIN! Here's how you can get a HAND PAINTED TIGER LOOK that's easy to apply yourself! Stripe your doors, your roof, your hood—even your entire car!"

But in Pontiac advertisements the tiger image conveyed a no-nonsense ferocious quality. An early GTO ad concluded, "Sample one of these here big pussycats," but later Pontiac ads capitalized on the tiger image by branding the opposition as pussycats. "To all the other cars from the GTO: 'What's new, pussy-cats?' . . . Wherever real tigers are sold."

Other manufacturers reacted to the tiger image. Ford showed its 1966 model with a tiger tail hanging from the hood and sweeping across the grille as if it'd been devoured. The caption read: "How to cook a Tiger," and the recipe that followed described the Fairlane GTA. Chevrolet described the 350-hp Chevelle as "a potent squelch to all those others who keep talking about lions, tigers, and such." The following year Chevrolet ads showed those lions and tigers in a cage and one said, "I'm glad there's a cage between us" with the threatening Chevrolet outside. The ad revealed that "The new Chevelle SS 396 wasn't named after anything you'll find in a zoo."

In 1965, Dodge ran anti-GTO ads which pictured a Coronet convertible on a banked track, invoking the competition image, with the caption "Animal Tamer." Two years later, Plymouth, moving fully into the muscle car field, ran full-page back-cover ads in magazines which, like some of the Pontiac ads, showed not a car but a place where a car might be—in this case a banked racetrack with the sun glowing through the trees at dawn. The headline was: "Where Tigers Fear to Tread." And the text continued: ". . . if the world of motor racing is a jungle—and most agree it is—why, then, is it so strangely devoid of animals, or rather, cars that purport to be animals?" This was a jibe at Pontiac's lack of a racing program, while MoPars were cleaning up in competition.

The tiger theme in GTO advertising was very successful, and helped to sell Pontiacs of all types, but eventually it ran into trouble when it was expanded to television. Pontiac, working with Uniroyal, developed a tire with a thin red line on the sidewall which was called the "Tiger Paw," and it was offered at first only on Pontiacs. To promote the tire Uniroyal ran an exciting New Wave animated TV commercial which showed a car increasing its speed until it slowly metamorphosed into a tiger, its claws gripping the road. This ad brought together subliminally both Pontiac themes: the tiger image and the Wide-Track image.

That animated version met with great success but another TV commercial offended, even enraged, some GM officials who wielded sufficient power to end the tiger campaign. John DeLorean recalled the situation: "[The ads] featured Barbara Feldon, later of TV's Get Smart, growling like a tigress as she extolled the virtues of Pontiac from a tigerskin rug. The dealers liked the campaign. . . . Un-known to me, however, Chairman Jim Roche was doing a slow burn over the advertising, apparently because he felt the tiger image was too vicious and unfavorable for the corporation. He called Ed Rollert, my boss at the time, who called me at home one night and said, 'John, get that goddamn tiger out of your ads.' That was the last Pontiac Division saw of the tiger."

CHAPTER NINE

Car Of The Year
1968

*T*he model year 1968 began with the GTO winning a major award only two months after it had been introduced: the *Motor Trend* Car of the Year Award. In May it came in second in the *Car and Driver* Fifth Annual Readers' Choice Winners in the Best Super Car division (behind the Dodge R/T Charger). In September it was named one of the Ten Best Test Cars of 1968 by *Car Life*.

These awards were the more public statements celebrating the success of the GTO, but it was a big year for Pontiac in general. This was the fourth time in nine years that Pontiac Motor Division had received the *Motor Trend* award, recognition that in sum Pontiac was the car of the decade. Indeed, as John DeLorean was quick to point out, three quarters of all General Motors developments from 1960-1969 came from Pontiac. In 1959, Pontiac had been honored by winning the *Motor Trend* award for its Wide-Track styling; in 1961 for the Tempest; in 1965 for "styling and engineering leadership"; and in 1968 for the GTO. This was an impressive number of wins. It consistently received lesser awards, too, such as first in *Car and Driver*'s Readers' Choice Winners in the Best Full-Size Sedan class with the Catalina, which was described by the editors as "America's answer to the Jaguar. . . ." Such recognition helped sales, and in 1968 Pontiac sold over 900,000 units for the first time in the company's history.

Car Life, when presenting its award, said that the GTO was "still hands-down leader of supercars," adding, "In looks, performance, and high resale value, the GTO has become a classic in its own time. It's an unmistakable car, slightly erotic, highly romantic, full of verve, optimism, grace and beauty."

Walt Woron, editor of *Motor Trend*, said, "Never before has an automobile been so successful in confirming the correlations between safety, styling and performance as the 1968 GTO."

The car was deserving of such praise, with an all-new body and frame. The body elements were nicely integrated, with a sleek front end incorporating the traditional two-piece horizontal grille split by the vertical nose, a return to the horizontally placed headlights (with optional, concealed headlights), a venturi Coke-bottle shape to the sides of the body and a roof which smoothed out the demarcation line between roof and rear quarter panel in the hardtop coupe (the sports

Styling photos showed what 1968 GTO might have looked like. Note parking light and grille insert possibilities. Endura bumper was a delete option, meaning one could buy a GTO with chrome LeMans grille, although few did.

1968 GTO had new 112-inch wheelbase chassis and new sheet metal; central styling feature was revolutionary Endura front bumper. Car had uncluttered front end, extremely clean lines.

coupe 'post' model was dropped this year). On the hood, for the first time, was the factory-installed tachometer, which sat slightly lower than the dealer-installed 1967 tachometer.

At the rear the taillights were moved into the wide chrome bumper, a change which made the uninterrupted sheet metal much cleaner. On both quarter panels were side-markers in the shape of the Pontiac crest; the die-cast emblems, which had been used since 1964, were replaced by larger-size GTO decals. General Motors had always been antidecal, but with the 1968 GTO it had succumbed to temptation.

The car was extremely smooth and flowing, offering no blunt surface other than the grille. It was lower and shorter than the 1967 GTO (the 112-inch wheelbase was three inches shorter, and the overall length was six inches shorter), and the Wide-Track was widened from fifty-nine to sixty inches front and rear. The styling emphasis was on the short deck and the long hood, made to seem even

Hurst floor shift for GTO with four-speed transmission.

Hurst Dual-Gate floor shift for GTO having automatic transmission.

1968 GTO convertible with hood-mounted tach and wraparound side-marker lights.

longer because of the twin air scoops, the concealed windshield wipers and the new Endura front bumper.

It was such things as the concealed wipers, which Pontiac had pioneered on the Grand Prix in 1967, and the Endura front bumper that Walt Woron was referring to when he said, "Pontiac has established new design standards and supplied the entire industry with a method for accomplishing them."

In retrospect, not everyone thought the concealed wipers a good idea. There were many complaints, primarily from people who lived in the North and Northeast, that the recess in which the wipers were concealed would fill with snow and ice. It was also suggested that the hidden wipers were adding to the cost of repairing a GTO with front end damage, and that they could be a real safety hazard.

Edward Daniels of the Automobile Club of Michigan said that studies had revealed that in moderate accidents there was a tendency for the hood corner to be driven back into the windshield, breaking the glass, which added approximately a hundred dollars to the cost of repairs. Earlier models, without concealed windshield wipers, had the cowl which would absorb this kind of a blow.

The Endura bumper was more than a styling innovation—it was the point of the car upon which the eye focused and from which the body elements smoothly flowed. It was also the first impact-absorbing safety bumper, and because of this bumper Pontiac was able to anticipate federal standards for low-speed collisions which said that a bumper had to have a "recoverable" quality. The Endura bumper had that quality; when struck, it would absorb the energy and return to its original

Optional GTO Rally Clock.

400-ci V-8 engine was rated at 350 hp, had compression ratio of 10.75:1, four-barrel carburetor. This one ran power steering, air conditioning.

Quadrajet manifold was made in two pieces, with heat riser cast separately. Shown with new 'Tunnel Port' head.

shape, without evidence of damage. Anyone who watched television in 1968 remembers the famous Pontiac commercial which showed John DeLorean striking the front of a new GTO with a sledgehammer to show that the bumper could withstand considerable punishment without adverse effects. The editors of *Motor Trend* performed their own test, equally dramatic, with similar results: "We dropped a bowling ball from a 5- or 6-foot height on one of the bumpers. The ball rebounded only about one foot, indicating that considerable energy was absorbed, but left no sign of impact. The same procedure with a conventional bumper left a healthy dent."

The bumper was able to survive this kind of treatment because it was made of a heavy-duty rubber plastic material—actually a synthetic urethane or ABS plastic (acrylonitrule, butadiene and styrene)—molded around a very strong C-shaped steel plate. It was a miracle material because it had a 'memory' ability to return to its original shape and this elasticity could be controlled, ranging from immediate action to a delay of many minutes. It was also fire-retardant and heat-resistant, unaffected by all of the common solvents such as gasoline, oil and acids as well as salt water and sunlight and it had a high tensile strength. At the time, it appeared that all cars would soon feature front and rear Endura bumpers as the answer to low-speed collision damage.

1968 GTO dashboard was redesigned. Note Dual-Gate Hurst shifter for new three-speed Turbo Hydramatic transmission.

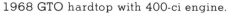

1968 GTO hardtop with 400-ci engine.

It is appropriate that the Endura material should first have been used on the GTO, as Pontiac had pioneered the use of modern plastics in automobiles, coming out with the first plastic grille in 1965, plastic fender liners in 1966 (some GTO liners were made of red plastic), plastic fan shrouds and plastic fender extensions on the big Pontiacs in 1968. The latter innovation blended various metal sections and made repairs, as well as yearly design changes, less expensive.

The Endura bumper was an integral part of the front end styling and, because it could be molded to any shape and painted the same color as the rest of the car, it offered many design possibilities. As amazing as the plastic, was the paint which had to be developed to cover it. Ordinary paints lacked flexibility, and would chip and crack upon impact. What was needed was a paint that would flex with the plastic and remain on the plastic when it returned to its original shape. This problem was solved when Pontiac developed a paint that could be sprayed on the mold and would adhere to the urethane when it was injected into the mold.

The Endura front end was as controversial as it was revolutionary. Pontiac surveys made during 1967-68 showed that there was sales resistance to the idea of a 'bumperless' car. As a result, General Motors design chief William L. Mitchell felt that the Endura front end wasn't right for the new Firebird, a decision he later reversed. Pontiac was prepared for this kind of reaction to the Endura front end and at the beginning of the 1968 model year it was offered as a delete option on the GTO. A small number of buyers opted for the chrome Tempest LeMans bumper and grille, with the GTO emblem.

An optional feature, which complemented the Endura bumper, was the concealed-headlight system. This worked with a vacuum power unit, and when the headlights were withdrawn the front end had a very clean and uncluttered appearance.

The 1968 GTO featured other, less obvious changes. There was, for example, a built-in electrical testing system called Sercon, developed in conjunction with Sun Electric Corporation, which incorporated an idea used on airplanes. Any Pontiac tune-up man could connect the car's electrical systems to his diagnostic

John Z. DeLorean beside a 1968 GTO with Endura front end.

Miss GTO graces the new car at a race gathering.

machine and, by observing a board of colored lights, could simultaneously check some three miles of wiring for malfunctions. There were also two new antitheft devices: a warning buzzer which, when you opened the door, reminded you that the key had been left in the ignition; and a plate molded to the top of the instrument panel, easily seen through the windshield, which contained the car's serial number. The latter item was federally mandated and used on all US-produced cars.

A limited number of GTO's were sold without the Endura bumper; these came with the conventional chrome front bumper and grille (delete option, Code 674, price $25) as were used on the LeMans. Retractable headlight covers were not available with this bumper option.

GTO three-spoke steering wheel, optional for 1968.

Morrokide interior. Note GTO crest on door.

Raymond Herman bought his GTO from the original owner in 1975; a California car, it is in mint condition. It has a 400 HO engine, four-speed transmission, Posi-traction, as well as such deluxe options as air conditioning, power steering, rear window defogger, AM-FM stereo, eight-track player.

There were structural changes, including those to correct what had been mentioned as a perennial problem seemingly inherent in the GTO since its inception: frame flexing and rear axle hop. An all-new frame was built for the shorter wheelbase (two frames, actually, since the four-door Tempests and LeMans used the 116-inch wheelbase) and it had the swept-hip configuration with two important advantages over the older frame: It was heavier, and the body sheet metal came down over the frame, so that the body contributed to the strength of the car. Within the doors were steel post reinforcements, to comply with federal safety standards, and these helped to also strengthen the body. New body mounts were designed on rubber cushions to cut down on road noise and vibration.

The GTO continued to use coil springs and differential control arms on the rear end, but to cure axle hop there was a new "computer-designed" four-link rear suspension system. This involved the four trailing suspension arms, two of which were angled to provide lateral location of the axle. In this sense they acted much like aftermarket traction bars. The spring rates were increased, and a larger-diameter front stabilizer bar was used to limit side sway. But, the GTO still lacked a rear stabilizer bar like the one used on the Oldsmobile 4-4-2 and, although the cars shared sheet metal and chassis parts, Oldsmobile's stabilizer bar could not be adapted to the GTO without a great deal of fabrication work. The result was a GTO with a firm suspension and wheel movement well controlled by heavy-duty shock absorbers. The car would lean on corners, but there was no sense of it wallowing or lurching.

Motor Trend's test driver liked the way the new GTO handled (in fact, he liked everything about the car with one exception: The ashtray, when open, interfered with the floor shift!). "GTO is a beautiful road machine. Speeds of 60 to 80 mph are as steady and firm as a drive through the car wash. Any reasonable speed won't upset its balance. We've had GTO's well over 120 mph—under controlled conditions—without noticing any skittishness.

"Handling maneuvers will make converts of anyone who ever doubted U.S. cars could go-around-corners. . . . Like the fabled tiger connected with the GTO,

Rear seat of Doug McGrew's GTO is done in white Expanded Morrokide, a very durable material.

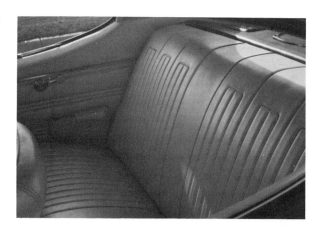

Interior of the door on McGrew's car also used the Morrokide material, in matching white.

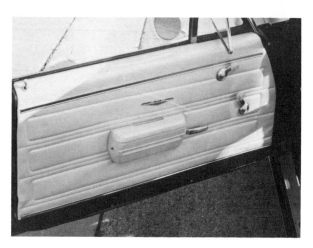

it paws around corners flat and true, then leaps through short straights, ready to have another go at a seemingly hard turn."

Car Life's driver was less poetic and less enthusiastic. He complained about the car's handling characteristics, mainly about the amount of understeer at low speeds, when it was complicated by the slow power steering, and at high speeds. This was compounded by having fifty-seven percent of the car's 4,000 pounds on the front wheels. "While it's predictable, the front tires scrub and slide like crazy, and the firmly suspended rear end jumps all around if the corner happens to be unsmooth." That driver's other complaint could be corrected. He felt that the car, with a 3.90:1 rear end was geared too low, and as a result the engine was turning 4000 rpm at 65 mph on the highway. He suggested that one try to talk the dealer into exchanging the 3.90:1 differential for a 3.23 or 3.26:1 rear end ratio.

Everyone was impressed with the GTO's power, even though the engines were similar to those offered in 1967. There were four 400-ci V-8 engines: the economy model with the two-barrel carburetor and Turbo Hydra-matic transmission rated at 265 hp; another with the four-barrel carburetor rated at 350 hp (the standard engine); another rated at 360 hp; and the Ram Air engine rated at 360 hp.

In mid-year Pontiac introduced the 1968½ Ram Air II engine with redesigned heads featuring round ports. This engine, rated at 370 hp, was the forerunner of the 1969-70 Ram Air IV. All of these horsepower figures were conservative, in keeping with Pontiac's policy, and it helped to placate insurance people. The Ram Air engine was reported by Pontiac to develop 360 bhp at 5400 rpm, but *Car Life* claimed that the actual horsepower would probably be one-third *more* than the factory's figure!

Motor Trend's test car was a Ram Air 400-ci V-8, with a four-speed and a 4.33:1 rear end. The car ran at the Orange County drag strip and turned 96 mph, with an elapsed time of 14.80 seconds, absolutely stock. With the air cleaners removed and a pair of Goodyear Super-stock 'slicks' on the rear, the car turned 98 mph with a time of 14.45 seconds. *Hot Rod* magazine ran its GTO test car at Irwindale Raceway and turned a high of 99.11 mph in 14.48 seconds. *Car Life*'s test car was almost identical except for gearing. Although most people agreed that one of the GTO's primary virtues was its gobs of low-speed torque, *Car Life*'s driver felt that the torque was relatively weak at low rpm, that it would rise above 3000 rpm, and that although the tachometer red-line was 5800 rpm the engine would turn 6000 rpm without any sign of valve float or lifter pump-up (this was with the 3.90:1 rear end!). The magazine calculated that at 5800 rpm in fourth gear the car's top speed was 112 mph. At the local drag strip it turned 0-100 mph in 14.6 seconds, and went through the quarter

1968 GTO on the assembly line being fitted with a grille.

in 14.42 seconds at a speed of 101.01 mph. All three cars were in street trim with all legal equipment, and these were engines with the anti-air-pollution calibrations.

Super Stock magazine's test car received the Bobcat treatment, which included the usual—reworked heads, headers, larger primary jets in the Quadra-carb and the advance setup on the stock distributor. Somehow it got a 4.33:1 rear end with the Ram-Air and four-speed combination, and ran G70-14 Firestone Wide Ovals on the rear. In this form, and with only 118 miles on the engine, it turned the quarter mile in 13.37 seconds for a speed of 105.80. During an afternoon of experimenting with rear-tire pressures and colder spark plugs the car finally attained a speed of 108.05 mph in 12.93 seconds—the NHRA B/s record was 12.43 seconds and 113.63 mph.

The GTO seemed to keep getting better. Or, as *Motor Trend* Editor Walt Woron said when he presented Pontiac with the Car of the Year Award: ". . . the 1968 GTO—a car that incorporates not only the best taste in GM's 'A'-body variations—and an excellent handling and performing package—but also the most significant achievement in materials technology in contemporary automotive engineering all combining to substantiate it as the outstanding intermediate of the year, and the outstanding car."

Less wordy was John DeLorean's summing up: "The success of the GTO has shown that many young new-car buyers desire a car that offers high performance, excellent handling with around-town suitability, distinctive appearance and moderately low cost." These qualities were what the GTO offered, and at least 87,684 people fulfilled their desires by buying 1968 GTO's.

OWNERS' COMMENTS

It's a very powerful car, handsome, yet practical for daily use. However, cornering ability does not match straight-line performance. Drum brakes all around are inadequate for the power involved. I can't deny the ego trip provided by this car. Often challenged by newer Trans Ams, Camaros, an occasional Corvette, the Goat takes them. The best part is not the victory but the fact that the Goat does the job so gracefully that the win appears to be easy. The car moves out without a great deal of smoke, roar and spin. I enjoy maintaining a relaxed position, maybe just steering with one hand, no sweat, as the Goat blows a challenger off the road, said JP, Vero Beach, Florida.

I have owned three GTO's since 1973. My 1968 has 180,000 miles and it looks and runs like it only has 50,000 miles. The car does not have a rattle in the body, and the engine only burns one quart of oil per 2,000 miles. They don't build 'em like that any more! commented RPH, Walnut Creek, California.

I like the GTO's styling and luxury. Stylists apparently worked overtime on '68 styling. However, the closing headlight system on 1968's and 1969's never has and never will work very well due to a lack of engineering. Until yours goes out or breaks you won't notice how the clutch linkage is over-engineered. A simple setup like Chevy's would be nice to work on and a lot less failure-prone. Ignition I think should be just single-advance instead of two-vacuum setups which are a pain. I have yet to see a high-mileage GTO in correct state of tune. DMG from Omaha, Nebraska.

CHAPTER TEN

The Competition

*I*n the mid-1960's a new term entered the language: the muscle car. The examples were seen everywhere—they roared along the freeway, sometimes slightly over the legal seventy-five-mph speed limit, low-restriction mufflers resonating against the asphalt; at night the drive-in restaurants tried to contain row after row of raked and scooped machines, drivers impatiently stabbing the gas pedal while the Lovin' Spoonful or Sam the Sham and the Pharaohs harmonized in the background.

By 1967 *Road Test* felt the term needed to be defined, and offered, somewhat tongue-in-cheek, its own definition. "What is a Muscle Car? . . . it is part and parcel of America's unending quest for youthfulness. It is a sexy car, in the Detroit sense of the word, though some of the cars lean toward the Rubenesque rather than the Hefnerian. But, most of all, the Muscle Car is Charles Atlas kicking sand in the face of the 98 HP weakling. It is the American man's answer to Susan B. Anthony. Wally Cox and Don Knotts reign supreme and Woody Allen *can* go home again."

The GTO combined a big engine with a light body, had extensive performance options and was clearly identified as the first muscle car. It enjoyed instant popularity because it was fast, fun and affordable. Almost every enthusiast wanted a dual-purpose machine like the GTO, a sensible, well-behaved family sedan which could compete with Corvettes and yet cost only $3,000!

The GTO was possible because of Pontiac's racing history, the performance equipment the factory had developed and the philosophy shared by many who were, in one way or another, associated with Pontiac. In spite of the GM ban on factory-sponsored racing activities, Pontiac advertising continued to emphasize the GTO's tire-spinning abilities.

The GTO *was* fast, a beneficiary of the horsepower race that had begun in the early 1950's. In 1964 there was no other car like the GTO; cars which could be considered comparable simply didn't have a chance. For example, the Chevy II Nova was a compact with a 283-ci V-8 which generated 195 hp; even with the optional four-speed transmission it didn't have the horsepower to be competitive. The Ford Falcon, with a 200-hp 289-ci V-8, was in the same situation; not even Mercury's Comet with the optional 271-hp high-performance package could compete. These were lightweight machines with fairly large engines, and while they could burn rubber at the stoplight their quarter-mile times were as much as 15 mph and four to five seconds slower than that of the GTO.

For example, a comparable intermediate car with GTO aspirations was the 1965 AMC Marlin, a fastback with interesting styling; it came with standard disc brakes, a big 327-ci V-8 with 9.5:1 compression, a mild cam and a Holley 3045 four-barrel carburetor. The Marlin turned the quarter mile in 17.40 seconds with a speed of 79 mph—almost 20 mph slower than a decent-running GTO!

The GTO was conceived as a car which would maintain Pontiac's image as a performance car, and which would compete with the new Mustang; it achieved both goals. It's interesting to note that although Ford had begun a long-range national and international racing program in 1963, two years passed before it had developed a GTO-type car. This is especially surprising since optional speed equipment was available for the Mustang as well as the Falcon and Fairlane.

The Cobra Performance Kit, for the 221-ci, 260-ci and 289-ci engines, included racing pistons, a high-lift cam and tappets and 'reworked' heads; the kit sold for $350. There were also single and dual four-barrel manifolds, and a tri-power setup. The killer was a special manifold that used four dual-throat Weber carburetors; it was, the ads said, "virtually the same as used on the Ford-powered Lotus at Indianapolis and the Cooper Cobra which took first at Riverside." The differences between the Ford Cobra kits and Pontiac performance options were that the Cobra kit was an aftermarket item developed by Carroll Shelby and sold through Ford dealers, it was available in limited quantity and it was expensive (the tri-power manifold cost $210 plus installation, twice the price of the Pontiac tri-power installed; the Weber carburetor setup cost $1,230, almost half as much as a complete GTO!).

A comparison of a GTO and a Cobra-equipped Ford is difficult to imagine and would be unfair since the latter was not an assembly-line car. The same is true

The Chevelle SS 396 came with either 325-hp or 350-hp engine. Shown here is a 1968 sport coupe.

of other cars which fall into the muscle car category but which were not readily available to the public. Examples that come to mind are the 1963½ Ford Galaxie 500 with 427-ci V-8 and four-speed transmission (only one hundred cars were built as part of Ford's racing program) and the 1969 Boss 429 Cougar (only two built). Because at least fifty identical models had to be built for a car to be eligible for NHRA S/S class, a factory would sometimes produce hundreds of the model, but it would still be a specially built, limited-production machine. Examples are the 1969 Ford Boss Mustang (859 built) and the 1970 Boss Mustang (499 built). These were hand-assembled cars built *by* the factory but not *at* the factory.

One of the triumphs of the GTO is that it was built on an assembly line by the thousands and yet each GTO was, in a sense, 'custom' built. This is an important point, because it's no problem for a manufacturer to produce a limited-production model and use that car in advertising, as if that exception represented the norm. In 1964 one could buy a Studebaker Lark Daytona, which was a Lark with a 289-ci V-8 rated at 225 hp; like the GTO, the Daytona had a list of options that included a four-speed transmission, Posi-traction, disc front brakes, heavy-duty suspension, power steering, bucket seats, and so on. There were also optional engines: the R-1 came with a 289-ci V-8 with a 10.25:1 compression ratio and a bigger four-barrel which gave it a rating of 240 hp; the R-2 had a similar engine equipped with a Paxton supercharger, which was rated at 289 hp; the R-3 had a 304-ci V-8 with 9.5:1 compression ratio, high-lift cam, bigger ports and valves and the Paxton supercharger, which gave it a rating of 335 hp.

These cars were developed by Studebaker and Andy (Mr. STP) Granatelli, who owned Paxton Corporation, and they were strictly limited-production machines. Advertisements for the Lark Daytona said that a "similar" car had been clocked at 150 mph, but did not state that the one for sale to the public would perform like that. The GTO, on the other hand, properly tuned, would do what the ads claimed, over and over again, car after car, without being fussy, cantankerous or undependable. For most GTO owners, it was as close to a real race car as they would ever get, but without the problems associated with race cars.

The simple but revolutionary concept of putting a big engine in an intermediate-size car caught everyone by surprise. As late as January 1964 the pundits said that the trend of putting the biggest possible engine in a full-size car would continue: Ford would put its 427-ci V-8 in a Galaxie, Chevrolet would put its Mk. II 427 Daytona engine in an Impala, and so on. It was assumed that all cars in S/S class would make extensive use of fiberglass and aluminum body parts to keep the weight near the minimum 3,200 pounds allowed by NHRA for cars equipped with 427-ci engines.

What a surprise it was when the GTO came out of the chute ahead of everyone with a hot 389-ci V-8 in a 3,200-pound car that had been put together in quantity on the assembly line! Not even the other divisions of General Motors had anything similar, nor the ability to produce a GTO-type car in short order.

Chevrolet was the first to respond. The company resented Pontiac's violation of the corporate rule stating that no engine larger than 330 ci could be put in an A-bodied car; it would not break this rule, and so it put the 327-ci Corvette engine in the Chevelle, gave it an optional four-speed and sundry performance parts. That engine, although smaller than the 389-ci Pontiac, was rated at 365 hp; the Chevelle was approximately 300 pounds lighter than the GTO. The Chevelle was perhaps the biggest immediate threat to the GTO in terms of speed; both cars could turn 0-60 in six seconds.

Months later, toward the end of 1964, Oldsmobile announced that its 1965 Cutlass coupe or convertible would have an optional 442 package (the following year, after some doubt that it would appear again, it appeared as the 4-4-2). This numerical sequence indicated that the Oldsmobile option had a four-barrel carburetor, a four-speed transmission and dual exhausts. The 4-4-2 could also be ordered with an automatic transmission.

Almost a year later Buick joined in when it announced the Skylark Gran Sport, which had a 401-ci V-8 with 10.25:1 compression ratio, four-barrel, dual exhausts and an optional four-speed.

The GM cars had a great deal in common, especially Buick, Oldsmobile and Pontiac which shared some sheet metal and structural components. The GTO and the Olds 4-4-2 had similar frames and suspension, the main difference being that the latter had stiffer springs and a rear stabilizer bar, which improved handling and curbed the tendency these cars had to pitch downward in front when braking. The Chevelle was the lightest, weighing approximately 2,900 pounds; next came the GTO at around 3,200 pounds; the Gran Sport and the 4-4-2 each weighed about 3,350 pounds. The three-speed manual used in the 4-4-2 and the Gran Sport—and in most GTO's—was the same unit and it was made by Ford. Like the GTO, the 4-4-2 and the Gran Sport used a two-speed automatic transmission with torque converter.

The GM cars shared similar faults too, such as rear axle hop on severe acceleration and braking, a loss of traction when accelerating from a standing stop, excessive weight on the front wheels and inadequate brakes for a muscle car (like the GTO, the other muscle cars in the GM line were hopped-up versions of standard models whose brakes were essentially unchanged; the 4-4-2 actually had less lining area than the GTO).

Of the four GM cars, the GTO stands out in terms of both appearance and performance. The Chevelle, because of its favorable power/weight ratio, could compete with the GTO; the 4-4-2 and the Gran Sport, while no slouchers, were not as fast. In the quarter mile, a tuned Gran Sport could come on strong, primarily because it produced maximum torque at 2800 rpm while the 4-4-2 and the GTO got maximum torque at 3200 rpm, but a GTO with four-speed, tri-power and Positraction was still the faster car.

There were other basic and important differences. Although these were all homologated production cars, the GTO *looked* like a special car. It seemed as though it had been planned rather than decorated. For example, the dashboards in the 4-4-2 and the Gran Sport were standard passenger car items, with nothing of the race/sports car appearance that the dash in the GTO had with its large round instruments and machined aluminum backing. Even though the material was not genuine aluminum, it gave the cockpit a business-like appearance. And while the GTO had its optional tachometer mounted in the dash, the 4-4-2 and the Gran Sport had theirs mounted on the console in an almost unreadable position. It had all the appearances of an added-on gadget. The GTO's hood 'scoops,' which could be made functional, made more sense than the 4-4-2's rear quarter panel 'scoop,' which was totally nonfunctional. The GTO sold for $100 more than the Chevelle SS, and $200-$300 less than the 4-4-2 and the Gran Sport, but that was because the GTO was an intermediate muscle car, not a luxury intermediate muscle car.

The GTO was outstanding not only because it was a performance machine but also because it was effectively promoted and clearly identified. As Roger Huntington said of the other would-be performance cars: "They didn't have the image . . . You had to have competitive performance, but if you didn't have the image you didn't have anything. That made all the difference in the world." The GTO had an instant image, and would maintain that image throughout most of its ten-year production life.

For two years the GTO was *the* asphalt burner, but by 1966, when the terms muscle car and supercar came into vogue, other manufacturers were building cars which were comparable to the GTO. They realized that there was a considerable market for homologated machines, and not only among young car buyers. To vie for a piece of that market there appeared, in addition to the Olds 4-4-2, the Chevelle SS and Buick Gran Sport, the Ford GTA, Plymouth GTX, followed by the Mercury Cyclone, Plymouth Road Runner, Ford Mach 1, AMC Javelin and

Advertisement for 1967 Ford GTA was aimed at beating the GTO; 'recipe' was a list of Ford options and attributes.

HOW TO COOK A TIGER

other cars designated by cryptic letters or cartoon character names. The competition on the street was reflected by the manufacturers' competition for sales.

The GTO continued to out-perform the Mustang, even as that car headed a new list of machines to be known as 'pony cars.' *Hot Rod* had race car driver Paul O'Shea wring out a new Mustang; it had a 289-ci V-8 rated at 271 hp in a car that weighed 2,935 pounds. With a four-speed manual the car turned 0-60 mph in 6.9 seconds, and ran the quarter in 15.5 seconds, performance which was considerably slower than that of the GTO. In Los Angeles, Carroll Shelby built the Mustang GT-350, a *Gran Turismo*-type car. Shelby's Mustang involved a complete rebuild of Ford's version, and it had performance equipment, modified suspension and brakes, roll bars, the whole works. Two versions were built, a street version with a 289-ci V-8 rated at 306 hp, and a competition version with a similar engine rated at 350 hp. The car weighed only 2,550 pounds, and turned 0-60 in 5.7 seconds; this was slightly faster than the GTO but the Ford Mustang GT-350 cost $4,500 for the street version and $6,000 for the competition model.

The GM muscle cars continued to get hotter and more sophisticated. By 1967 Buick's GS-400 had a 340-hp version of its 400-ci V-8, with a compression ratio of 10.25:1, four-barrel and dual exhausts. The next year it had the Cool Air induction system which took in air through two flush scoops in the redesigned GS hood; the factory did not change the horsepower rating. Buick also offered that engine in a Stage I option; this included a special camshaft, carburetion, fuel pump, heavy-duty cooling system, special dual exhaust system with Stage I mufflers and two-and-a-half-inch tail pipes and a revised lubrication system, which resulted in 365 hp. In 1970, when GM relaxed its ruling against engines over 400 ci in A-bodied cars, Buick bored out its 400-ci engine to a total of 455. A GS-455 Stage I turned 0-60 in 6.5 seconds and the quarter mile in 14.6 seconds at a speed of 95.2 mph.

In 1967 the Oldsmobile 4-4-2 had a 350-hp 400-ci V-8 which pulled 440 pounds-feet of torque at 3600 rpm. In addition to a compression ratio of 10.5:1, this engine had a high-performance camshaft, reworked heads with bigger valves (2.06-inch intake, 1.629-inch exhaust) and dual exhausts with "low restriction mufflers." Kibitzers began to claim that GTO meant Go To Olds; and by mid-1967 *Car Craft* could report, "The Olds 4-4-2 is starting to give the Pontiac GTO a real run for its money in stock class competition at some of the leading dragstrips. A

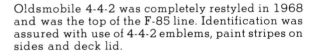

Oldsmobile 4-4-2 was completely restyled in 1968 and was the top of the F-85 line. Identification was assured with use of 4-4-2 emblems, paint stripes on sides and deck lid.

check of Midwest drag strips reveals that the Oldsmobiles are starting to take trophies for that class away from the formerly almost unbeatable GTO Tigers."

Two years later Oldsmobile brought out the Cutlass S W-31, a hot car that joined the trend toward smaller engines. It had a 350-ci V-8 rated at 325 hp at 5400 rpm. It developed this horsepower through the use of high-compression heads and a four-barrel Rochester Quadrajet carburetor; it had a high-lift cam with exceptional overlap, that caused it to run rough at low speeds but to rev forever. Standing starts had to be made at 3600 rpm or the engine would balk; shifts were made at 5500 rpm and the engine would turn an honest 6000 rpm. *Car and Driver* said: "The Cutlass S works. It is fast, not fast enough to be a hairy-chested street racer, but it won't have to hide from touring Ferraris and GTOs either. . . . Best of all, the Cutlass is neither an exotic nor an expensive automobile." The Olds W-31 turned in some hairy-chested times: 0-60 in 6.0 seconds, a speed of 97.2 mph in 14.5 seconds in the quarter mile and it had an estimated top speed of 132 mph.

The year before had seen the development of a beautiful and fast limited-production Oldsmobile. That was the Hurst Olds, a car developed by Jack 'Doc' Watson and George Hurst and built by Demmer Engineering in Lansing, Michigan, the city where all the other Oldsmobiles are built. Watson said he wanted to build a car that would perform and handle well, and to offer it to the more affluent buyer. This would be a car that would have "Poise, Personality and Performance," he said.

Not bound by the GM ruling against engines over 400 ci, Watson replaced the 400-ci 4-4-2 engine with a 455-ci V-8 with force-air induction. The engine was completely reworked, with special head work, a high-lift, long-duration camshaft, enlarged carburetor jets, a specially machined crankshaft and an improved distributor curve. The finished engine generated 390 hp at 5000 rpm. To handle this power effectively, Watson reworked the Turbo Hydra-matic extensively and equipped it with a Hurst Dual-Gate shifter. The car was distinctive with its silver and black paint, hood scoops, spoiler and conical exhaust pipes. The Hurst Olds was expensive, selling from $4,500 to $5,000, but it had all the luxury options because Watson said he wanted a car that could be raced while the driver sat in air-conditioned comfort. And go it did, hitting between 97 and 100 mph in the quarter

1969 Ford Torino fastback has traces of Mustang styling, also 'GT stripes,' GT emblem on hubcaps. Stock engine was 302-ci V-8, options ranged to Cobra Sportsroof, the NASCAR-inspired model with 428-ci engine, with Cobra Jet Ram Air, four-speed transmission, competition suspension.

—without air conditioning. With air the speeds were approximately four mph slower. But with or without air the Hurst Olds would give a Judge a good run!

Also highly competitive was the Chevrolet SS 396. The standard engine was a 396-ci V-8 which was rated at 325 hp at 4800 rpm, and developed 410 pounds-feet of torque at 3200 rpm. The optional engine was a 396-ci V-8 that developed 350 hp at 5200 rpm with 415 pounds-feet of torque at 3400 rpm. Both engines had a 10.25:1 compression ratio, four-barrel and dual exhausts. The big difference was internal: The 350-hp engine had high-strength castings, extra-thick bulkheads above each crankshaft bearing and wide-base bearing caps. The 'porcupine' heads —so-called because valve stems protruded in various directions—had individual inlet and exhaust ports, larger valves (2.06-inch intake, 1.72-inch exhaust), a high-lift cam and hydraulic lifters good for 6000 rpm. A third version, rated at 425 hp, was primarily developed as a competition engine for the Corvette. That engine had 11.5:1 compression, a hotter cam with solid lifters, huge ports and valves, and a big four-barrel carburetor on a special aluminum intake manifold.

The Chevy 396 in any form was an impressive engine; its power was so great that it, like the GTO, was honored with a song. "SS 396" was written by Lou Adessa and Vince Benay and recorded on Columbia by Paul Revere and The Raiders.

> *Forget about your hemis and your GTOs*
> *I got a new machine that really goes*
> *When I get you on the drag strip you'll know darn well*
> *You've been beaten by Porcupine Chevy Chevelle*
> *Packing it up now, you better be quick*
> *Nothin' can outrun my SS 396*

To be fair, however, the SS 396 enjoyed a performance option now denied the 4-4-2 and the GTO. In the middle of the 1966 production year GM banned the use of the tri-power setup for A-bodied cars, which meant that GTO's and Oldsmobile 4-4-2's could no longer be equipped with this option. On the other hand, Chevrolet had just brought out a new three-carburetor manifold for the Corvette which, with very little port work, would fit the Chevelle SS 396. This was just what the NASCAR and S/S class drag racers had been waiting for, and soon GTO owners, limited to a single Quadrajet, found themselves competing against Chevelles equipped with legal triple-carbureted engines.

Gran Turismo muscle cars were everywhere. Ford came out with the GTA and announced a line of Ford accessories with which you could "Give your car a GT flair!" There were the Plymouth GTX, the Dodge Charger fastback coupe and the Road Runner R/T; the Chevrolet SS 427; and the Buick GS-340, a detuned version of the GS 400. There was a whole new line of pony cars, including the Camaro Z-28, the Firebird HO and 400, the Cougar XR-7 and a new Shelby Mustang called the GT 500. None had existed before the advent of the GTO and now all, directly or indirectly, competed with the GTO.

Pontiac's Firebird Ram-Air 400 was a pony car with a shorter wheelbase, yet had the same wide track and 400-ci engine as the GTO. The Firebird would turn the quarter mile in thirteen seconds, with a speed of 106 mph. A companion GM pony car was the Chevrolet Camaro Z-28 ("Z is for Zap!"). It had a much smaller engine, a 302-ci V-8, but it was rated at 325 hp. This engine had forged crank, rods and pistons, dual-quad Holley carburetors, a cold-air induction system and a wild cam with mechanical lifters which allowed it to rev to 7000 rpm. The GTO success story was repeated when Pete Estes, who had overseen the development of the GTO and was now general manager at Chevrolet, said, "We only planned on selling about four hundred Z-28's in 1968, but instead we had 7,000 orders."

In 1957 American Motors had complained loudly that performance should not be a criterion in promoting and advertising cars, and its complaints led to the Automobile Manufacturers Association ban on factory-sponsored racing activities. Now, ten years later, Victor G. Raviolo, a new vice president at American Motors, said, "We'll be building in the direction of the GTO with our new AMX," which he called "The Walter Mitty Ferrari." In a sense, AMC in the mid-1960's found itself in a position similar to the one Pontiac had been in a decade earlier; to improve its market image and to boost sales it moved into the muscle car field.

The Javelin was a perky, short-wheelbase machine with two optional engines, a 290-ci V-8 and a 343-ci V-8. The latter was rated at 280 hp, and although the car handled well, coming off the line without traction problems or wheel hop, it turned a speed of only 93.26 mph in the quarter and required fifteen seconds to cover the distance. Nevertheless, the red, white and blue cars called attention to AMC's performance program.

Next to be developed was the AMX, described by the factory as "the hairy little brother of the Javelin." Dick Teague, AMC's vice president for styling, explained something about the car's origins. ". . . we decided to do a really hot 2-place car—one like Ferrari would do, but instead of 10 a year, design it so we could build 10,000. I said one of the things I'd like to see in a car was a rumble seat. . . ." The AMX did not have a rumble seat, but it was a snappy little two-seater hardtop with a short wheelbase and a big engine. It weighed only 3,035 pounds and had a 390-ci V-8 rated at 315 hp at 4600 rpm; the compression ratio was 10.2:1; and the engine was fitted with a four-barrel Carter carburetor and dual exhausts. *Motor Trend* tested one in this form with a four-speed manual transmission and recorded 0-60 mph in 6.9 seconds, 0-75 mph in 9.9 seconds and a quarter-mile speed of 92 mph with an elapsed time of 15.2 seconds.

In addition to the Javelin SST there was the Rambler Rogue; once a staid family car with a 128-hp 199-ci engine, it was GTO-ized by replacing that small engine with a 343-ci 280-hp Typhoon V-8 and offering a list of performance options. In 1969 the engine size was increased by using the AMX 390-ci 315-hp V-8; it also had an optional four-speed, disc brakes, Twin-Grip (Posi-traction) rear end, Hurst shifter, mag wheels, a very awkward hood scoop and special paint. On the strip it was giving GTO's a run for the money by turning the quarter mile in 14.14 seconds at a speed of 100.44 mph.

When the GTO appeared in 1964 it had to first confront, and vanquish, the lightweight MoPars, and it did. By 1966 the hot MoPars were beginning to gain lost ground on the street and on the strip. In 1965 Eric Dahlquist wrote in *Hot Rod* magazine, "Up to September of this year, the ranking order (of hot cars) was pretty much established as to who was top dog, or maybe top tiger would be more appropriate, but then a hemi was loosed by Dodge and the order of command was knocked into a cocked hat."

Dodge had never admitted that it *had* lost ground; only months after the GTO was introduced, a Dodge ad showed a Coronet convertible circling a banked racetrack, with the caption: "Animal Trainer." The text was: "Bring on the Mustangs, Wildcats, Impalas . . . we'll even squash a few Spyders while we're at it." At the end the ad read: "Build Coronet the way you want it: Street or Strip. And then go tame a few tigers."

The MoPar strategy was akin to the GTO's strategy, but it lacked promotion and a sense of identity (which it got some four years later, when it was called Road Runner, Super-Bee, Charger, and everyone had a disease called 'Dodge Fever'). The Coronet was the intermediate 117-inch-wheelbase car which had as its standard engine the 272-ci V-8. Optional engines were the 318-ci and 361-ci V-8's, and after that things got interesting: There were the high-performance 383-ci V-8, the 426-ci street engine and the Hemi Charger 426, which was a wild engine to be used in a family car! Options included Sure Grip (Posi-traction) rear end, four-speed transmission, a console with tachometer and more.

The Plymouth line was similar; it included a Fury with an optional high-performance 383-ci V-8, equipped with four-barrel and 10.1:1 compression ratio, and an optional street version of the wedge-head 426 V-8. The Belvedere line had four optional V-8's from 273 ci to 383 ci, plus a street-tuned 426-ci V-8 and two versions of the ram-inducted maximum-performance 426-ci V-8.

Chrysler continued to develop its fleet of muscle cars, often interchanging parts, and by 1968 they ranged from the Barracuda to the Charger. The Plymouth

Famous Boss 429 Ford V-8 was a large-block lightweight engine, had aluminum hemi-type heads with 'stagger-valve' arrangement. In Thunderbird it developed 360 hp at 4600 rpm, pulled the heavy car to 123 mph; NASCAR version would generate 650 hp on gas with single four-barrel carburetor, and engine was built to allow shift points up to 9000 rpm!

Barracuda had a 383-ci V-8 which was probably underrated at 280 hp, and a 340-ci V-8 which was clearly underrated at 275 hp (NHRA gave it a rating of 310 hp). Like the GTO, this car had a number of performance features, some standard, some optional. There was a four-speed transmission, disc brakes, the Formula 'S' suspension package and Firestone Wide Oval tires. A light car, at 3,400 pounds, with a cam that gave it a characteristic rough idle, it was one of the best accelerating sedans. With a three-speed TorqueFlite, it could travel from 0-60 mph in 7.8 seconds and cover the quarter in 15.5 seconds at a speed of 92 mph. *Car Life* tested one with a manual four-speed; it turned the quarter mile in 14.95 seconds with a speed of 96.63 mph. *Hot Rod*'s tester got a better speed from a similar car; it went 99.10 mph with an elapsed time of 14.22 seconds. *Car Life* credited the Barracuda with a top speed of 119.6 mph at 6200 rpm. In spite of its performance, Barracuda sales were poor.

The Dodge Charger R/T, which resembled a 1968 GTO with a 1967 GTO roofline (it was even available in a GTO green), had as its standard engine a 440-ci Magnum V-8, and as its optional engine a 426-ci Hemi-head V-8. *Car Life* declared that the Dodge Charger 500 with Hemi-head, two four-barrel carburetors and four-speed was "the fastest test car" when it turned a time of 13.68 seconds in the quarter mile. The magazine also called the car "a disguised NASCAR racer," which it was (it was designated the Dodge 500 because NASCAR rules dictate that a manufacturer must build at least 500 units of any model). The Charger 500 also had certain unique aerodynamic styling features, such as a grille that was flush with the front edge of the hood, and a non-fastback rear window.

The Dodge Charger caught on immediately. *Motor Trend* said "The Charger was the success story of '68, sprinting out 437% of '67 and accounting for 15.5% of all Dodge sales." During 1968, a total of 85,000 Chargers were sold.

Motor Trend tested a 1968 Magnum 440 and a Hemi 426 in Dodge Coronet 500's, and was impressed in spite of the fact that both cars were California models and had the CAP (Clean Air Package) emission controls. It found that the CAP restriction affected the Magnum more than it did the Hemi V-8, mainly because it required that the primary carburetor venturis be made thirty-six-percent smaller. Nevertheless, the Magnum turned the quarter mile in 15.4 seconds with a speed of 94 mph. The Hemi, which developed its torque after 3000 rpm and therefore had less wheel spin when coming off the line, had a time of 14.9 seconds and a speed of 98 mph.

The MoPars were terrifically fast, with awesome amounts of brute power, but some points should be made when comparing them to the GTO. First, body modifications on the Dodge Charger 500 were done at locations other than the factory. Second, the car was not inexpensive; a Charger with a Hemi V-8 cost $5,300. Third, the Hemi engine required a good deal of maintenance, and some were known to use a quart of oil per tank of gas. As a result, it had a limited warranty. As Jim Wangers said, "The Hemis would go like crazy on the strip, but they had trouble getting there and back, while the GTO never had any problems in traffic."

The GTO had the engineering built into it so it was able to go fast but handle well around town without lugging, overheating or loading up. In his road test with the Dodge, Eric Dahlquist had some of these problems. His 426-ci street Hemi had dual Carter 3140 AFB carburetors, and he noted that the engine would conk out occasionally when gas sloshed in the float bowls, and that it would "sputter mo-

1970 Oldsmobile 4-4-2 sport coupe was a clean machine; Olds enthusiasts insisted that GTO meant 'Go To Olds.'

mentarily" when he braked for a light. For all of these minor, but annoying problems, the car turned the quarter in 14.60, a speed which the dual-purpose GTO had often beat.

In 1968, Dodge began a media blitz, with TV commercials and eight-page, full-color signatures in the popular automotive magazines announcing that "Dodge Fever" was sweeping the country and that the only cure was to see "The Dodge Boys." The ad campaign, which recalled the 1965 GTO campaign in its scope and intensity, used a combination of hillbillies, leggy blondes and Southern sheriffs to remind the observer that this was NASCAR country. Also introduced was the Scat Pack, which included "racing stripes" to give the MoPars a racy appearance as well as an identity. This was the lesson learned from the GTO. No longer would a Dodge be called something mundane like the Coronet. MoPars would have fancy, supercharged names like Charger, Super Bee and Super Bird (with its two-foot-high spoiler); they would be known as "The cars with the Bumblebee stripes."

A car which met with instant success, and which definitely cut into the GTO market, was the Plymouth Road Runner, introduced in 1968. This was the economy muscle car that The Judge had wanted to be and that buyers had waited for. It was a low-priced Belvedere two-door with a big engine and catchy identification markings. As the ads claimed, ". . . we kept the frills to a minimum. So we could do the same with the price." It was a plain-Jane two-door, with a plain interior, reminiscent of a police cruiser. Under the hood was a 440 Magnum V-8 rated at 375 hp, developing 480 pounds-feet of torque, with a long-duration cam, a four-barrel carburetor and dual exhausts. There was only one optional engine: the 426-ci Hemi V-8. With this kind of power in a 3,400-pound car Plymouth had an instant winner. Some of the other muscle cars, including the GTO, were getting bigger and heavier. They were becoming loaded with options which had more to do with comfort than with performance, and the prices were getting uncomfortably high. The Road Runner had a couple of other things going for it too: It had colorful decals of the cartoon character for which it was named, and it had a horn which sounded the familiar "beep beep" which was that cartoon character's only line of dialogue.

In 1969 the market for muscle cars seemed unlimited. Engines intended for hot sports cars like the Corvette found their way into intermediate sedans. For example, the L-88 Corvette, a genuine 150-mph car which would cover the quarter mile in ten seconds at a speed of 133 mph, had a 427-ci V-8 which, although produced in limited quantity, was placed in street-driven Chevelles. One of the fastest sedans was the 1970 Chevelle LS-6 with a 454-ci engine; its quarter-mile speed was 104 mph with an elapsed time in the high thirteens. It should be pointed out that the LS-6 Chevelle was not a real production option, but a special-order car and only a few hundred were built.

By 1971 the bottom had fallen out of the muscle car market. High insurance rates, emission controls and safety legislation affected all makers equally as they tried to produce low-compression engines which would pull a heavy sedan down the quarter mile with some agility. There were bogus muscle cars, such as AMC's Hornet SC/360, but it was clear that the era of real muscle cars was over. The Dodge 440 and the Plymouth GTX continued to be offered with a 10.3:1 compression ratio and the famous Six Pack (tri-power) manifold through the 1971 model year. After that last remaining example of sheer power, there was the energy crisis, downsizing and the universal mini-car. But, for many, there were good memories of cheap gasoline, burning rubber and horsepower ratings.

CHAPTER ELEVEN

"Heah Come Da Judge" 1969

Although the 1969 GTO was virtually identical to the 1968 Car of the Year, sales declined seventeen percent. This decline would continue steadily for the five years that remained of GTO production. In fact, eighty-five percent of all GTO's were sold during the booming first five years of production.

One reason for the sales decline was the high cost of insuring a GTO. The youth market was there, the car had appeal, but insurance premiums had skyrocketed—when insurance was available. Many insurance companies refused to insure anything bearing the name GTO, and they were equally leery of terms like four-speed, Ram Air and Posi-traction.

Another reason for the drop in sales was the plethora of muscle cars. Where once there had been only the GTO, there was now a fleet of cars with tough-sounding names, bucket seats and Hurst floor shifters. All of these competed with the GTO for the diminishing market, and the GTO now even had to compete with its brother, the Firebird pony car. When the Firebird was introduced in February 1967, it was accompanied by an ad campaign that proclaimed the car to be "a European-style GT car," which was remarkably close to calling it a GTO. It leaned on two of Pontiac's best-known images, performance and the GTO, by using a Pontiac front end and drive train, and the 400-ci Ram Air engine. While John DeLorean no doubt intended the Firebird to be in direct competition with Ford's Mustang, he must have known that it would cut into GTO sales. Perhaps he had something up his sleeve for the GTO, like the installation of the 428-ci V-8, when he said: "A car like the Firebird may lead to a greater differentiation between the Sprint and the GTO."

The Firebird drew the eye away from the GTO, and automotive writers soon began to compare the GTO with its younger brother rather than the other way around. When *Hot Rod* magazine tested the new GTO, it praised the car indirectly: ". . . it's hard to tell whether it's a Firebird or a Tempest; the Tempests look that trim. . . . Firebird-like hood scoops, outside tach, Ram Air and steel wheels that look like mags. . . . So here's the new GTO. Last year you would have thought it a Firebird. In fact, you might think so this year. . . ."

The Firebird was even promoted in much the way that the GTO had been. Such promotions and advertising cut into GTO sales, but there was still hope. Rumors abounded that Pontiac had plans for a new version of the GTO, one that would focus attention on the original muscle car idea and would thus increase sales. The word was that the car would be powerful, would be painted a bright color (probably orange) and would, in its basic form, be inexpensive. An economy supercar! Such rumors made the GTO fanatic's pulse quicken. But the 1969 GTO was essentially a 1968 model with minor trim changes.

As before, it was offered in both a hardtop coupe and a convertible, and had the same long hood, short deck, Endura front bumper and optional concealed headlights. The grille pattern was changed slightly to a mini-egg-crate design with a bright center strip added to emphasize the horizontal Wide-Track look. Square parking lights, similar to those in the 1968 model but larger, with a more emphatic 'bomb-sight' appearance, were set in the ends of the valance panel. A minor but striking change was the absence of vent windows, which gave the car an open and uncluttered look. For those who found the air stuffy without the vent window there was a new "upper level ventilation system" which brought air from the outside. If you needed more air—for a flat tire, for example—there was an option called Instant-Aire, which was a portable air pump driven from the intake manifold vacuum. Last, but not least, there was factory air conditioning.

Other changes were brought about in part because of the new emphasis on safety, as outlined in the growing list of federal standards. Inside the car were padded headrests, more padding on the dash and less wood trim. Outside there were round side-markers on the lower edge of the front fender ahead of the wheel open-

1969 GTO with Endura front end, optional concealed headlights and hood-mounted tachometer. Letters on front fender replaced traditional GTO emblem.

ing, and a new GTO crest side-marker at the rear. The 6.5-litre front fender emblems were also replaced with die-cast GTO emblems.

A new antitheft device locked the steering and transmission by requiring that the driver put the gear shift in park (automatic) or reverse (manual) before removing the key. There were many reports of problems with this system, including those experienced by the *Car Life* testers who had to lock their GTO in a garage at night with the key in the ignition because they couldn't get the car into reverse.

But the GTO was only mildly changed. The use of Endura plastic did not extend to rear bumpers as had been hoped; the 1969 GTO had a traditional chrome rear bumper. However, vinyl roofs grew in popularity, and one of every two new GM cars had one this year—GTO's included.

These styling changes were not enough to build an ad campaign around, especially when the competition included Road Runners and Ramchargers. And so, the GTO's biggest change was under the hood.

Although transmission and rear end combinations remained the same, there were new engines which could be coupled to them. The standard engine was the 350-hp V-8 with a four-barrel carburetor, and the optional engine was the 265-hp V-8 with a two-barrel. The earlier 400 HO had been increased from 360 to 366 hp and, equipped with functional hood scoops, became the Ram Air III.

A new engine, evolving from 1968's Ram Air II, was rated at 370 hp and was called the Ram Air IV, not only because it was fourth in line but also because it made use of four cold-air intakes. It had a pair of functional scoops on the hood which could be opened or closed by a cable-operated valve at the driver's discretion. There were also two ducts to the carburetor behind the grille with traps for dirt, snow and other foreign materials. Decals on the hood scoops identified these Ram Air engines.

The Ram Air IV was really a super engine, with redesigned round port heads, forged rather than cast pistons, polished valves and a high-rise aluminum manifold. It had a wilder cam, with a duration of 308 degrees on the intake and 320 degrees on the exhaust, and a lift of 0.520 inch on both intake and exhaust. The rocker arms had a 1.65:1 ratio. This was a very strong engine, and the factory horsepower rating of 370 was grossly understated.

Meanwhile, rumors circulated concerning the "new version" of the GTO. It was rumored that this GTO would be a "new thin-pillar coupe," that it would be a

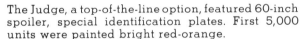

The Judge, a top-of-the-line option, featured 60-inch spoiler, special identification plates. First 5,000 units were painted bright red-orange.

"budget GTO," an economy supercar that would compete with the new Plymouth Road Runner which had established itself as an economy muscle car the year before. The rumor was that the new car would have all-GTO suspension and performance equipment, including the Ram Air systems. It might also have something novel, like a rear deck spoiler; and, as mentioned, the first cars would be painted a distinctive color. The special GTO would have all this, but at a price intended to be lower than that of the regular GTO. As yet the car had no name, but a contest was planned to name it, and there would be prizes and television fanfare and lots of advertising and once again, it was hoped, the GTO would be America's number one muscle car!

There was no contest, and there was no budget supercar. The plan to introduce the car in early fall was delayed. An announcement was issued by Pontiac saying that there would not be a budget muscle car but stating no reason for the car's cancellation. Then, suddenly, a sneak preview was held for the automotive press and they were introduced to The Judge, the new GTO which was at the top of the line in price and, the factory hoped, in prestige.

On December 19, 1968, Pontiac announced to the motoring public that The Judge would be introduced in January, and it said that the car "goes one performance step further in the popular muscle car field, a field and market Pontiac had opened up five years ago with the GTO." The news release went on to say that The Judge would have as standard equipment the 400-ci V-8 with 366 hp, which featured a compression ratio of 10.75:1 and the four-barrel Quadrajet carburetor (the engine which became known as the Ram Air III). Also standard would be dual exhausts, a three-speed manual transmission with a floor-mounted Hurst T-handle shifter and a 3.55:1 rear end. The interior would feature Morrokide bucket seats, "driver-oriented instrumentation," and a shallow-dish steering wheel.

Close-up of GTO emblem on fender, replaced the 6.5-liter GTO fender emblem.

Colorful logo appeared on glovebox and spoiler; also on front fender.

Decal on side of scoops identified car as having new Ram Air IV engine; 400-ci 370-hp engine was optional on GTO and The Judge.

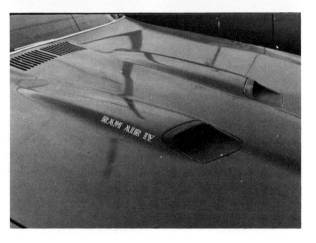

When The Judge became available, it featured all these things and more. The Judge package added $332 to the GTO's base price and, in addition to the above, included low-restriction mufflers, a blacked-out grille, a rear deck spoiler, G70x14 glass-belted blackwall tires and Rally II wheels without trim rings. Options included various rear axle ratios, a hood-mounted tachometer, a Rally gauge package and the Ram Air IV engine.

There was also an elaborate identification package. The GTO's past success had depended on its image and the manner in which it presented itself for easy identification by the public. While other manufacturers seemed to almost *conceal* the identity of their limited-production hot cars, the GTO was clearly visible. The entire legend of the GTO stands behind the letters seen on each grille, fender and deck. By 1969 the necessity of product identification was apparent to the makers of other muscle cars—and some that were not so tough—and so they appeared bedecked with decals, stripes, spoilers and bolt-on scoops, like fighters sporting their trophies. The Plymouth Road Runner had a decal showing the well-known cartoon figure. In 1968 Oldsmobile built a limited-production Cutlass called the Hurst Olds, with special paint and scoops, which was, in a way, a direct forerunner of The Judge. It was this kind of car that The Judge had to compete with.

Pontiac was acutely aware of the development of muscle cars by the competition; hence, the birth of The Judge. On June 27, 1969, on an inter-organization letter form, a PMD official cited the registration figures for the GTO, LeMans and "competitive makes" during the first four months of 1969:

LeMans	30,031
GTO	20,517
Total	50,548
Road Runner & GTX	26,103
Torino GT	25,301
Charger	22,454
4-4-2	9,175

Sales promotion illustrations of the 1969 hardtop coupe and convertible.

GTO HARDTOP COUPE

Those who were promoting The Judge were aware of the necessity of image; not only would they have to make it stand out from the other muscle cars, they would have to make it uniquely different from the GTO. The front was distinguished by the Endura bumper, a black grille, the Ram Air hood scoops and the hood-mounted tachometer. The rear end was even more striking with its sixty-inch floating deck airfoil, or spoiler. The first 5,000 Judges were painted Carousel Red, a shade of bright orange, and were easily recognized well before you got close enough to see that spoiler or Endura bumper. The Judge was available in other colors. Of The Judges built during 1969-70, 6,833 were painted Carousel Red (later called Orbit Orange by Pontiac), 1,244 were orange, 1,067 were blue, 951 were yellow and 535 were black.

To make The Judge even more distinctive, it had a three-color slash stripe on the upper edge of the front fender running back to the door, and the car was liberally sprinkled with The Judge name plates—there were decals on the front fenders

Main instrument panel gauges for the 1969 GTO.

Stylish interior of the 1969 GTO.

Lee Meyer's GTO breaks traction as the result of heavy foot on the go pedal. Smoke piles up behind rear tires—just like in the ads!

and on the spoiler, and an emblem on the glovebox. The slashes came in black, blue or olive with bright, contrasting colors. The black slash was outlined in yellow with a thin red stripe; the blue slash was outlined in red with a yellow stripe; and the olive slash was outlined in yellow with a white stripe. The logos' colors matched the slash used. These colors, when placed against the background color, were *vivid*! They recall the idiom of the late 1960's, psychedelic.

The colors were like a comic-book page designed by Peter Max, and in this context it's important to remember that the car's name came from a line uttered by a character on the highly popular Rowan and Martin *Laugh In* television program. "Heah come de Judge" caught on and was one of those lines that people said to one another for whatever reason. Like the television program, the car was highly visible, and with the *Laugh In* line echoing, some people felt that The Judge was itself a joke, perhaps a spoof on muscle cars, with its decals and bolt-on spoiler.

Camshaft of Ram Air IV engine has stout lobes, big distributor gear.

Ram Air IV piston. George DeLorean said it was a "pretty good" piston.

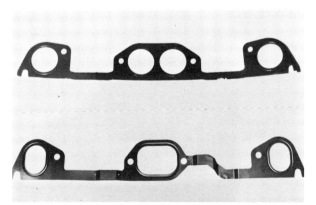

Manifold gaskets for the Ram Air IV (top) and the Ram Air III (bottom).

Cylinder head for the 1969 Ram Air IV.

To a degree the externals concealed what had been lost. The car had grown heavier (3,800 pounds), fatter and slower; and was often saddled with options like electric windows, power steering and a power assist for the disc brakes. But The Judge was still a performer. Heavy-duty springs and shocks gave the weighty car a firm ride. The three-speed THM transmission with 5200-rpm shift points was available as were wide- and close-ratio manual four-speeds.

Hot Rod magazine tested one of the first Judges to come off the assembly line. It featured the 366-hp engine coupled to a four-speed transmission and a rear end with a 3.90:1 ratio limited-slip differential. The car was tested in showroom condition, and the driver made no adjustments to the engine, nor did he experiment with tire pressures or spark plugs. The car wound to 6000 rpm easily and, the driver noted, on two occasions the engine turned past that point with no damage except for a slower elapsed time. The best time in the quarter mile was 14.41 seconds with a speed of 99.55 mph.

As with previous GTO's, the Bobcat package was available for The Judge. This consisted of having the combustion chambers cc'ed to assure equality, and any variation in spring height was corrected. The rockers were fitted with posi-lock adjusting nuts so that valve action could be adjusted, which allowed the engine to rev to speeds over 6,000 rpm without valve float. The distributor had heavy-duty points installed, and a Mallory condensor was substituted for the factory condensor.

Super Stock magazine pitted a Judge with a 366-hp Ram Air III engine with a Bobcat package against a GTO with a 370-hp Ram Air IV. Both cars had the close-ratio four-speed transmission, Schiefer clutch, pressure plate and flywheel assembly and 3.90:1 Safe-T-Track rear end. In addition to the Bobcat package on The Judge, both cars had aftermarket headers which ran back to a pair of dual pipes made of two-and-a-half-inch tubing. The Judge had Corvair Spyder mufflers, which were described as being "not too loud or blatty, but very metallic and business-like." The GTO had glass-pack mufflers which were described as just being "loud."

1969 GTO hardtop with Ram Air IV engine.

Close-up, front suspension (including heavy-duty stabilizer bar), 1969 GTO.

In this form, and running stock wheels and tires, The Judge turned a top speed in the quarter mile of 107.91 mph in 13.57 seconds. With wider tires and a pressure of 12 psi, the car turned an amazing quarter-mile speed of 109.75 mph in *under* thirteen seconds (12.96)! The nearly-stock GTO with the Ram Air IV engine turned even more amazing times: 108.04 mph in 13.06 seconds; with slicks on the rear and the headers opened, the GTO turned 111.38 mph with a time of 12.63 seconds!

In May 1969 Pontiac announced a new engine. There were expectations that Pontiac would develop an ohc V-8, because of the success it had had with the ohc six-cylinder and because Malcolm McKellar had appeared on the cover of *Hot Rod* with five experimental engines, two of which were ohc V-8's; but this engine was based on the 400-ci engine. Called the Tunnel Port, or Ram Air V, it was a production performance engine, *not* a limited-production engine. It was available from the dealer in component form by special order for only an extra $389.

The Tunnel Port engine was based on the Ram Air IV; it featured identical cam timing specifications, but it used mechanical valve lifters. However, the valves were larger, having been increased to 2.19 inches, and the exhaust valves remained at 1.77 inches. The valves were also lighter, having been tuliped, and the hollow stems were chrome-plated. These opened onto a precisely machined combustion chamber via large ports—hence the name, Tunnel Port.

400-ci Ram Air engine with Quadrajet carburetor.

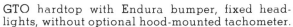

GTO hardtop with Endura bumper, fixed headlights, without optional hood-mounted tachometer.

Good breathing and volumetric efficiency were the keynotes of this engine, and it featured an aluminum intake manifold with the big four-barrel Holley 800 CFM carburetor. The entire lower end was redesigned: The web areas were stronger, and featured four-bolt main-bearing caps. The main-bearing journals were cross-drilled, the connecting rods were much heavier and the pistons were the pop-up type. The compression ratio was a whopping 11.0:1. Final horsepower figure was approximately 425, but others estimated that the engine could develop something closer to 500 hp. With this kind of power the GTO/Judge was still very much in business! Unfortunately, fewer than 200 engines were produced by Pontiac.

Aesthetically, the spoiler was the focal point of the car. Extending across the rear deck, supported by a pair of stands, the fiberglass spoiler gave a slightly Can-Am appearance to the car. It fit close to the deck, and the ends turned down to meet the rear fender extensions. This gave a smooth, finished appearance but created a potential problem because if someone were resting his hand on the fender with the trunk lid up—fingers could get smashed when the trunk lid was closed.

1969 GTO convertible, with standard cornering lights.

Clean 1969 GTO hardtop rear end.

The spoiler gave the impression of speed and it was soon found on other cars. The Judge spoiler was similar to the Firebird Trans Am spoiler and would fit perfectly on the Pontiac Firebird, as well as on the 1968 GTO. Dealers were soon filling orders for this item to be adapted to other models.

The 1967 Camaro had a small duck-tail spoiler, and larger spoilers had appeared on a handful of American Motors Javelins in 1968. The Javelins had been set up for Trans Am racing, and the spoilers were actually rather primitive wind deflectors. They were intended to function, said an observer, as "more art than science . . . [they] were pivoted for best aerodynamics by guess and brawny mechanic muscle-power." To support his thesis he mentioned the following incident involving the well-known driver Peter Revson: "It is safe to say that the airfoils are still in the experimental stage. During practice, Revson came into the pits and asked that the deflector be adjusted to provide a few pounds more pressure. The obliging mechanic didn't whip out slide rule and protractor, nor did he even bother with the adjustment nuts. He laid hold, and with his bare hands deflected the deflector until it looked right to him. Revson made no further suggestions." (*Road Test*, August 1968)

The Judge's spoiler was not adjustable, and some found it simply decorative, or even ostentatious; others saw it as being attractive and useful. *Hot Rod* magazine's driver claimed that it was functional because ". . . its rear placement on the car adds weight to the tail end, desirable for weight transfer on acceleration." The benefits of a spoiler at low speeds are, one understands, negligible, but increase at higher speeds.

Herb Adams, a Pontiac engineer at the GM Technical Center, performed wind-tunnel tests with a Judge, and reported that at 100 mph the deflected wind placed a one-hundred-pound downward pressure on the rear end, thereby assuring better

License plate on Paul Bergstrom's Judge says it all.

Rick Lam's clean 1969 GTO. Wheels were an aftermarket item.

traction and stability at that speed. Unlike Plymouth, which claimed that its huge (twenty-five inches tall) airfoil on the Super Bird became functional at speeds in the 120- to 130-mph range, Pontiac made no claims that the spoiler was engineered to aid the aerodynamics of the car or that it helped in any way; it was simply there ("The 60" spoiler"). Pontiac, in fact, said nothing even when rumors circulated that the wind-tunnel tests had shown that the airfoil had exactly the opposite effects than were desired—it tended to pull *up* rather than push *down* at high speeds.

An independent test was done by *Car Life* magazine. The cars tested were a Judge, a Javelin and a Camaro Z/28. The tests were elaborate, and conducted in a scientific manner with precision instruments which measured any change in the car's configuration at 65 mph, 85 mph and 115 mph. The testers found that the spoiler on the Camaro helped, the one on the Javelin made no difference and that the one on the Judge had a negative effect. "The tail-mounted, elevated spoiler on a Pontiac Judge actively works *against* high-speed control, by adding front lift force instead of producing rear downforce. The faster the car goes the more the car is jacked up."

They also discovered that "Without [the] spoiler, the GTO Judge developed lift at front and rear. The increase was gradual and in the proportions that will keep the car in an understeering attitude. Without [the] spoiler in place, the Judge had reduced lift in back. But the front tipped up too far. The rear spoiler did more to raise the front than it did to lower the back. . . . The GTO Judge's spoiler affected both front and rear ends—to the overall detriment of its aerodynamics. While the spoiler reduced the tail lift to about 75 lb. at 115 mph [versus 105 without the spoiler], the resulting change in attitude shoveled air under the car's nose, and gave the front end a whopping 375 lb. lift. Total: 95 lb of extra, unwanted lift. This is too much of a good thing. The reduction of rear lift is a benefit, but the increased front lift is much more than a car needs. Front tire grip is supposed to lighten some, but not as much as it did." Pontiac attempted to correct the front end lift problem in 1970 by adding a front air dam to The Judge.

In spite of the results of this authoritative study, the spoiler concept would continue and grow. Not only did the 1970 Judge have one, but other cars followed suit, such as the 1970 Mercury Cyclone whose body shape—the rear roofline slope, the quarter panels, overall profile in spite of its enormous hood and front and rear overhang—strongly resembled the 1969 GTO configuration, which indicates that the GTO was still worthy of being copied by the competition.

OWNERS' COMMENTS

When I bought my Judge convertible through a classified ad, I knew I had run across a unique automobile. After joining the Pontiac-Oakland Club I was surprised to find out how rare it was: only 108 produced. I like the excellent performance features offered by the Pontiac 400, superb handling characteristics, comfort and the luxury of many accessories available in '69. My convert has air conditioning, power steering and brakes, factory 8-track, etc. I have traveled extensively with my Judge—west to Colorado, south to Florida—and have found it a dependable (though not too economical) automobile, said PB, Fridley, Minnesota.

The front fenders rot out by the water drains . . . leaves and twigs fall on the windshield and then down behind the fender and collect there, holding the water in, keeping it constantly damp. Also, a big problem in maintaining the car is in getting gasoline. Now that high-test is no longer available, we have to use a mixture of high unleaded and regular to get high enough octane to keep the car from pinging, running on and to get decent gas mileage—and to get decent performance. MM and LM from Roselle Park, New Jersey.

Best feature is the Ram Air IV option—or Ram Air V. Only two problems: For some reason I can't seem to keep the rubber on the rear tires for long!! And I had trouble obtaining *all* the rare options, which I eventually achieved!! KN, Troy, Michigan.

CHAPTER TWELVE

"For People Who Think Driving Should Be Fun" 1970

With the advent of a new decade, Pontiac continued to emphasize the *fun* of driving, but the winds of change were blowing from every direction and one thing they seemed to indicate was that whatever else driving might be it was no longer fun. It was necessary, it might even be a means of escape, but driving was not *fun*. Sometimes it was hard to recognize the pleasure principle or apply it: The war in Vietnam raged, and there were massive demonstrations against it by Americans who en masse had grown serious about the excesses of power. Many of those people, Americans in Vietnam or in the demonstrations at home, were examples of the 'youth market' at which the GTO and the other super-cars were aimed; for many, such cars seemed to represent another excess of power. Now, fun was rock music and drugs, and Woodstock was the big event of 1969. The radical change in the public attitude toward cars could be seen as people converged on Woodstock in revamped Divco milk trucks and VW buses with old Eugene McCarthy stickers and flowers painted on the sides. Performance was unfashionable, and a high-performance car was considered to be an example of materialism. In 1970 the word 'ecology' gained popular usage; Earth Day was celebrated on one California campus by the students digging a hole and burying a brand new Chevrolet, as if by this action they could exorcise the demon of the freeway.

Other examples of change, unrelated to the above, were the departures of the two key men associated with the GTO: John DeLorean left Pontiac in February 1969 to become general manager of Chevrolet, and Jim Wangers left MacManus, John and Adams and the Pontiac advertising account to do free-lance consulting work. Both men were crucial to the GTO's lifeblood. It's not possible to overemphasize how important they were to the development and the success of the GTO. Perhaps they saw the writing on the wall and realized that the GTO, the 'fun car' of the 1960's, would be unable to survive in the new decade.

Others continued to work on the GTO, and from their public comments we can infer that they remained enthusiastic about the car and the potential market for the car. James McDonald, then vice president and general manager of Pontiac Motor Division, now president of General Motors, stressed the integrity of the new GTO and the history behind it: "I think right from the beginning the GTO was designed to be a muscle car for the highway. And that says a lot. It says it's got to be

455-ci V-8, rated at 360 hp, was a bored and stroked 428, with new crankshaft, modified 428 camshaft and heads.

1970 GTO had clean, flowing lines especially when viewed from rear, side. Taillights were built into bumper for smoother appearance. GTO emblem has given way to decal.

tasteful, it should have honest performance and it's gotta be the kind of muscle car a guy would be proud to drive. . . . I think all of us at Pontiac feel that Pontiac has had and must maintain a performance image. We've got to keep energizing our performance image. There is no question about it."

Actually, there was some question about the GTO's image as a performance car, for in order to make driving *fun* the factory had to make concessions, and the GTO became a performance/luxury car. The problem was that old shibboleth, compromise. The performance image was giving way to the comforts of easy living: air conditioning, electric windows, power disc brakes, power steering and stereo sound systems. The result was that in six years the GTO had become a thousand pounds heavier, acquired a middle-age spread and lost some of its quickness. It could still turn a fast quarter mile, but, as one driver said, the car "was far better suited to cross-country touring or sporty commuting."

Typical interior of a 1970 GTO Judge.

An excellent view of the spoiler on a 1970 GTO Judge hardtop. Note spoiler, striping and decals are body color.

Perhaps it was the times, the change in public attitude or perhaps it was the change in the GTO. Whatever the reasons, the effect was a drastic decline in GTO sales, dropping to a total of slightly over 40,000 units, which was approximately forty-five percent of the previous year's production. Of this total, 32,737 units were hardtop coupes, 3,615 were convertibles, 3,629 were Judge hardtop coupes and only 168 were Judge convertibles, a very rare car today.

From the beginning the GTO had helped boost the sale of other Pontiac models, but now that performance image seemed to be having a negative effect. In 1970, Pontiac sales dropped by 200,000 cars and the company fell from third place, a position it had held since 1961.

But the GTO was still a very impressive car. Even though it had lost the lean look of youth it had a new and distinctive beauty, a sense of maturity, perhaps,

Bill Crain's all-original Judge is Starlight Black with yellow and blue Judge decals. Fender slashes have psychedelic shifting colors. Has Ram Air, and over 100,000 miles on odometer!

Only 168 Judge convertibles were built in 1970. Ron Torland bought this one from original owner; it's now completely original and unrestored, has only 49,000 miles.

with its expansive hood whose gentle curve was only slightly interrupted by the sculpted twin hood scoops and the tachometer housing. The grille vaguely recalled the egg-crate grille of the Ferrari. And The Judge option was even more colorful, looking like a gentleman uncle in a new seersucker suit. For many, the GTO represented the epitome of motoring, the car which *did* make driving fun. Ron Aungst remembers coming home after four-and-a-half years of military service and celebrating his return with the purchase of a new Judge, a car which he still owns:

"When I was shopping for a new car, I stopped at the local Ford dealer. The friendly salesman told me that he could have the Mach 1 of my choice for me in *one* week. I chose to wait *ten* weeks for The Judge of my choice. I remember pacing the floor and spending a lot of time looking out the windows of my home, waiting and waiting and waiting. . . . When it finally did arrive, what a beautiful sight! Worth every week of waiting.

"One of the most memorable days of owning my shiny new Judge was shortly after my marriage in 1970. I took my beautiful young bride to the premier showing of *Two Lane Blacktop* at the local drive-in theater. It was one of the proudest days of my life. When we drove past all the other cars lined up row after row, I could see and sense the feeling of awe in the other people as they watched us drive by. I then realized that this was just the beginning of a long and lasting relationship between

Exhaust splitters were standard; Cordova vinyl roof, available in five colors, was optional. Original Morrokide interior is elegant, long-lasting. Note GTO identification plate over glovebox.

1970 GTO hardtop; emerging from a dip?

man and machine. The movie was inspiring too, since one of the principal characters drove a new 1970 Judge."

The car that inspired such enthusiasm and loyalty was a combination of toughness and luxury; a boulevard cruiser that could still get it up. One saw first the smooth front end, the redesigned Endura bumper which, because it was the same color as the car, blended neatly into the sheet metal. The two-part grille was split by a protruding fin which tapered into the hood center where it passed between the two air scoops. The grille was rubber-mounted on a steel base. It was recessed six inches, and each grille section was banded by a wide piece of chrome trim.

This styling theme was repeated in the headlight surround, a new styling term to describe the quad light system. Each of the four headlights had a wide chrome bezel, with the light recessed, which gave them a Frenched-in appearance. Once again the squarish parking lights were set low in the valance, with a wide air intake below the grille. The overall result was a front end which had a more massive appearance than the previous GTO front ends which were uncluttered and delicate in design.

A major change in styling was the return to exposed headlights; the concealed headlight option was no longer available. There had been problems with the system that couldn't be solved. The hidden quad headlights on the GTO used a vacuum-operated vertical door which was raised when the lights were turned on with the engine running, and was dropped when the lights were turned off or the engine stopped. Ice and snow would get packed around the lights, interfering with the up or down movement of them; the vacuum reservoirs mounted behind the grille blocked the circulation of air through the radiator; vacuum lines leaked. The GTO headlight covers could not be moved away by hand, unlike the system on Ford cars, and if the vacuum reservoir ran out, the headlights remained hidden. Pontiac could have developed an electrical system to cover and uncover the lights, but that would have been more expensive than the vacuum system.

Another argument presented, quite seriously at that, against concealed headlights was that the driver of a car coming from the opposite direction was unable to tell whether the car with concealed headlights was moving toward or

1970 GTO Judge hardtop; here with spoiler and decals painted flat black.

away from him. This was, of course, the same argument that was raised when the 1947 'backward' Studebaker appeared!

Automobile styling seems to follow two evolutionary patterns, and often the two occur together: a movement toward bigness, as if a big car simply grew from a small one, and a movement toward surface decoration. The GTO had grown larger and heavier, but it had not been restyled by the addition of chrome trim. It's true that The Judge featured fender slash decals and nameplates, which some people considered excessive, but the GTO always had a clean appearance.

By 1970 the 'GT look' was everywhere, extending to cars like the new Honda coupe. And the 'look' was usually applied to otherwise unremarkable machines in the form of decals, appliqué 'racing' stripes, airfoils, dams and scoops. Some examples were the result of factory options, others were aftermarket accessories. The 'GT look' was popular and suspect at the same time because it was, in a way, aesthetically pleasing but gimmicky and nonfunctional in cars which were, by definition, functional. An example of this kind of styling was the Barris Instant Kustomizing package, conceived and marketed by George Barris, which turned the new Oldsmobile 4-4-2 into the Pulsater. The package included a bolt-on rear spoiler, side scoops, paint accent stripes and "simulated" outside exhaust collectors.

What the GTO had inspired had caught on like wildfire. As Brock Yates wrote of the phenomenon which came to a head in 1970: "[Detroit has] now escalated the super car concept to the point of absurdity; 450 cubic inch engines are common, 'shaker hoods,' cornball, 1956-vintage racing stripes are everywhere, and you can get NASCAR-type hood pins and bogus-mag wheels on practically every brand of automobile except the Checker Marathon."

Detroit seemed to be going through another phase, much like the one which, in 1957, inspired Alfred P. Sloan, Jr., president of GM, to say: "They're not making cars anymore, they're making fins."

Not that the addition of decals and bolt-ons to the GTO didn't occur to the people in charge. In 1970 James McDonald said: "We have often talked about adding racing stripes to the GTO. We've looked at it with stripes and we still feel that this car is so tastefully and distinctively designed that they don't do anything for it. You really don't need them, we think, to make it alive. . . ."

Bill Mitchell, then vice president in charge of GM's Styling Staff, added: "This car had an image from day one. It started off that way. It isn't vogueish. Vogue is a

1970 GTO hardtop and Pontiac Motor Division companion.

popular form of temporary usage and if you do some berserk things you might like it one year and you can't wait to get it out of the room later."

The new GTO was sleek and uncluttered, and had that 'blacked-out' look that Pontiac had encouraged for the past decade. Every surface had exactly the right amount of curvature, and the parts blended perfectly. Even the GTO medallions, so important to product identification, were removed and replaced with decals, which, although the change had been motivated because it would save money, contributed to the car's uncluttered appearance. The radio antenna was now concealed within the windshield glass, a styling breakthrough developed by John DeLorean and pioneered by Pontiac the year before on the senior series. The rear deck and fender line were unbroken by any ornament or trim distraction; the taillights, which resembled those on the 1968 Grand Prix, were placed within the bumper and followed its curve where they served as side-markers. This might have weakened the bumper structurally but it solved the problem of how to present a smooth, unbroken rear deck area.

The interior of the 1970 GTO conveyed a luxury-car image with padded dash and large bucket seats; it was spacious, having more room than the Grand Prix. As usual, the rolled and pleated Morrokide was attractive, and has proven to be long-lasting. The standard steering wheel had shock-absorbing qualities, but it was not nearly as exciting as the optional Custom Sport wheel, which had a simulated wood rim and three stainless steel spokes.

The dash panel was very readable, with three large instruments: a speed-ometer, a tachometer and a gas/oil pressure/water temperature gauge. If you had a hood-mounted tachometer, the dash space could have been used to house a Rally clock. The water temperature and oil pressure gauges must have had many people worried. They read in reverse of the usual gauge; when the temperature

Spoilers, splitters and decals were stock, original items.

Judge has 400-ci V-8 with Ram Air, produces 366 hp.

and oil pressure went up the needles dropped, and this situation could, at times, create a panic. The gauges were set in a simulated wood dashboard, with the ventilation and heater controls to the right; a simulated metal-turned panel held the radio.

Then there was The Judge. Roger Huntington's verdict was: "That was his [Wangers's] idea. It was a failure I think." If The Judge seemed excessive, with its decals, vivid paint and spoiler, this excess was intentional. It took its name from a silly television show and, apparently, not even those in charge were serious about the car; it has been described as a 'spoof' and a 'put-on,' an imitation of the hot street car. It was conceived as a car which would have instant appeal to those who were interested in such things as psychedelic paint and spoilers. In spite of the stylists' lack of seriousness, The Judge succeeded: It did give the GTO a temporary shot in the arm, and, in the tradition of the GTO, it was fast!

Shortly after The Judge came out, Bill Collins, assistant chief engineer at Pontiac, said: "The Judge has really exceeded our expectations. . . . We wanted

Ron Aungst bought his Judge new in February 1970. Car has 38,000 miles, and is in showroom condition.

New side-guard door beams, introduced on 1970 Pontiac.

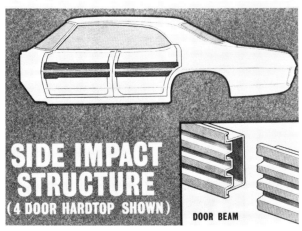

to get something out there that was really almost a put-on for Woodward Avenue. Those of us in the marketing group conjured up that car. . . ."

And years later Jim Wangers said: "The Judge was a spoof on muscle cars that ran like gangbusters and sold better than anyone could have guessed." He told me, laughing, that The Judge was "a spoof, an exaggeration . . . it included everything they could think of that was outrageous—and that orange paint! But it worked. It called attention to itself, and it gave the GTO the shot in the arm that it needed. The Judge had instant appeal, and it also had certain sexual connotations. Some Judge drivers saw the car as an act of defiance. The upshot was that the joke backfired—The Judge had terrific power, it was a fast car!"

Pontiac may have grown more serious about The Judge's possibilities when it saw the sales chart. As James McDonald said in 1970: "An interesting percentage of sales is The Judge . . . it has been running slightly above fifteen percent of all our GTO's [for 1969], and that is strictly a hot car."

And at the same time there continued to be plans to build a budget supercar, which was what The Judge was originally intended to be. Steve Malone, Pon-

Tempest two-door coupe with the GT-37 option, which gave buyers an alternative to paying ever increasing insurance rates for The Judge. Options included hood locking pins, special body striping, white letter tires, dechromed Rally II wheels, dual exhausts with chrome extensions, and GT-37 identification.

tiac's chief engineer, commented on Pontiac's plans for a budget supercar, ". . . Some of our competitors have come out with a bare body shell and a big engine to appeal to that segment of the market . . . The Judge isn't really that kind of a car, it's got a few more features on it. . . . We've given a lot of consideration to putting out a bare-bones-type car, in other words, a better car with a performance engine . . . we've got a marketing group looking over the potential in this area. . . ."

But for now Pontiac was committed to a car which would be a compromise between performance and luxury. An interesting effect of this compromise was improved handling; the new GTO had a ride which was firm but not choppy. This was the result of softer springs and, finally, a rear sway bar; the GTO had never had a rear bar because John DeLorean didn't believe in them. With DeLorean's move to Chevrolet, the GTO could finally receive what it should have had years earlier.

The stabilizer bar, similar to the one which had been used on the Oldsmobile 4-4-2, was ⅞ inch in diameter in standard form, but a bar 1⅛ inches was available

Palamino Copper GTO convertible, owned by David Thommen, has aftermarket wheels and Dunlop radial tires.

1970 GTO hardtop owned by Paul Rader, vice president of GTO Association of America. The car is all-original, has factory-optional stamped-steel Rally II wheels.

for both the front and the rear with the optional handling package. This package included variable-ratio power steering, larger tires (G60-15) on seven-inch-wide rims, special springs with increased spring rate and heavy-duty shocks. This package was a compromise, but it greatly improved the GTO's handling and ride; because the heavy stabilizer bar controlled body roll it was now possible to use softer springs. "You don't want to raise spring rates," said Herm Kaiser, the executive chief engineer, "but you do want to increase shock valving. Even race cars have gotten away from the very hard springs. There's no reason for a car to go bouncing down the road."

Car and Driver's test driver found that the new GTO still suffered from axle hop, but said that the car generally handled well and that it rode with a degree of comfort seldom experienced in performance cars. "Even with the rear bar the car very definitely understeers, particularly with the extra weight of the air conditioner on the front wheels, but it is a very satisfactory compromise for almost any situation you will ever encounter on public roads. Also to its credit the GTO manages to handle well without having a teeth-chattering ride. It is on the stiff side but it lacks the sharp harshness that characterizes other, particularly non-GM, performance cars. This is just one of the many factors that tends to make the GTO a satisfying car for a broad range of buyers."

Another factor was the GTO's power. For 1970 the small engine was dropped and other engines were introduced as the trend toward more cubic inches continued. The former standard 260-hp two-barrel engine was discontinued (as was the ohc 6 in the Sprint). The standard engine remained the 400-ci V-8 which, with a four-barrel carburetor and a compression ratio of 10.25:1, developed 350 hp at 5000 rpm. Optional engines were the Ram Air III, which developed 366 hp at 5100 rpm, and the Ram Air IV, which was rated at 370 hp.

Then there was the optional 455-ci V-8! For the first time the GTO had an engine larger than its basic 400-ci engine, a move made possible because General Motors had suddenly lifted its ban on engines larger than 400 ci being placed in the intermediate-size cars. Now that Buick, Oldsmobile and Chevrolet would use larger engines in their intermediate-size cars, Pontiac wanted to have a big engine also; it took the 428-ci V-8 used in the senior series, bored and stroked it, and developed the big 455-ci engine. In addition to more cubes, it had four-bolt main bearing caps, bigger valves and the camshaft from the 1969 Ram Air 400.

The man responsible for that cam, Malcolm McKellar, Pontiac's chief engineer, said: ". . . Certainly this 455 engine is going to make this the most pleasant, powerful car which doesn't require a higher numerical axle ratio to achieve its performance. I think this is certainly going to broaden the market for the GTO. With the larger engine, professional people who want air conditioning, for instance, will have a better-feeling car."

The 455-ci engine was rated at 360 hp, which was odd because two of the 400-ci engines exceeded this horsepower figure. The fact is the 455-ci V-8 was intended for the big Pontiacs, and not for the performance model; it had lots of cubic inches, a good deal of torque, but like all Pontiac engines it had required

Classic stance of the 1970 GTO hardtop.

emissions controls. It had a tach red-lined at 5100 rpm, and it was, as McKellar said, a good engine for a car with air conditioning. *Car and Driver* ran one through the quarter mile and turned 96.5 mph with an elapsed time of 15.0, and came to the conclusion that "It was a decidedly non-racer kind of car."

But Pontiac played on the GTO's racer image. The advertisements emphasized power, and called the 455-equipped GTO The Humbler because it would humble the competition—or at least it *sounded* as though it could. "You'll get the message when you hear the new, low-restriction, performance exhaust you can order. Kind of like a 30-inch woofer having a field day with a grumbling bass sax." The source of this sound was an interesting option which resembled the old (and illegal) aftermarket device called an exhaust cutout; in this case a vacuum-operated exhaust system bypass allowed the driver to control the flow of exhaust gases past the muffler chambers, which sounded wild and helped reduce back pressure.

But even with this option Pontiac was playing the popularity game in trying to appeal to as wide a buying public as possible. Some wanted a quiet exhaust, others wanted the rumble which indicated throaty, uncontrollable power. The buyer could have it both ways. While the original GTO was designed to appeal to a limited number of people, the new GTO was designed as a *compromise*, a car which would appeal to everyone. As with any compromise, something was gained but, too, something was lost. Pontiac seemed to realize this when it began its advertising campaign for 1971 by striking a nostalgic note. . . . "It was back in 1964 when it all began. Out of a shop in Pontiac, Michigan, swaggered a car with a slightly ungainly name . . . and a legend to build."

OWNERS' COMMENTS

I bought this Judge four years ago without knowing what I was getting into and became so attached to it that I couldn't sell it if I had to. Its best features are: 1) acceleration power; 2) styling; 3) comfort; 4) reliability; 5) handling. Faults: 1) excessive fuel consumption (but I don't consider this a fault since these cars were designed when this wasn't a factor), 10-15 mpg; 2) back window area susceptible to rust-out; 3) manual steering can be a pain. Another virtue: I would say ninety-eight percent of GTO drivers are cool so there is so

Mike DeFazio's 1970 GTO has 455-ci V-8 engine, four-speed, Posi-traction rear end. Spoiler was factory option. L-60 street tires gave better traction; fit under fender without jacking up suspension.

Mike DeFazio's 1970 on the move!

137

much more to the car than just transportation. BC, Austin, Texas.

Perhaps somewhat unusual is the fact that my car (1970 Judge convertible) was purchased new by a lady; maybe not so unusual, considering that by 1970 the GTO had passed the peak of its popularity . . . considering that the car had turned into a jazzed-up convertible with automatic transmission and a clock where the tachometer belonged. Don't misunderstand; I love the car. Underneath the garish trim it's still a solid GTO. RT of Tualatin, Oregon.

The car's best feature is highest quality of excellence in the restyling of the '70 Judge, giving it an identity of its own. The awesome classic supercar look and aerodynamic styling. Rubber-like bumper integrated with body design that no other car had. Last but not least, its high-performance Ram Air engine. . . . To be alone in my garage with The Judge is a sense of tranquility, of happiness and satisfying relaxation, pure bliss—like being with a two-hundred-dollar-a-night hooker—worth every penny—unbelievable. It doesn't talk back either, said RA, Altoona, Pennsylvania.

My 1970 GTO convertible is, by today's standards, a true land yacht—smooth, sleek and powerful. Every cruise with this car is a definite ego trip as well as an exciting driving experience. The unique combination of styling, appointments and performance seems equally at home on Woodward Avenue or on Worth Avenue! commented EM, Atlanta, Georgia.

CHAPTER THIRTEEN

"Pure Pontiac"
1971

As the new decade began, Pontiac, like other American automobile manufacturers, found itself poised on a fulcrum, trying to balance the desire to build a car which was fast with the need to build a car which would comply with the federal safety and emission requirements.

On the one hand, there were still persistent rumors of a new ohc V-8 engine for the GTO. Horsepower figures were not released, but the rumor reported in *Hot Rod* was that one of the sohc engines had been tested "in the neighborhood of 620 hp (on gasoline) with an rpm limit of seven grand." As readers envisioned one of these engines in a GTO, the article ended with the question: "Is it going to be offered as a production V-8? Pontiac wouldn't say . . . But you can just bet that it's going to happen. Probably not in 1969, but hazarding a guess, we'd say maybe the 1970 models."

Such rumors were given credence when, in October 1970, *Hot Rod* did another cover story on a Pontiac experimental engine, showing a beautifully 'styled' Hemi-head ohc engine with aluminum block and fuel injection. Unlike the earlier engines, this one was built on a special die-cast 427-ci aluminum block. Rated at 640 hp at 7500 rpm, it was capable of running in excess of 8000 rpm. In addition to the power such an engine would be capable of, it would also save weight. Pontiac's Chief Engineer Steve Malone was quick to point out that the new GTO was almost identical in size and weight to that of the 1964 Grand Prix, and he said that Pontiac was eager to get the intermediate car back to where it had been.

So much had happened in the world, both the automotive world and that larger world, since the GTO had been introduced it's debatable whether it could ever return to where or what it had been. Weight reduction would be a step in the right direction, of course, and the introduction of an option like an exotic overhead cam engine would certainly be welcome, but even as these hopes were circulating the bottom fell out of the factory high-performance program.

General Motors told its divisions that all the new GM cars would have to be equipped to run on low-lead or unleaded gasoline; to accomplish this it was necessary to drop the compression ratios on the high-performance engines. On an engine like the 455-ci V-8 this meant lowering the compression ratio from 10.25:1 to 8.4:1 on the HO engine, and to 8.2:1 on the lower-horsepower 455 (8.2:1 on the 400-ci). The result was a horsepower loss of from five to ten percent, a drop in torque and a severe restriction on the engine's efficiency. Moreover, the effect of this single memo was to terminate the concept of the high-performance engine—with a return to relatively low compression ratios it was futile to think in terms of wilder cams or multiple carburetion.

In addition to drastically lowering compression ratios, Pontiac made other changes to comply with the federal standards as spelled out in the Clean Air Act of 1970. It fixed (neutered, some said) the idle mixture limiters on all carburetors; the idle mixture was preset at the factory so that the mixture couldn't be adjusted without breaking a seal. An aluminum die-cast choke housing was mounted on the intake manifold so that the choke coil could sense engine temperature more accurately, causing the choke to turn off more quickly. The distributor cam lubricator, used previously only on high-rpm engines, became standard for more precise timing. And, finally, an evaporative emission-control system was put on all Pontiac engines.

With regard to these changes, James McDonald, Pontiac's general manager, was optimistic in the face of an obvious compromise between performance and

Rear-end styling followed that of previous year. Only 661 GTO convertibles were built; only seventeen Judge convertibles, car is so rare that the factory doesn't have a photo of it!

emissions controls. "All of our engines for 1971," he said, "comply with the strictest pollution regulations without sacrificing performance." This might be true—it depends upon one's definition of 'performance'—but it was clear to everyone else that performance as it had been defined by the GTO, a car which could turn a thirteen-second quarter mile, was now in the past. As evidence of this, Pontiac decided in 1971 to terminate the high-performance catalog that it had been publishing for years.

In 1971 GTO and Judge were very similar to the previous year's models; even though the factory literature referred to the new Pontiac as being "distinctly stylized." The major styling change was the new grille, which was a cluttered version of the previous grille. The Endura bumper was retained but greatly changed; it was less well integrated, and seemed almost to have been added on.

The nacelle section butted to the hood rather than flowing into it with the sculptured ridge of the previous year, and the nacelle tapered into a bumper on each side. The front end again featured quad headlights set into chrome light surrounds. The grille featured a wire mesh similar to that used in the 1967 GTO but because the surface area was so much larger it looked even more like a fence.

Below the bumper were round parking lights, a departure from the square 'bombsight' lights of the past several years, and on the front of each front fender were twin side-markers which flashed with the directional signals. Above the grille openings, on the leading edge of the hood, were two wide air scoops, distinctly different from previous scoops in appearance, and baffled to prevent rain, snow and foreign materials from entering.

While the front end was cluttered, from the cowl back through the rear deck area the '71 GTO had the same clean, flowing lines of the 1970 model.

Also identical were the transmission combinations, steering and suspensions. The rear axle ratios were increased to the next lower gear ratio to prevent the engines from being noticeably lower in power. The car used the same 112-inch wheelbase, and was again available in a two-door hardtop and, for the last time, in a convertible model.

This 1971 GTO convertible has hood tie-downs for high-speed safety.

The standard engine was the 400-ci V-8 with four-barrel carburetor which was rated at 300 hp at 4800 rpm, and with 400 pounds-feet of torque at 3600 rpm. This year, for the first time, manufacturers were required to cite *net* horsepower ratings also, which was determined by measuring horsepower with the engine in the car and all road equipment attached. This method helped to control inflated figures, and it also helped to deemphasize horsepower figures in general. The GTO's 300-hp engine, for example, had a *net* horsepower rating of only 255.

An optional engine was a 455-ci V-8 which was rated at 325 hp at 4400 rpm (260 net hp at 4000 rpm) and which developed 455 pounds-feet of torque at 3200 rpm. The 455 HO V-8 engine was standard on The Judge and optional on the GTO. It was rated at 335 gross hp at 4800 rpm (310 net hp), and had a slightly higher compression ratio and a slightly wilder cam (288 degrees duration versus 273 degrees).

An indicator of how Pontiac's performance image had diminished was the termination of the two Ram Air engines. Another deletion, one which certainly had symbolic meaning, was the lack of chrome rocker arm covers, air cleaner and oil filler cap, dress-up items that had been standard equipment on the GTO since its inception.

The ultimate GTO engine, the Ram Air V, was never released to the general public; how different might the history of the GTO have been if that engine had been offered as a production-line option. It was truly a high-performance, streetable engine; if it had been made available on a limited basis a GTO with a Ram Air V engine would be a valuable machine today.

George DeLorean, who was responsible for the development of the Ram Air V, told me how the project blossomed, then died. He had raced Pontiacs successfully until the GM ban on racing was imposed in 1963; when performance parts became unavailable he switched to Mercury, although his interest in Pontiac remained high. One of the Ford factory-sponsored cars had a 427-ci V-8 built by Holman and Moody. DeLorean, fascinated by this powerful, high-revving and durable engine, persuaded the driver, Benny Parsons, to lend him the heads, valve train and camshaft. He took these to the Pontiac engineers in charge of experimental engine development and they studied the parts closely. The result was the Ram Air V.

The engine was designed during 1966, and the first one was completed in December 1966. George DeLorean estimates that five hundred Ram Air V engines were built and tested during 1967; the first one hundred engines were 428-ci V-8's with dual four-barrel carburetors, and the remainder were 400-ci V-8's with a single four-barrel.

In spite of the GM ban on racing, the odor of competition lingered in the garages of Pontiac Motor Division like exhaust tinged with castor oil and alcohol. Ford Motor Company had sunk millions of dollars into its racing program; there were people at Pontiac who wanted to see their employer get back into racing, even if it was on an unofficial basis and with an engine design pirated from Ford. George DeLorean recalled that the engineers in charge of the Ram Air V project were "pleased" when they got the first dyno reports: The 428 with dual four-barrels and a compression ratio of 10:1 generated 510 hp. The engine used the one-hundred-

Although never released to the public a limited number of the Ram Air V engines were built. Shown here is its intake manifold and four-barrel carburetor.

eighty-degree dual quad intake manifold that DeLorean had helped to design, but the engineers had rejected his camshaft. Instead they used the Ram Air IV camshaft (which DeLorean described as "junk") and solid lifters. The factory built in limited quantity a beautiful exhaust manifold; it used equal-length, curved tubes with a diameter of four inches. This manifold was used only on the Firebird, for some reason, and when George DeLorean put a Ram Air V in a GTO he built a set of tube headers.

DeLorean and the engineers in charge of this project were ecstatic about the engine and its racing potential, but they had to be realistic in order to get it past the front office and into production. The dual quad 428 engine was pretty wild, so they developed a single four-barrel 400-ci V-8; it was a streetable engine that they felt would get the okay. Then, in late 1968, John Z. DeLorean was transferred to Chevrolet, and the new head of Pontiac, John MacDonald, terminated the limited performance activities.

George DeLorean recalled the importance of that engine, and how the future of the Pontiac image, the future of the GTO, depended upon the Ram Air V. "We seemed to be gaining momentum, it seemed a reality," he said. "I was desperate to save that engine, I tried everything to keep it active." His program to save the engine wasn't limited to Pontiacs. Jaguar of England was having difficulty meeting the American Clean Air Act standards with the cars that it exported to this country. George DeLorean and a friend, Bob Lawrence, attempted to import engineless Jaguars and fit them with Ram Air V engines. That ingenious project, born out of desperation and love, failed, as did other attempts to save the engine.

The Ram Air V was never released to the general public. What, then, happened to the five hundred engines that were built? George DeLorean said that "ninety percent of the engines were gifts, given to people who used them on the oval track, and ten percent were hung around." All the 428-ci engines are gone, he said, but an unknown number of the 400's are still around. "There are some at the road test garage in Milford, and every once in a while someone will pull in (to Leader Automotive) with one in the back of a truck." Even today he intensely regrets that the factory didn't release some Ram Air V GTO's; that, he said, would have been a true collector car.

In addition to lowering the gear ratios, to give the GTO better acceleration, changes were made in the engines to compensate for the loss of compression. The 455 HO engine used the round port heads and the high-rise aluminum intake manifold from the now-extinct Ram Air IV engine. Modifications to the four-barrel carburetor included changing the secondary air valve opening time on the Quadrajet carburetor from 2.5 seconds to one second for faster throttle response, and increasing the air capacity on the 400-ci and 455 HO engines equipped with manual transmissions for improved starting and acceleration. All 400-ci and 455-ci engines had valves identical to those in the earlier high-performance engines, with 2.110-inch intake and 1.770-inch exhaust valves.

There were other changes, such as the Rally Sports shifter with the single-stage upshift feature for use with the automatic transmission, the self-regulating integrated-circuit alternator which did away with a separate regulator, and the maintenance-free battery which Pontiac got first because it had paid for most of

Shown here is a side view of the 1971 Ram Air V engine.

the battery's development costs. While these were interesting and practical changes they contributed nothing to the GTO's performance image. That was fine with Pontiac, for although it could reminisce in its advertisements about the "car with a slightly ungainly name . . . and a legend to build" it sensed or perhaps knew that the days of the true performance car were over.

Pontiac, like the other automobile companies, had never faced the dual threat of public opinion and federal legislation. While politicians had held hearings about auto safety in previous years, those committees seemed ineffectual; now the government had drawn up a list of requirements, requiring the automakers to build their cars the way Congress wanted them built, and it was implementing legislation. A popular joke was that a politician had seen a GTO, noticed the tachometer on the hood, and flew back to Washington to draft legislation which would require that *all* cars be built with their dashboards placed out on the hood! A far-fetched, but not impossible, example of the kind of power that Washington was exerting and that the auto makers were trying to comply with.

Nowhere was this attitude of accommodation seen more clearly than in the GTO advertising: no more color layouts of a spinning, smoking rear tire. Speed and performance were out the window. The emphasis now was on safety and socially-redeeming values; and within a couple of years the emphasis would be on economy.

The third and final year of The Judge option saw the performance car maintaining a brave, even flamboyant, attitude in the face of adversity. This was the car that had evolved during the fifteen years that Pontiac had stressed performance, and now, like an unwanted relative, it kept hanging around the house, speaking in a voice that was too loud, wearing clothes that were too gaudy, calling attention to itself when Pontiac preferred that it maintain a low profile.

Like the GTO, The Judge was essentially unchanged from the previous year. The front end was restyled, and The Judge option included functional air-intake hood scoops, a heavy-duty three-speed transmission with a floor-mounted Hurst T-handle shifter, a black textured grille, a rear deck spoiler (optional black when ordered with the white car) and Judge stripes, decals and emblems, now described as coming in "some of the keenest colors this side of a light show."

The standard engine on The Judge option was the 455 HO V-8, and the standard transmission was the heavy-duty Muncie three-speed. With 335 gross horsepower and a stick shift The Judge would still move out. And with the special handling package, which included wider Rally II wheels, G60x15 tires, heavy-duty shocks and sway-bar, it *would* handle. Pontiac advertised it as "the ultimate road car" and stressed the handling abilities of the GTO and The Judge. In 1971, the factory coined a term, "ridge-nibble," to describe the effect of a tire running on an uneven surface and said that the "GTO's front suspension geometry is now designed to overcome this problem and make the car go exactly where you point it. Not off in some direction of its own. For proof, just try to nibble a ridge sometime. Or go through a turn. GTO has a way of Wide-Tracking around it like the car was locked in a slot."

The factory's other key phrase in 1971 was "tractive force," a term used to explain how the low-compression engine could perform as well as the high-compression engine. "You see, what comes out of the crankshaft is only one function

1971 GTO was only slightly changed from previous year. Changes were in grille and bumper, round parking lights, wide scoops at leading edge of hood.

144

of a car's performance. Even on the straightaway, a car's performance is determined by the net result of all its drive-train components. And that's what tractive force is. The force exerted by the turning of the drive wheels."

Hot Rod magazine tested a Judge fitted with "the ultimate optional suspension pieces, identical to those found on the T-A Firebird," and found that it handled exceptionally well. It was then tested on the track against a Firebird and the "lap times . . . were almost identical." Considering all the attention which was being paid to the Firebird, this comparison was high praise.

But in spite of this praise, The Judge was doomed. Even in an ordinary year it probably would not have survived because sales were dismal. Only 357 Judge hardtop coupes and seventeen Judge convertibles were sold! In fact, the GTO did not do well either, selling a total of only 10,532 cars; of these 9,497 were hardtop coupes and 661 were convertibles. That's a decrease of some seventy-four percent from the previous year, which was also low.

Part of The Judge's problem was that it was the terminus of a line that began with the Tempest and continued upward through the LeMans, the LeMans Sport, the GTO and, finally, The Judge option. As a buyer worked his way up the price range he now found himself stopping somewhere along the line rather than paying the full sum for The Judge.

There was another reason for buyers stopping at the LeMans level and that had to do with the cost of insurance; it cost a great deal more to insure a Judge than it did to insure a LeMans or Tempest, and part of the reason was the increased horsepower, another part was simply the car's name. Insurance rates for muscle cars, which had been increasing steadily, now rose to new heights, and although the insurance companies admitted that the higher rates were based on losses due to theft rather than accidents they were apprehensive about insuring any car with a performance image.

Ray Brock editorialized about the cost of insurance for muscle cars and revealed that he had got hold of an insurance company "confidential 'hot' sheet," which he called a blacklist, a term conjuring up the McCarthy era. Insurance companies, he said, circulated these lists among themselves, listing undesirable models. Included were the GTO and The Judge, other muscle cars and just about everything capable of turning a quick quarter mile *except* for the Corvette. The sheet went on to talk about the language of advertising and to cite other dangers; it warned against insuring cars equipped with "Radials, Wide Ovals, Posi-traction, Hurst Equipment."

Mr. Brock said: "The above words and definitions show the stupidity of at least one insurance company and indicate how tough it will be to do business with them. Other words on their lists which I suggest you avoid mentioning within earshot of an insurance agent are: mags, slicks, racing cam, solid lifters, blueprinting, traction bars, four-speed, scattershield, spoilers, ram air, headers, high-speed rear end [?], and slap stik [sic]. All the above words mean that cars so equipped are bad risks for insurance coverage with all too many companies. Beware!"

1971 GTO Judge hardtop, with 455 HO engine.

In response to Brock's editorial, Dean Jeffers, president of National Mutual Insurance Company, wrote saying that his company was increasing rates on "super-powered" cars by no less than fifty percent. He said ". . . these cars are not conducive to moderate drivers" and the reason for the increase was "to discourage their appeal." The editor of *Hot Rod* replied, "It's extremely difficult to figure out why an insurance company should concern itself with discouraging the appeal of something the public evidently wants."

And that was only the beginning. Before long, various schemes were concocted to put pressure on muscle car owners by making insurance for such cars either terribly expensive or impossible to get. One such scheme was devised by Iowa State Insurance Commissioner Lorne Worthington, who proposed 'banning' muscle cars, lowering speed limits and not licensing *any* car which could accelerate from 0-60 mph in less than nine seconds, was capable of speeds over 80 mph or came equipped with a speedometer which calibrated speeds over 80 mph! The proposal didn't pass, but it reveals much about the mood of the times.

As an answer to the insurance problem and, in a way, as an example of the budget supercar that had been mentioned for several years, Pontiac introduced the GT-37 in 1970, an innocuous nonname which would not appear on any insurance company's blacklist. The Tempest name was gone, having been replaced by the designation T-37, the internal code number for the intermediate hardtop body. The GT-37 was an option package available for any V-8 LeMans coupe or hardtop. It was mainly a trim package, featuring a manual transmission with a Hurst shifter, a set of Rally II wheels without trim rings, G70-14 tires, hood pins, dual exhausts, D-98 vinyl body stripes (identical to those on the 1969 Judge) and special GT-37 identification decals (which from the distance of a few feet looked like they said GTO). There was nothing here that an insurance man could object to.

And yet the GT-37, with any of the five engines available, from the 350-ci engine with a two-barrel carburetor to the 455 HO engine, was a car reminiscent of the 1964 GTO. The Pontiac advertisements picked up on this theme: "There's a little GTO in every GT-37. And you don't have to be over 30 to afford it!" That kind of approach was intended to appeal to the youth market and others who wanted a supercar but were operating on a low budget. Another ad appealed to the latent racer; it showed a GT-37 in a garage, and the car had NASCAR-type hood locks. The caption claimed: "It's Pure Pontiac!"

A basic GT-37 cost $2,800, a reasonable price in 1971, but with the big V-8 and a few options the price rose to around $4,000. As with the GTO there was an option list which included a tachometer, a thick-rimmed Formula steering wheel and honeycomb mag-type wheels. In fact, the GT-37 could be ordered with all GTO options with the exception of The Judge package.

Hot Rod magazine tested a GT-37 with a 400-ci V-8, a wide-ratio (2.52:1 low gear) four-speed transmission and a 3.55:1 rear end. The testers complained about a lack of power, which they attributed to the low-compression engine (8.2:1), and about the feeble clutch, but the car turned the quarter mile in 14.5 seconds for a speed of 96.87 in stock form. They removed the air cleaner and got a speed of 97.50 with an elapsed time of 14.40 seconds. They compared the handling qualities of the GT-37 with those of the early Road Runner because it also had high-rate springs and lacked a rear stabilizer bar. The latter, they pointed out, could be adapted from the GTO (". . . it's a bolt-on"). And if this were done the advertisement would literally be true: There would be a little of The Great One in the GT-37.

OWNERS' COMMENTS

When Pontiac first produced the car (the GTO) I was impressed with the styling and performance. Even though I was not old enough to drive at that time I knew one day I would own one. From the first year to the last the GTO has always been an eye-catcher and in my opinion king of the streets. JB of Cincinnati, Ohio.

My GTO is a Judge with the 455 HO low-compression engine. I like to see the reaction people give, and when you say Judge they know there is nothing on the street better or faster. I didn't know what I had until I joined the GTO club. JN, Dorchester, Massachusetts.

CHAPTER FOURTEEN

On Borrowed Time
1972-1974

LEMANS IN DISGUISE: 1972

In the world of 1972 the GTO concept was clearly an anachronism; federal legislation regarding safety and emissions standards, high insurance rates, crowded roads and a public attitude which eschewed speed indicated that the GTO's time was nearly over. Pontiac had changed its attitude toward performance machinery and, turning its back on the performance image it had worked fifteen years to build, it responded to the series of obstacles by instituting a revisionist policy.

The first step was to terminate The Judge; this was the supreme Pontiac supercar, and it was too flamboyant for a company that wanted to keep a low profile in regard to supercars. Second, it terminated the GTO convertible; it was the next most ostentatious model. Third, Pontiac terminated the GTO as a separate model and, as it had begun, it again became an option in the LeMans series.

To further diminish the GTO's separate identity, the GTO front end became an option available on the LeMans two-door hardtop and the sport convertible. The irony was overwhelming: One could not buy a GTO convertible, but one could, this last year anyway, buy the LeMans convertible with the GTO front end, big V-8, three-speed manual transmission with Hurst shifter, dual exhausts and other options. It was not a GTO, but for a few it was a satisfactory GTO substitute.

Given the fact that the GTO was competing with the LeMans models and the Firebird, as well as with the remaining muscle cars built by other companies, it's no surprise that once again GTO sales were depressed. Although the base price was a reasonable $3,100, a total of only 5,800 GTO's were sold. As an indication of how GTO sales had diminished, 1972 sales were approximately half of 1971 sales, which represented a quarter of 1970 sales, which were approximately half of 1969 sales. The downward spiral was consistent and seemed irreversible.

Because the 1970 GM strike had delayed the all-new GM intermediate car for one year, the 1972 GTO was essentially the same as the 1971 model. It retained the Endura front end, with the energy-absorbing bumper, twin grilles with the same wire-mesh material and twin scoops at the leading edge of the hood. Changes were limited to the 'air extractors' in the front fenders, and at the rear was a rare option,

In addition to usual gauges this owner installed a column-mounted tachometer in his '72.

Close-up of twin scoops at leading edge of hood.

Optional honeycomb wheels for 1972 used Goodyear Neothane bonded to steel disc welded to wheel rim. Also seen here are side splitter exhausts.

a spoiler which had become integrated with the deck lid, much like the duck-tail spoiler seen on the Camaro years earlier. The exhaust was rerouted into splitters which, as on the 1964-65 GTO, exited behind the rear wheels rather than from under the bumper. Even this minor detail was brought up in the sales literature to recall the glory days of the past; the exhaust splitters "... help make sure GTO's classic burble is on pitch."

Engine options were limited. Standard was the 400-ci V-8 which, with four-barrel carburetor and dual exhausts, was rated at 250 net hp. The optional engine remained the 455 HO with slightly higher compression, Ram Air heads and cam, dual exhausts, four-barrel carburetor and was rated at 300 net hp.

A special handling package was also optional. It included fast variable-ratio power steering, G60-15 white-lettered tires on 15x7-inch wheels (the standard tire was G-70x14), high-rate springs, heavy-duty shocks and larger (1⅛-inch) front and rear stabilizer bars.

The GTO was fairly fast and handled well, although by this time it was no match for the Dodge 440, which featured the famous Six Pack (an induction system similar to the old GTO tri-power setup) and a 10.3:1 compression ratio. Perhaps the Pontiac's best feature was that you could tell your insurance man that you had a LeMans, which gave you much lower premiums than if you told him that you had a GTO.

This trend in naming, or not naming, was happening with other makes, too. Chevrolet simply called its muscle car the Chevelle, without citing the SS option, and Oldsmobile's 4-4-2 was called the Cutlass. Plymouth dropped the GTX model identification but continued to offer the Road Runner; Dodge dropped the R/T designation but continued to offer an optional Rally package (its 440 model was listed but not advertised or promoted). Again, such marketing was a compromise:

Front fender air outlet appeared on only 1972 GTO.

1973 GTO featured new energy-absorbing front bumper, louvered quarter window, new body with traditional two-piece grille. Optional accent stripe came in red, black or white, unified disparate body sections.

The factory wanted to offer as much performance as it thought it could sell, but to sell it under a name or designation which would allow the buyer to get it insured at a reasonable rate.

There was a market for performance cars, but it was diminishing each year. Pontiac, hoping to anticipate the next buying trend, offered a new model, the Ventura II. This was a sporty compact, slightly smaller than the GTO, with a wheelbase of 111 inches. The Ventura's standard engine was a 250-ci six-cylinder, and the standard transmission was a column-shift three-speed manual. But it had an optional 307-ci V-8 and the Sprint package which included a three-speed manual floor shifter, a custom steering wheel and a blacked-out grille. Even with its optional folding vinyl sun roof it seemed to recall the original GTO, an association which no doubt took sales away from the current GTO.

YEAR OF THE BUMPER: 1973

The industry was now building cars which would conform to the ever-changing federal guidelines, but in spite of these limitations it realized that it could continue to build a decent muscle car. There was also an indication that the public was showing a renewed interest in such cars. In 1973, muscle cars and pony cars accounted for only four percent of the total market—down from ten percent in 1967—but sales were picking up. Larger engines like the 455-ci V-8 were available and, once shorn of their antipollution equipment, they had a great deal of potential. The cars themselves were larger; gas economy was not yet a real issue with either the manufacturer or the buyer.

The new laws and guidelines were extensive. Some were easier to meet, like the requirement that interiors had to have a maximum burn rate of four inches per minute; others were more difficult, like the new bumper requirements. The result was that manufacturers began an intensive campaign to standardize their cars; when they had solved a problem they applied the solution to the other models under their control. For example, the federal government required a 50,000-mile durability run for each engine/transmission/rear end ratio and car model combination; the factories were in a mad race to make these tests and to meet production schedules. Once they had tested and approved a certain combination they used this combination in many models. Instead of spending money in testing and modifying a dozen engines, the factory got one accepted and offered that engine in a dozen models.

This 1973 GTO is owned by Tony Bastien, president of the GTO Association of America. Bastien's GTO is original, has optional Rally II wheels rather than spartan disc wheel, moon hubcap.

This standardization was also true of chassis design. The GTO was one of the all-new '73 GM intermediate lines; these cars were supposed to be the 1972 models that the GM strike of 1970 had delayed for a year. For the first time the GM intermediates all used the same chassis: a new 115-inch wheelbase chassis which was used for both the coupe and the sedan models (the intermediate convertible had been terminated this year). The body changes were much more than a facelift; with the new frame, new sheet metal had to be designed, and all this restyling was due, in large part, as a result of GM's attempts to meet the federal Motor Vehicle Safety Standards (MVSS).

The new chassis was required because this was, as someone tagged it, The Year of the Bumper. For 1973, all cars had to meet these federal requirements: The front bumper had to withstand a 5-mph barrier crash test without damage to safety-related items, and the rear had to withstand a 2.5-mph barrier crash test with the same minimal damage. In the front end this meant that the hood latch, the headlights, parking lights and turn signals would not be rendered inoperable; and, in the rear, that the taillights, turn signals and backup lights, plus the fuel-tank filler system would not be affected. Manufacturers would literally have to design the car around the front and rear bumpers. Not only would the bumpers themselves be fairly massive and separate from the body, but also the side sheet metal would have to be designed to accommodate the protruding bumpers.

For the GTO, this required a return to the pre-1968 steel bumper. The Endura front end, with its amazing resiliency, could suffer "a deflection of one-half inch under a 1000-psi. load, with complete recovery in 24 hours after depression by a 4000-pound load for eight hours" but it could not survive a 5-mph crash test with such admirable results. The replacement bumper on the 1973 GTO was a massive chrome-plated steel unit. It featured a new energy-absorbing frame mount which could compress three inches and return to normal position. The unit used heavy telescoping steel chambers, pressurized gas and hydraulic fluid to absorb the impact. The rear bumper was also massive, but it was nontelescoping. It was backed up with steel-boxed beam reinforcement and supported with flexible steel bars which acted like mild springs. To protect the chrome plating, an optional rubber rub-strip could be affixed to the leading edge of both bumpers.

These bumpers passed the respective 5- and 2.5-mph tests, but they also completely changed the now-familiar GTO front end design. The Endura bumper was more than a buffer against other cars; it was the styling frontispiece around which the entire front end was designed. It not only allowed for, but was in some ways the *raison d'être* for, the peaked grille divider which flowed smoothly back to the twin hood scoops and from which the hood and fenders flowed.

The new front bumper seemed almost separate from the rest of the car. In order for the telescoping mechanism to have room to operate, the bumper was positioned several inches ahead of the front end sheet metal; the parking lights and

1973 GTO Colonade coupe with 400-ci engine.

dual cold-air intakes were neatly located in the lower half of the bumper, but from the side the unit looked stepped, like the front porch to an elegant house. In addition to aesthetic considerations, the federally legislated bumpers were heavy and expensive to replace when damaged.

This disjointed effect was evident throughout the car's design. The 'Colonnade styling' resulted in a car which had the appearance of having been designed by a number of people who were not on speaking terms. The front half had a squared-off appearance, with a flat grille and square headlight housings; while the rear section was curved, coming to a sharp point at the back bumper. These halves met at a roof which seemed to have been designed simply as a middle ground, and the doors had the outline of vestigial pontoon fenders similar to those found on the 1946-47 Cadillac. The helter-skelter effect was accented by the quarter windows which were covered by louvers, and by the NACA-designed hood scoops which were twin triangular shapes vaguely similar to the Pontiac medallion, cut out of the hood. The latter were really pretty strange—like the eyes of a jack-o'-lantern, two tri-shaped holes made by a cookie-cutter.

In spite of the confusion of styles, the car managed to have an element of credibility: It looked mean, as if it had been backed into a corner and suddenly decided that it had been pushed around long enough. The effect was due to the plain grilles, the change from quad to dual headlights, the plain seven-inch steel wheels, G60-15 black tires and moon hubcaps. It recalled the 'chair cars' of the 1950's, an unpretentious sedan that the police wouldn't notice but which housed a full-race engine. In other words, it had a no-frills racing look; it was a sleeper.

The list of options diminished since the GTO became an option in the LeMans line, as a LeMans sport coupe or Colonnade. The options were essentially limited to appearance items: the blacked-out grille, twin "NASA type" hood scoops, GTO decals on the front fenders and deck lid, blackwall tires, moon hubcaps and dual exhausts with chrome extensions. Bucket seats and a Ram Air system were available as well, although the latter is *very* rare. There were also optional vinyl accent stripes which came in a variety of colors; these began near the front of the hood and broadened into a spear on the doors and ended at the rear fender kickup. They added color, and helped to unify the disparate body elements.

There was also a heavy-duty handling package, consisting of stiffer shock absorbers and bigger stabilizer bars (1.25-inch front and 1.0-inch rear). These, coupled with the new perimeter frame and the four-link coil rear suspension, did improve the car's handling abilities. In addition, all the GM intermediates had the new Accu-Drive, where the suspension reacted to neutralize side movement.

In keeping with the trend of offering a limited number of engine and drive train combinations, the GTO came with only the 400-ci V-8 and three-speed heavy-duty manual transmission with floor shifter (the same engine and transmission which came as standard equipment on the LeMans sport coupe). The major option list didn't even include a four-speed transmission!

Actually, with a little work, or with a dealer who was willing to deal, it was possible to develop your own option list. The Muncie M-20 four-speed or the Turbo Hydra-matic three-speed transmissions would fit in this car, as would the 455-ci V-8.

The factory promotional literature announced that there soon would be an optional engine available—the 455 SD (Super Duty) V-8 which was an option on

Adding striping and decals is precision work.

the Firebird and was being extended as an option on the GTO. This engine was rated at 310 net hp, which made it the most powerful domestic engine available in 1973. The Super Duty engine was described as a high-performance engine which had been detuned for street use in order to pass emission standards. News that such an engine was available was greeted enthusiastically by the avid street racer.

The Super Duty parts, interchangeable with the earlier 455 HO engines, included four-bolt main caps, nodular iron crank, forged-steel connecting rods, heavy-duty oil pump, forged-aluminum pistons and other goodies. And the engine had even greater potential: It produced 310 net hp at 5000 rpm and was capable of turning in excess of 6000 rpm. It was easy to see that head work or the use of high-compression pistons could raise the compression ratio from 8.4:1 to something around 10.5:1, and if the camshaft were changed horsepower could be increased to 400-425 hp.

And if that wasn't enough to make the dyed-in-the-wool Poncho racer's heart beat faster there was also the news that an aluminum block would soon be available. It was designed by Pontiac but was sold through Reynolds Aluminum, and came as a blank which could be bored to the desired size.

But such dreams were not to be. The aluminum block idea vanished almost immediately. And the 455 SD engine, which was "On hold pending acoustical development," was limited to approximately 120 units before it was killed. *Hi-Performance Cars* said that it had tested such a car. The magazine raved about the 455 SD GTO's performance and handling abilities and, although it awarded the car the Top Performance Car of the Year cup, it released no data on the test. Without such evidence it was difficult to accept or dispute the editor's assertion that "The 1973 GTO . . . is better than the original Tiger in every conceivable way. . . ." What *was* indisputable was that only 4,806 GTO's were sold, a figure lower than the one the factory grudgingly allowed for the GTO back in 1964.

ECLIPSE OF THE GREAT ONE: 1974

Performance diminished even more in importance with the sudden 'energy crisis' of 1973. Companies now had a third problem: how to build a car that was safe,

1974 GTO, described in factory advertising as "Pontiac's tough little road car," was actually a Ventura with trim options.

wouldn't generate excessive pollution and was also economical. As Martin Caserio, general manager of Pontiac, said, "One-third of our engineering dollar is going into engine and emissions work."

At the end of the year, James McDonald of Chevrolet spoke for the industry when he acknowledged this problem: "The American automobile market is undergoing a marked change toward smaller cars. Since last February, when the fuel shortage became a matter of public discussion, the small car end of the market has really boomed. Buyers are not only concerned with lower purchase price; they want lower operating costs as well."

The nature and scope of the manufacturers' problems were reflected by the progressive growth of the authority of the Environmental Protection Agency (EPA). At first the EPA was concerned only with regulations dealing with clean air. Then it began publishing the figures indicating the relative exhaust emissions put out by the various domestic and foreign cars. Next, it began publishing fuel economy figures obtained during emission tests. Finally, it forced manufacturers to label their various models with the average gas mileage for cars with a specified weight, along with the mpg of that particular car. This was a situation that the manufacturers had never before faced, and the published statistics, whether accurate or inaccurate, had an effect upon the car-buying public.

It's no surprise, then, that the final GTO became a down-sized version of the 1973 GTO.

Although the LeMans and LeMans sport coupe models would continue to be manufactured until 1977, the GTO option was dropped on that line after only one year and was assigned to the compact Pontiac model, the Ventura. In the early 1960's the Ventura was the full-size model, or more accurately it was a trim package based on the Catalina line. In 1971 it was introduced as a separate line, a compact model developed to compete with Chevrolet's Nova (the Nova and Ventura used the same body). Now the GTO option was available on the Ventura, the Ventura custom coupe and the hatchback models.

For the true GTO aficionado the new GTO was seen as a joke—if The Judge had been a spoof on muscle cars, a parody, this version of the GTO was simply a bad joke. They felt that it really wasn't a GTO at all, but merely a trim option on the Ventura. But some felt that the new GTO bore considerable resemblance to the original GTO; and hoped that the car's evolution had come full circle, returning to its roots. They pointed out that the Ventura was short (actually shorter than the 1964 GTO: 111-inch wheelbase versus 115-inch), with less overhang (199 inches versus 203 inches) and with the clean lines of the original.

GTO differed from Ventura Sprint in that it had parking lights in grille, 'shaker' hood scoop, GTO identification decals. It was available as a coupe or hatchback.

The Ventura seemed like a scaled-down version of a 1970 GTO. It continued with the traditional two-piece horizontal grille, with a black wire mesh inset behind a chrome strip and, like the 1966-67 GTO, the parking lights were bolted to the grille. The headlights used a surround almost identical to that found on the 1970 GTO, but on the smaller car the lights had a massive appearance. The grille center came forward in a peak which continued down the middle of the hood. Most notable of both the front and the rear of the car were the chrome energy-absorbing bumpers, which were large and set well away from the sheet metal in order to allow the bumpers to telescope. The bumpers' faces had optional rubber rub-strips, as did the vertical bumper guards. The front bumper had openings which served as air intakes.

The GTO option consisted of a new blacked-out grille with parking lights, Mag-type Rally II wheels without trim rings à la Judge, dual exhausts, GTO decals and outside sports mirrors. It also included what the factory described as a "tough-looking shaker hood that scoops up cold, dense air," a phrase that recalled the early Ram Air advertising. The functional scoop on the hood of the new GTO faced backward, and was taller and less graceful than the earlier scoops. Additional options were bucket seats, sport steering wheel, power front disc brakes and the Rally gauge cluster with either a tachometer or a clock (available when you ordered bucket seats and console).

As an indication of how much things had changed, there was only one engine available: the 350-ci V-8 with a four-barrel carburetor. The standard transmission was the three-speed manual, but available as options were either the four-speed or the Turbo Hydra-matic three-speed with Hurst floor shifter.

Also available was the optional Radial Tuned Suspension system, a product of the computer age. This package consisted of 'tuned' suspension parts, including Pliacell shock absorbers, heavy-duty stabilizer bars, 'tuned' suspension bushings and jounce restrictors, and FR78-14 steel-belted radial tires. Cars with this suspension package were identified by a special RTS plate on the instrument panel. Once again the GTO was a small car with a big engine, but now the old handling problems were being dealt with. Of this handling package the factory said, "The RTS objective is to give the Pontiac driver increased steering response with controlled vertical motion and a minimum of impact harshness. Improved roadability and traction are the results of Radial Tuned Suspension."

The new GTO did handle well and, with the front disc brakes and radial tires, it stopped in a shorter distance than had the original GTO. The decals seemed too large for the car, but otherwise there were only a couple of chronic problems: The inside door handles tended to break off easily, and on the hatchback model the rear door fit poorly and would rattle.

Pontiac projected a sales figure of 10,000 GTO's, which might have been optimistic in view of the previous year's sales figure which was less than half of that. In fact, sales of the new GTO rose sharply, increasing some forty-three percent over 1973, and a total of 7,058 GTO's were sold. This was actually a rather high figure considering that 1974 was a terrible year for the automobile industry, as it continued to suffer from the economic recession and react to the energy crisis.

A Pontiac 350-ci V-8 engine being dynamically balanced at the factory.

The latter situation, which had a number of causes but which could be said to stem directly from the 1973 Arab oil embargo, saw the price of gasoline increase one hundred percent overnight. This drastic increase in the price and availability of gasoline, of course, adversely affected what market remained for supercars. Even this down-sized GTO, with the 350-ci V-8, got only 9.9 mpg.

The 1974 GTO wasn't fast enough to be considered a true supercar, or agile enough to be a sports car and it got such terrible gas mileage it couldn't be considered an economy compact. At what market did it aim? Most of the advertising emphasized safety, 'accident prevention' and antitheft devices, elements of motoring which previous GTO advertising had largely ignored. A notable advertising theme called the GTO "Pontiac's tough little road car," but that could have been said of the LeMans or the Trans Am Firebird. The fact was obvious: The GTO had succeeded because it had a clear sense of identity. It had an image, and because of this image the car was able to create a market; the down-sized Ventura/GTO lacked an image, and therefore it lacked a market. The image-market situation was complicated by the problems of meeting federal safety and emission requirements, the high cost of gasoline and insurance and the declining interest the public showed toward a machine built on the image of power. But these were problems Pontiac could have confronted if it had been committed to the concept of the GTO. Instead, it decided to promote the Trans Am as the factory performance machine and, ten years after its birth, the GTO was terminated.

It's symbolic that shortly after the GTO was dropped from Pontiac's line, the building at 196 Wide-Track Boulevard—the place from which all the factory photos, posters and free GTO materials flowed—was demolished. Today, you'll find a parking lot at this address.

APPENDIX I
Goodies For An Old Goat

The Pontiac V-8 as used in the GTO is a strong-running and long-lasting engine. It requires only normal maintenance and tune-ups to provide years of dependable transportation, and it's not uncommon to find a GTO engine with over a hundred thousand miles which has had neither the heads nor the pan removed. For example, Charles Price has 135,000 miles on his 1964 GTO and the only problem is a front bearing/seal oil leak. Charlie Bowers bought his 1966 GTO new and says "The car has 180,000 miles on it and runs as good as ever. The motor has never been overhauled."

It's still a strong-running engine, as fast today as it was in the 1960's; a fifteen-year-old GTO that has been maintained and kept in tune will still spin a hundred miles of rubber off the back tires in one quick acceleration run. In spite of the national 55-mph speed limit, most GTO owners cite the power of the GTO as their primary reason for owning one. As cars get more anemic this pleasure undoubtedly increases; the GTO is an anachronism, a rocket from the past, and you cannot buy that kind of power off the showroom floor anymore. To compare the new and the old we need only look at a recent movie, *Smokey and the Bandit II*, and the 1980 Trans Am Turbo with a 301-ci V-8 used in the action sequences. The first film had lots of tire-spinning chase scenes, an important element in such films, and the director wanted more of the same in the sequel. But the turbocharged car lacked the low-speed torque to spin its tires! The company had to fly two men from California to Georgia to install a nitrous-oxide injection system—and then it would smoke the tires only on wet pavement! That little demonstration says a great deal about how things have changed.

However, even a GTO engine may need to be rebuilt eventually. Nearly twenty years have passed since the advent of the GTO but finding engine parts is not a problem. The corner auto parts house has, or can order, such items as a gasket set or rings and bearings at a reasonable price; any good machine shop can boil out the block and heads and do a competent valve grind. If the owner has time and is inclined to get his hands dirty he can accomplish an engine overhaul with the aid of a factory or aftermarket workshop manual. The Pontiac V-8 is not an exotic engine, and if a machinist checks the cylinder walls, crank journals and rods for wear and sets the engine up according to factory tolerances it should be good for another hundred-thousand miles.

The only qualification that needs to be added here has to do with the tri-power. Factory literature on this subject is almost non-existent, but carburetor rebuild kits are available and a tune-up shop should be willing to do the job. The real problem is trying to straighten out the plumbing that's been added during the past dozen years! If you want that aftermarket fuel block and neoprene hose off your otherwise original GTO you'll have to find someone with an original tri-power in order to see what you need (the reproduction linkage is available, and the GTO Association of America recently published a series of articles on how to restore a tri-power in its newsletter, *The Gas Can*).

If your goal is to have a smooth-running, stock GTO you ought to consider rebuilding the original distributor to insure a hot spark, to avoid point float and to be certain that the mechanical advance is fully operational. A kit with special weights, springs and advance-limiter bushing is

455-ci V-8 had chrome rocker arm covers, chrome aftermarket performance air cleaner. Tube in cleaner led to Spearco water injection unit, helped high-compression engine run on lower-octane gasoline.

available at most speed shops; this kit speeds up the rate of centrifugal advance and limits it so the initial advance is increased. This kit, along with Mallory H-D points and Mallory Voltmaster coil, will insure a hot spark and a full advance curve.

If you're less of a purist and more interested in performance, the next step would be to consider a set of exhaust headers. The factory manifolds are comparatively restrictive, and free breathing is the key to performance. The first Ram Air engines had their exhaust ports increased by nearly thirty-four percent over the standard ports, and headers take advantage of that larger opening. Factory cast-iron headers can sometimes be found at swap meets, but most likely you'll want to buy preformed tubing headers from an aftermarket dealer.

With a hot ignition, headers and rebuilt carburetor(s) your GTO should be moving out better and with improved gas mileage, but if you're still not satisfied you ought to consider a Bobcat kit. Nearly all the GTO's tested in magazines had the Royal Pontiac Bobcat treatment, which was one reason they turned such terrific times.

Royal Pontiac no longer exists, but the Bobcat kit can still be ordered from George DeLorean at Leader Automotive in Troy, Michigan. Because the octane rating in today's gasoline is much lower than it was during the heyday of the GTO, he tailors the kit for a particular engine. Whether the kit will be used on a pre-1971 high-compression engine or a later low-compression engine, George DeLorean said that "It's still the Bobcat kit, but it's a custom kit rather than the basic kit we used to sell everybody." The Bobcat kit comes in stages, which can be purchased separately. There is the carburetor kit, the distributor kit, the valve kit, the tune up kit and the cylinder head kit. "We still package them and send them out, but we don't sell that many anymore," said George DeLorean. "The whole package is right around $99," he said, which is approximately what the basic kit cost a dozen years ago.

1968 Tunnel port head (top) has breathing advantages over older square port head.

Engine in Tom Tilton's GTO uses earlier 326-ci block bored 0.030, with 10.5:1 pistons, TRW double-moly rings, TRW double-roller timing chain, Crane camshaft, lifters, push rods and valve springs. Uses 1969 400 HO heads with 62-cc chambers. Entire assembly has been balanced.

A favorite with serious racers is this Doug Nash tunnel ram manifold which uses two four-barrel carburetors. Made of magnesium alloy, it is very rare and expensive; sells for around $600 now.

The Bobcat kit doesn't visibly change the car in any way, and this is in keeping with the wishes of most GTO owners today who want to keep their goats as original as possible. Besides, most of them find 300-360 hp to be sufficient for their driving needs. But for the person who buys a GTO without an engine, or who is unable to find the correct engine for a particular year/model GTO, or who desires to fulfill that impulse to own a faster, more powerful GTO, the answer can be found in that popular adage of the 1950's: There's no substitute for cubic inches!

The first possibility is to find a later-model 400-ci engine (or bore the 389-ci block .060 inch); not only is it a larger engine, but there are other advantages. The post-1966 GTO engines are better, the ports are visibly larger on both the intake manifold and the heads, the manifold runners are straighter and the valve size has been enlarged to 1.923 inches for the intake and 1.643 inches for the exhaust. Previous engines needed to have a set of screw-in rocker arm studs adapted; the post-1966 engines come that way stock. Also, previous engines suffered excessive push-rod wear because of the essentially guideless head, but the post-1966 heads have a stamped steel guide for perfect push-rod alignment. For 1967-68, the heads had the valve spacing shifted from 1.82 inches to 1.98, and the valve angle was dropped from a twenty-degree to a fourteen-degree inclination. The result is that those heads resembled the 1962-63 Super Duty heads; they'll bolt on pre-1967 engines without any problem.

It would be better, of course, to use the 1969-70 Ram Air IV heads, as those were completely redesigned: reworked

Cast-iron factory optional GTO header.

John Biro, Jr., owns this wicked-looking modified GTO. The car is essentially a 1967, with 1967 Tempest hood fitted with Moroso scoop. Front wheels are 14x6 Cragar reverse with D70x14 Super Charger tires; rear wheels are 14x10 Cragar standard with N50x14 Mickey Thompson tires. Side pipes are 3.5-inch Cyclones.

Engine is 1969 400-ci from Biro's GTO, fitted with earlier tri-power setup, Mickey Thompson rocker arm covers. Transmission is 400 Turbo-Matic with Dual-Gate floor shifter. Rear end is 10-bolt 3.23:1 Posi-traction.

combustion chambers, tuliped valves, larger push rods with internal restrictors and larger, round exhaust ports. In these heads the valves had been moved to a position directly in the center of the combustion chamber, a design similar to Ford's NASCAR 427 engine, and the two center ports have been moved apart. This change nearly tripled the diameter of the intake port and spaced the exhaust port so that fuel flowed directly into the chamber through 2.19-inch-diameter valves and exited through 1.73-inch exhaust valves. The cam (#9794041) for this Ram Air IV engine had a .480-inch lift and was the first cam ever designed by computer.

The installation of these Ram Air IV heads and cam will boost the horsepower by about twenty and increase engine speed by about 300 rpm. The use of the Ram Air IV lifters and springs will increase engine speed to approximately 6000-6200 rpm as opposed to the stock limit of 5500 rpm because these lifters have a higher leakdown rate and the springs have considerably more tension. The use of RA IV lifters and springs is almost mandatory because the quicker lift rates of the RA IV cam will trigger valve float earlier.

Apparently Pontiac designed a limited number of RA IV cams for use with mechanical lifters; these had a lift of .520 inch, with a duration rate of 308 degrees intake, 320 degrees exhaust, which was a little radical. McKellar preferred a milder grind, a cam which followed a good torque curve and which allowed the engine to idle, and he preferred hydraulic lifters, even though he recognized their limitations, because he felt that a street engine so equipped would stay in tune longer.

If you're interested in cubic inches, the next step up would be the fabulous 1961-63 Super Duty 421. These engines, however, have always been extremely rare; they were actually factory blueprinted engines from the good old days when Pontiac was actively engaged in racing. They came equipped with a McKellar #7 or an Iskendarian E2 cam with solid lifters, and they were underrated by the factory at 348 and 363 hp. Dick Jesse of Royal Pontiac ran a "nearly stock" Super Duty 421 in his 1965 GTO funny car; it regularly turned 7500 rpm, and covered the quarter mile at 136 mph on a nitro fuel mixture.

Since those engines are so rare and expensive, one might as well think in terms of a 428-ci V-8. This engine, the big brother of the 400-ci, will bolt into any GTO without the need to change motor mounts or purchase an adaptor, and it weighs almost the same as the smaller-displacement engine. The 428-ci V-8 is a high-torque engine of almost square dimensions, having a bore size of 4.12 inches and a stroke of 4.0 inches; it has a big five main bearing crank, and a compression ratio of 10.75:1. With a single four-barrel carburetor it is rated at a whopping 390 hp at 5200 rpm.

In 1968 Royal Pontiac began to perform this engine swap in GTO's, and the exchange price in those days was only $650! That price included the Ram Air tub, open hood scoop(s) and engine modifications. Royal raised the compression ratio by milling the heads .025 inch and using a thin head gasket to raise it even more. That was when you could buy high-octane gasoline for thirty cents a gallon; given the nature and price of present-day gasoline you may want to skip that modification.

To avoid valve float Royal increased spring tension by slipping .060-inch shims under them; with this alteration the engine would turn 5700 rpm—200 rpm over the factory's maximum—before the hydraulic lifters would begin to pump up. Royal also removed the vacuum-advance control on the distributor and reworked the centrifugal advance for a sharper curve, with maximum advance set at thirty-five degrees before top dead center. The carburetor was subjected to minor but crucial changes: bigger jets to enrich the primary mixture, and an adjustment to the air flap on

The engine in Dennis Cook's 1965 GTO is later-model 400-ci V-8, with 12.5:1 TRW pistons, Cloyes roller chain, TRW high-volume oil pump.

Valves have 1.77-inch diameter exhaust, 2.11-inch diameter intake, have been swirl-polished and tuliped. 1967 heads have been cc'ed. Heads use Crane outer valve springs, Engle inner springs, titanium valve spring retainers, Crane lifters, chrome moly push rods.

the secondary throats so that they wouldn't tend to starve out.

These changes, although minor, boosted horsepower to well over the 400-hp mark and allowed the big engine to perform smoothly at all speeds. Royal claimed that its GTO-428 conversion would go from 0-60 mph in 5.2 seconds, would cover the standing quarter mile in 13.8 seconds with a speed of 104 mph, had an estimated top speed of 117 mph and got 10-13 mpg.

If the 428-ci V-8 is good, the 455-ci V-8 could be better. This engine has the same outside dimensions as the 389/400-ci V-8 engines and will drop into the space they've vacated; the same motor mounts and transmission as well as the old water pump, harmonic balancer and fan assembly can be used. The stock exhaust manifolds will also fit, but because exhaust breathing is crucial it's suggested that aftermarket headers be used on this engine. Some headers require that a small section of the fenderwell be cut away;

but otherwise there is no need to make any changes under the hood—the big, big V-8 bolts right into a GTO.

Royal Pontiac made a number of these swaps also, putting the 455-ci V-8 in 1964 and later GTO's as well as in Firebirds. Royal used a factory short-block (#483393), stock Ram Air IV heads and special Pontiac super-duty rods (#529238); aftermarket equipment included Forgedtrue 12:1 pistons, General Kinetics cam with hydraulic lifters, JR headers and an Edelbrock manifold with a single four-barrel 1050 cfm Carter Thermo-Quad carburetor. The entire crankshaft, rod and piston assembly was balanced. This engine, in a Firebird equipped with Turbo Hydra-matic and a 3.90:1 rear end, turned the quarter mile at a speed of 121.78 mph with a time of 11.68!

The changes outlined above give the GTO plenty of power for all kinds of driving, they don't affect its dependability and they are changes which can be undone if one wants to return the car to its original state.

APPENDIX II
Herding Goats

The Pontiac GTO died in 1974 but like the archetypal heroes in classical mythology, who must die in order to be reborn, like the Phoenix rising from its own ashes, the GTO will rise again! Because it is more than a car, because it represents the spirit of great times gone by, muscle car aficionados continue to hope that Pontiac will retool and produce a car which is at least similar to the old GTO. Rumors abound: The Second Coming seems imminent to the true believers— even though the name has been used in vain on puny imitators like the Colt GTO from Japan and the Puma GTO from South America, a car that uses Chevrolet "Opala" parts and that bears no resemblance to *the* GTO.

Officers of the GTO Association of America were told by "a former Pontiac engineer" that there was a GTO-X car on the drawing boards and, excited by this prospect, they took a survey to get their members' reactions, some of which were published in the association's newsletter. A member who was in favor of the new GTO described his version of what the car might be like: ". . . a small car (Sunbird hatchback), modified with fiberglass panels, a 301 4.9 turbo, automatic and three letters to make it go, GTO."

Others were less enthusiastic. "For God's sake—let's let the name GTO die proudly—do you realize the farce it would be if some smog-motored box with the name GTO were to appear?"

"I give Pontiac credit for not bringing the name back. What resemblance would a 1981 GTO bear to the original, anyway?"

In response, Tony Bastien, the president of the association, came up with what seems an excellent and possible solution albeit one which would cost about $200 million; he suggested that "they [Pontiac] start a subsidiary in Mexico, and build *real* GTO's which we could then bring into the US, quite in the same way that 150-mph Lamborghinis are still being imported." The fact is that federal emission laws and safety standards prohibit an American manufacturer from building a car even vaguely similar to The Great One, and high gasoline prices would limit sales to such a small group of dedicated drivers that gathered together in a supermarket parking lot they could hardly start a good-sized club. And someone has pointed out that if Pontiac *did* build a GTO like the original, with the performance equipment, options, high-quality materials and finish, the car would cost between $20,000 and $25,000 in 1982!

It's not surprising, then, as American cars have been progressively down-sized, and all cars have merged into one anonymous universal car which has the shape and personality of a shoe box, with an eye dropper for a fuel pump, to find that the demand for older GTO's has increased greatly. They are desired as machines, as artifacts, as symbols. "I own a GTO," says Dennis Bornhorst, "because . . . it represents an era gone by, one which lives on in fond memories."

Charles Price appreciates the car's sheer power: "The car's best feature is power—screaming acceleration!"

Richard Buss owns a GTO because it is both realistic and fantastic transportation: "It's like having two cars in one—a good-looking touring car and a muscle machine, a kind of Dr. Jekyll and Mr. Hyde combination."

Otherwise stock 1965 GTO owned by James Croteau has air-brush detailing on deck lid. Note license plate.

For John D. DeFelice, a deputy sheriff, the car is better than a psychiatrist's couch: "My '64 GTO does for me today what it did then [in the late 1960's]. Whatever adult traumas I might worry about disappear when I drive my GTO."

Christine Kirkpatrick feels so strongly about her GTO that she ranks it with essential human relationships: "There are three things in my life . . . my daughter, my boy friend and my GTO. As long as I keep these three I have everything."

The GTO is desired for reasons that have to do with sentimentality, transportation, ego, machine-worship—and as a good investment. The GTO is a driveable, fun car which has steadily appreciated in value. In 1970 Brock Yates, writing about a handful of cars which he felt would be worth collecting because of their investment potential, prophesied that a $400 GTO would in the next ten years appreciate tenfold. Mr. Yates chose the right car, but because of the rate of inflation he somewhat underestimated its worth.

The 1982 *Old Cars Price Guide* singled out the GTO for a cover story entitled "GTO Pricing Profiles." The suggested price of a 1964 GTO coupe ranged from a low of $900 for a rough but restorable car to a high of $6,100; a 1964 GTO convertible ranged from $1,000 to $7,600. A decent driveable example of these models ranged from $3,700 to $5,050; ten percent should be added if the car has tri-power, and $200 should be added if the car has mint exhaust splitters. A 1966 sport coupe ranged from $670 to $4,000; a hardtop coupe from $700 to $4,100; a convertible from $1,100 to $5,000. Even the later models command a good figure. A 1970 hardtop is worth from $700 to $3,400, and a convertible from $850 to $3,600; it's suggested that you add twenty-five percent for The Judge option.

The Judge has rapidly increased in value, as have GTO convertibles. In his book, *Production Survival Source: The Investor's Illustrated Guide to American Convertibles and Special-Interest Automobiles, 1946-1976*, Charles Webb suggests that out of a total of 62,147 GTO convertibles made in eight years there are only 18,250 left.

Ron Aungst, who bought a 1970 Judge when it was new and who has not the slightest desire to sell it, was curious what his car might be worth and so he checked with Automotive Information Clearinghouse, one of several such agencies that have sprung up in recent years. The agency informed him that an average Judge was worth $2,005, a well-maintained one was worth $3,255 and an excellent example was worth $4,610. He was told that the car's rate of appreciation in 1980 had been 7.7 percent, while it would appreciate 12.6 percent in the upcoming year, a hefty increase.

During the past several years, for better or for worse, many people have seen antique and classic cars as a speculation and investment market; they may not care about the car per se but they do care about a return on their investment so they've jacked the price of Duesenbergs and Cords and vintage Mercedes to that financial limbo somewhere between $100,000 and $200,000. Even Fords of the 1930's, which ten years ago sold for under $1,000, are now selling for upwards of $25,000. Could a GTO ever be worth that much?

Factory tri-power setups, offered for GTO from 1964 to mid-1966, are desirable items and turn up at swap meets. They sell for $75-$125, will bolt to later heads.

A pseudo-GTO? In 1971-72, factory offered Endura Styling Option which included hood, air scoops, valance panel, parking lights, air extractors, fiberglass headlamp panels. Option here is fitted to 1972 LeMans Sport HT.

Perhaps—at least certain models. Robert Gottlieb wrote in 1981 in *Motor Trend*, "Too many Mustangs were built to permit them to ever reach astronomical prices . . . [but] muscle cars are in tremendous demand. . . ." Quantity dictates a car's potential price, and while all GTO's are desirable certain limited-production models are seen as especially good investments. For people who have extra money lying around, The Judge convertible has the investment potential of a Matisse painting. Only 276 were built during 1969-70, and only seventeen were built in 1971! The latter is so rare that the Pontiac factory does not have a photograph of it! Three years ago a 1971 Judge convertible was advertised for $17,500 firm, and one can assume that the price has now risen to around $25,000. Of the sixteen remaining examples, only four have been located; if it could be established that the others have been junked the five known 1971 Judge convertibles would rapidly rise in value.

Fortunately for those of us who exist in less rarified air GTO's are still affordable. They are listed for sale in the classifieds in large city newspapers, sometimes under the Antique and Classic Cars heading, sometimes under the Pontiac heading by an owner who doesn't consider it a special car. They are advertised on cards placed on bulletin boards in supermarkets and laundromats, especially in college towns, and in the free newspapers given over to advertising. Sometimes they can be found for a very reasonable sum in the back row of a used car lot. In the past three years many people have traded their big car for a small one; this has happened on the West Coast at an alarming rate, and while I sometimes feel anxious over the future of *any* full-size American car I do see it as a transitional period when one can buy a large car for a nominal sum, and this includes GTO's. In fact, one can buy a GTO which will appreciate in value, and buy *another* to use as a parts car, and yet *another* which, combined with the second, would make a good car for the spouse, and. . . .

Jeff Tillman looks at The Judge hardtop parked on the packed dirt driveway, as if appraising its value, and says, "I just had to have that one, too." It's late fall and the clear sunny day has a chill which would knock the leaves from the trees, if there were any trees. Instead there is the unbroken horizon and, to the east, the freeway leading to Dayton, and all around, brown fields, plowed right up to the area around the house where the tires of many cars have packed the dirt flat. Parked in the driveway, on the flattened dirt to the north of the house, in the back around the barn are cars, all of them GTO's. Jeff Tillman owns "around" twenty-five GTO's—he's not even certain of the number. He apologizes unnecessarily for not having more of his cars at home, and explains that he has several at his "other place" in Anna, Ohio, and a few at the houses of friends.

Jeff Tillman is twenty-six and has owned GTO's for the past ten years, with the exception of a two-month period

Console-mounted vacuum gauge is pre-GTO item, had been on Catalina and Grand Prix, was GTO option at least until 1967.

GTO shift knobs: 1964 (left), 1966 (right), 1967 Dual-Gate (center). They're in demand to replace lost, broken knobs; some go for as high as $50 (NOS).

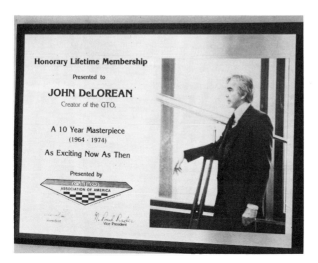

Plaque presented to John Z. DeLorean by GTO Association of America in appreciation for his development of the GTO.

after his marriage. "Since I was going to be the family type of husband I decided to give up on cars. I sold my second GTO and bought a nice, large family-type Chevy Caprice. I went about two months without a GTO but I began to get withdrawal symptoms. You know, can't sleep, stomach cramps, headaches. It was awful." He healed himself by buying a black 1965 GTO, just like the other two he'd owned. That was eight years ago, and he still owns it. Plus two dozen others.

"I bought a white '64 GTO," he says, kicking his heel into the packed dirt. "From then on, I more or less lost track of what happened. GTO's began springing up all over. I had them in the garage, on the street, in my yard, in my neighbor's yard. Any relative who said he had a little extra room in his driveway got one of my GTO's."

The town officials got complaints about Jeff's cars and after trying unsuccessfully to get them all hidden from sight he gave up and last year he bought a small farm where there is no zoning law against unlicensed automobiles and where there's room for even more cars. "I'm not much of a farmer," he says, "but I like raising Goats. Now that I have more space I think the herd is going to expand quite rapidly. Seems to me like the devils are starting to multiply faster than rabbits now."

Jeff knows GTO's thoroughly—knows their mechanics, their quirks, their history. He's the organizer and president of the GTO club, known as Goats Through Ohio, and he's the GTO Technical Advisor for the Pontiac Oakland Club International. Like other GTO owners he loves the car for what it is, a car, but it's also *the* car. "I've owned about every other type of muscle car. None of them compare. The only people that say that the other 'muscle cars' "—and you can hear the quotes around the words as he says them—"are better, are people who have never owned a GTO. Remember, GTO'S means Godfather of The Other Supercars."

A gust of wind blows across the barren, plowed field, raising a narrow dust cloud, bringing a northern chill; with this reminder of the changing season, the impending winter,

Jeff points to the concrete slab and the fresh studs pointing skyward. He tells me that he plans to open a used car lot, which is surprising since the location seems remote from anything except other farms and the only traffic seems to be on the freeway a few miles to the east. It's also surprising since I get the idea that he doesn't want to sell his GTO's. Nor does he seem to want to sell GTO parts except perhaps to a friend or to help another GTO owner. He mentions that a friend needed a fan assembly and Jeff offered him one for ten dollars; when the guy tried to beat him down Jeff kept the part. This was between friends, the price was lower than what a junkyard would charge and, anyway, he didn't *need* to sell the part. He doesn't *need* to sell anything. He'd prefer to acquire more—you can never have too many GTO's or parts, according to Jeff.

He mentions that he does do business with GTO owners around the country. His 'Texas pipeline' is a friend who moved from Ohio to Texas and who steers Jeff toward rust-free cars, of which Texas has many, in exchange for GTO parts and optional factory equipment, of which Ohio has many. He has a contact in Pennsylvania who deals in GTO options, and another in Florida. "But," he says, "there seems to be the most interest in GTO's in Texas and Montana—I guess because of all that space, and you can drive fast. A lot of people in those places want a fast car like the GTO."

So he is a cog in the national network of enthusiasts who keep GTO's running. He also attends local swap meets and national meets, like the *Car Craft* Street Machine Nationals, held last year in Indianapolis, where he trades and sometimes sells GTO parts. Now, as we walk past three Judges, their spoilers pointing skyward in an attitude of expectant flight, Jeff mentions some of the items that are especially desirable. The Judge glovebox medallion, for example, is hard to find and is worth money to The Judge owner who lacks one and the GTO owner who wants to convert his GTO to The Judge option. "There are lots of fake Judges running around," Jeff says. It follows that the Judge spoilers would be in demand too. "An original spoiler sells from $250 to $700

1973 GTO owned by Richard Aukerman has unusual configuration due to black and gold Imron paint applied by Ron Gibson at his Show Art Customs in Kalamazoo, Michigan.

Terrence Traynor describes his 1969 Judge convertible as a 'Replica.' Two years were spent gathering new old stock parts to turn GTO into a Judge; includes new spoiler, hood tach, glovebox emblem, stripes and authentic paint.

for a new old stock. But now they're making reproduction spoilers and they're better, smoother than the factory ones." He mentioned that factory spoilers are rough, brittle and they sag; probably a result of having been exposed to the elements for years. Those with proper care should still look good.

Of course the Ram Air IV engine is in demand, but so is the 1964 GTO engine. Jeff says that many GTO owners want their car to be as original as possible, and it's hard to find the early engines. Tachometers are also in demand. "Almost none of the hood-mounted tachs work," Jeff says, "the plastic faces get cloudy and the internals corrode." With the eye of a connoisseur he notes that the rarer 1967 tachometer is slightly taller than the 1968-69 model. And the 1965-67 air cleaner is in demand, not only by GTO owners but also by Corvette owners; it is a wide, flat, thin air cleaner with louvers around the side, stamped steel but otherwise identical to the cast-aluminum Corvette air cleaner.

There is a demand for these and other GTO parts, which is one reason Jeff has collected the nonrunning GTO's which are parked by the barn. One has been in a collision, but the others seem complete, even restorable. Where does he get them? He finds them, he says, or a friend tells him about a GTO sitting in a garage or behind a house, or someone driving past, attracted by the row of GTO's out front, will stop to look them over and before leaving will mention that he has a GTO or knows of someone who has one. Jeff follows up as many leads as he can; sometimes he'll purchase a GTO for little or nothing, but other times he'll pay high dollar. "If it's a convertible or if it has options, like that one," he says, pointing at his wife's 1969 GTO convertible.

"Options are really important," he says, as we walk back to the house. Naturally, his garage is filled with GTO parts, as is his basement, and some parts spill into the living room where his small sons are drawing crayon pictures of —what else?—GTO's. He returns from the basement with a huge box filled with small parts—dash knobs, carburetor linkage, inside door handles and window rollers and a hundred pieces of metal that only Jeff could identify. There's an early console-mounted vacuum gauge, a T-bar shift handle, and numerous gear-shift knobs. He holds up a wooden shift knob and says, "People are paying up to $150 for these—they break, or are stolen, and have to be replaced."

One feels that Jeff has an almost unlimited supply of such items but in spite of the high prices he's not selling. Instead, he's getting more. He goes to the desk in the living room and picks up a cardboard box which has *brand new* factory Judge decals. Where's he find them? "You can get them from individuals for about $200 a set, or sometimes from a dealer for $80 a set. I have a dealer ask the factory, and sometimes they come through. These stripes are important —they create the image. Some people paint them on, I've seen that, and they look bad." Those are for his 1969 Judge that he's restoring, and when it's done it'll be all original, with all the correct options, and it'll look good.

Jeff says that the people he knows who own GTO's are "psychologically into them," meaning that the cars are more than transportation, they're a way of life. The GTO was designed to appeal to the young driver but now, Jeff says,

he gets inquiries and offers to purchase his cars from older drivers. "Most of the guys are in their thirties and forties who want to buy them. A lot of the guys are Vietnam vets who were in the service when the GTO was new and who feel like they missed out on something—it's that kind of nostalgia, nine times out of ten. Interest is booming! It's a revolution! It's like the 1955-56-57 Chevy thing. . . ."

For Jeff, buying GTO's is also an investment—after all, he has a good deal of money and time tied up in this activity—and he points out that even the bank recognizes his cars as an investment which will continue to appreciate. For that reason the bank is willing to lend him money. Ultimately one feels that he considers his fleet of GTO's to be more than a monetary investment—they represent another kind of security against the unknown future. Like many other GTO owners, Jeff has contemplated a time around the turn of the next century, less than twenty years away, when he envisions a world without GTO's. The Great One will have disappeared. He says he wants his sons to be able to enjoy the car that he has enjoyed. Barring a world without gasoline or governmental legislation banning muscle cars, he has insured their future pleasures by herding together a flock of goats and enough spare parts to last his and his sons' lifetimes.

Jeff Tillman's impulse to acquire a number of GTO's is something we can all understand, but most of us have to settle for one GTO, and not a $25,000 Judge convertible either.

That it can be done, and on a limited budget, is evidenced by Matt Harshaw, who bought his 1965 GTO hardtop in February 1979 for $200. It didn't run, but it had the original paint, interior, motor and the tri-power. Matt got it running and spent a year doing little things to the car while he drove it. In July 1980 he had it painted the original color, Teal Turquoise, and it looks like new; now he's in the market for three rebuilt carburetors and a four-speed Muncie transmission. Stories like Matt's are not uncommon, and while it's possible to invest $10,000 in a GTO it's also possible to have a sharp-looking GTO in running condition for a tenth of that amount.

It's not difficult to locate a GTO, unless you're a purist. Many GTO's were jacked up, had the fender wells enlarged, had fiberglass tilt front ends installed, and were, in general, hashed up. It's hard to find an original car, and especially hard to find a GTO that wasn't driven with a heavy right foot.

You probably won't find the GTO of your dreams by standing on the corner watching traffic. Check the classified ads of your local paper; your best buys might be found here. Also check the ads in magazines such as *Hemming's Motor News* (Bennington, Vermont), *Cars & Parts* (Sidney, Ohio) and *Car Exchange* (Iola, Wisconsin); the prices here may seem inflated since these publications deal with the collector market. The cars may be located half a dozen states away from where you are, but at least you can get an idea of what's available.

An excellent source of cars, parts and information is *The Gas Can*, the publication of the GTO Association of America. In defining the publication's editorial stance, the editor, Tony Bastien, says: "Our main objective, then, is to

GTO's have always done well at the drags. Dennis Cook uses his 1965 GTO for street, show and strip; turning around 12.50 seconds, feels he could get into the 11.00's with set of Ram Air V heads.

help you preserve [the GTO]; and to provide for the exchange of views, parts, ideas, information and friendship amongst those of us who are lucky enough to own a GTO and a part of the greatest automotive era the world has ever known."

To meet this objective members contribute invaluable information; for example, it published a series of articles on how to rebuild a basket-case tri-power to a state of original condition. As editor Tony Bastien says, ". . . the factory shop manuals hardly ever mention the tri-power, much less show you how to put one together." The association also has a large library of technical publications, including body and service manuals, and will photocopy needed information for a nominal fee. Whatever problems can't be solved there, have a good chance of being solved in the section where readers answer other readers' questions, such as, "Will a cruise control work with a tri-power unit on a 1966 GTO?"

The newsletter also has a large Wanted and Unwanted section which lists GTO cars and parts, and there are reproduction items, such as the 1969 Judge spoiler, The Judge glovebox emblem, and the tri-power linkage.

Other enthusiast publications are the *Classic GTO Newsletter*, a monthly publication similar to *The Gas Can*, and *Thunder Am*, a slick monthly magazine which has one article in each issue about the GTO.

A nice feature of owning a car like the GTO is that it's essentially a Pontiac LeMans and, with the exception of the hood, trim and engine, it uses parts which can be found almost anywhere. In fact, many parts can be found on any of General Motors's intermediate cars; for example, a tilt wheel option from a LeMans or a Chevelle will fit a GTO. Other parts such as radiators, the 398-ci, 400-ci, 428-ci and 455-ci engines, the various transmissions and rear end assemblies will also fit in many cases.

In regard to the latter, for those who are purists, the ratio and type of rear end is clearly stamped on the rear of the right-hand axle tube adjacent to the carrier or on the left rear brake drum surface. The first letter of the code identifies the type of rear end: W = standard; Y = Safe-T-Track; X = standard with metallic brakes; Z = Safe-T-Track with metallic brakes. The second letter indicates the ratio: B = 2.56; D = 2.93; E = 3.08; F = 3.23; G = 3.36; H = 3.55; K = 3.90; L = 4.33. To find what parts will fit your GTO it would be a good idea to buy, or at least have access to, the *Hollander Inter-change Books*. These books list over a million interchangeable parts, and in them you can discover whether a cluster gear for a Muncie transmission interchanges with that old Chevrolet three-speed lying beside the garage.

Be prepared to make certain basic repairs on your GTO. For example, if you buy a 1968-69 GTO with the disappearing headlights option you can expect them to malfunction due to vacuum leaks and deteriorating rubber parts. On cars equipped with the Ram Air option the hoods tend to buckle due to a lack of structural support. Those are engineering problems, but other problems have to do with time and the nature of metal. On GTO's 1964-67 (especially the 1967's) the gas tank support straps rust prematurely, releasing the gas tank, and the 1969 GTO rear bumper ends also seem to rust out quickly. The 1970-71 GTO rear bumpers rust and pit from exhaust residue buildup. In those states where road salt is used, the corner pocket of front fenders, the lower edge of the doors and lower rear quarter panels seem especially prone to the salt's corruption (although I don't think GTO's, or even Pontiacs, could be said to be singular cases).

Rust around the rear window, however, seems to be a problem peculiar to the GM A-body cars. It's the result of water being trapped under the molding, and it can be cured by removing the molding, drilling a hole beneath it and letting the water run out.

Another problem common to early GTO's is that the ignition locks become worn and a pin in them causes the cylinder to lock up in the off position so that the car won't start. Randall Grider, a Pontiac mechanic, suggests, "All GTO's 1964-67 should have the ignition assembly checked over by an experienced locksmith."

Some problems are common but minor in nature. For example, the anodized strip over the radio in GTO's quickly discolors. Other common problems are much more serious. The GTO came from the factory with a nylon timing gear; after 40,000-60,000 miles the gear can break up, going into the oil pan where the parts enter the oiling system, plug lines and cause premature engine failure. A serious problem with a simple solution: Use a metal replacement gear.

But overall GTO owners report that they have fewer problems with their GTO than they have had with other cars. This is in spite of the fact that the GTO, because of its awesome power, is usually driven harder and faster. The GTO

GTO's have always been distinctive, lately have become truly special-interest cars. Here among antiques and classics, a 1966 GTO is being polished for judging.

is a long-lasting and forgiving car and, unlike the big MoPar Hemis, it stays in tune.

The GTO even seems to surpass other Pontiacs; Ron Torland has owned a Judge and a Firebird for many years and is able to make a valid comparison. "I'm pretty sure that my '70 GTO convertible with its Ram Air engine would easily outrun the smaller and lighter [1969] Firebird. Even though I did much more 'highway' driving with the Firebird, it required much more frequent tuning of the engine and carb overhauls to maintain its performance than the GTO requires."

Ron Aungst has kept a careful record of repairs made on his 1970 Judge since it was new and it adds up to: four tires, one battery, one radiator hose, one water pump and a Ram Air seal between the engine and hood. That's affordable—and Ron has spared no effort to keep his car in mint original condition.

GTO ownership has other fringe benefits. The car probably gets noticed more today, among long lines of drab, perfunctory traffic, than it did when it was new. People like to see a sharp GTO—even those who do not know what the name means or what the car represents. While it's annoying to have to search all over town for a source of leaded-premium or high-octane gasoline, the pleasures of a Sunday cruise outweigh the annoyances.

With a GTO you have a car which can be used for daily transportation, but which can also be used for special events —events for which you would be ineligible if you drove a Ford Pinto or a Datsun. To get the maximum pleasure from a GTO, most owners join a GTO club and spend time meeting with others who are passionate and knowledgeable about their cars. Members share information, tools and parts; they take cruises together, and many attend the GTO National Meet held in conjunction with the Street Machine Nationals. They exhibit GTO's in the plethora of car shows which allow mixed makes and special-interest automobiles, and sometimes a group of GTO owners will even stage its own show at a park or in a supermarket mall.

Ron Aungst describes the pleasures of exhibiting his car: "I display my Judge at numerous antique and classic car shows throughout the state. The enthusiastic response from the public has been overwhelming. A lot of people I meet talk of once knowing someone who owned a Goat or a Judge, but do not know what happened to the cars. I've found that GTO's are a rare breed at shows and are a welcome and popular addition. The trophies and awards I receive at shows are also proudly accepted."

Today, more than ever, the GTO is an exciting mode of transportation, and John DeLorean's retrospective evaluation, made shortly before he went to Chevrolet in 1969, rings with truth: "It was an exciting automobile to drive but, more important, it was useful for everyday driving. Everyone who drove it loved it. . . . Most people want distinctiveness. In these cars, you combine unique appearance and performance. Their market is here to stay. Too many people like to drive them for it to disappear."

Sometimes GTO owners just like to get together and go for a drive. Here are three: Tommy Webster owns the 1966, Jimmy Craighead owns the 1967 and James Webster owns the 1968 GTO.

GTO RESOURCE PEOPLE
AND ORGANIZATIONS

CLUBS

Classic GTO Club
(Publishes the *Classic GTO Newsletter)*
P.O. Box 392
Dallas, TX 75221

GTO Association of America
(Publishes *The Gas Can)*
Box 20614
Billings, MT 59104

Pontiac-Oakland Club International, Inc.
(Publishes *Smoke Signals and Silver Streak News)*
P.O. Box 5108
Salem, OR 97304

SOURCE PUBLICATIONS

Hemmings' Motor News
Box 380
Bennington, VT 05201

Car Exchange
Iola, WI 54945

Cars & Parts
P.O. Box 482
Sidney, OH 45367

Thunder Am
Quicksilver Communications
167 Terrace Street
Haworth, NJ 07641

Antique Automotive Color Reference Service
Bob Reed
P.O. Box 1053
Highland, NY 12528
(Paint chips, 1964-74 GTO)

Dave Fiedletz
2222 Autumn Way
Richmond, IN 47374
(Reproduction tri-power air cleaners)

Bob Antelman
9727 Mt. Pisgah Road
Apt. 103
Silver Springs, MD 20903
(Reproduction GTO decals; body patch panels)

Custom Automotive
Box 24
Chesterland, OH 44026
(Body patch panels)

Leonard Wenske
Box 1643
Lovington, NM 88260
(Headliners and carpet material)

Artistic Metalizing
Restoration Division
Box 8571
Long Beach, CA 90808
(Rechrome plastic parts)

E & V Plastic Plating Co.
13000 Haggerty Rd.
Belleville, MI 48111
(Rechrome plastic parts)

SOURCES FOR PARTS
AND REPRODUCTION ITEMS

Dale and Ray Hunt
Mid-America Speed Center
238 Wayne Road
Westland, MI 48185

Helm, Inc.
Publications Division
14310 Hamilton Ave.
Highland Park, MI 48203
(Body and chassis shop manuals)

Bob Black
S. 4th St.
Jeanette, PA 15644
(Used shop manuals)

Dick Boneske
Box 234
Butte Des Morts, WI 54927
(Reproduction tri-power linkage)

Classic Motorbooks
P.O. Box 1
Osceola, WI 54020
(Automotive literature)

Classic Auto
Kenny Kneringer
2210 W. Raleigh
Milwaukee, WI 53209
(Reproduction Judge emblems, spoiler)

Dennis Kirban
1482 Sugarbottom Road
Furlong, PA 18925
(New and used parts)

Sources for Pontiac Speed Equipment
and Information

George DeLorean
Leader Automotive
1207 Wheaton
Troy, MI 48084

Herb Adams VSE
125 Ocean View
Pacific Grove, CA 93950

H-O Racing Specialties
P.O. Box 429
Hawthorne, CA 90250

Mid-America Speed Centers
238 Wayne Road
Westland, MI 48185

Nunzi's Automotive
1419 64th St.
Brooklyn, NY 11219

APPENDIX III
Production Figures

Abbreviations Used
    STD—Standard engine
    2BBL—2-barrel carburetor
    3X2—(3) 2-barrel carburetors
    4BBL—4-barrel carburetor
    HO—High Output
    RA—Ram Air (I & II)
    RAIII—Ram Air III
    RAIV—Ram Air IV
    SPT—Sports
    MAN—Manual transmission
    AUT—Automatic transmission
    LM—Option on LeMans
    VT—Option on Ventura

MODEL YEAR	COUPE	HARDTOP	CONVERTIBLE	TOTAL
1964	7,384	18,422	6,644	32,450
	(8,245 with 389 3x2)			
	(24,205 with 389 4BBL)			
1965	8,319	55,722	11,311	75,352
	(56,378 with MAN)			
	(18,974 with AUT)			
	(20,547 with 389 3x2)			
	(54,805 with 389 4BBL)			
1966	10,363	73,785	12,798	96,946
	(61,279 with MAN)			
	(35,667 with AUT)			
	(19,045 with 389 3x2)			
	(77,901 with 389 4BBL)			
1967	7,029	65,176	9,517	81,722
	(39,128 with MAN)			
	(42,594 with AUT)			
	(751 with 400 RA)			
	(13,827 with 400 HO)			
	(2,967 with 400 2BBL)			
	(64,177 with 400 STD)			
1968		77,704	9,980	
		757—400 RA MAN	92—400 RA MAN	
		183—400 RA AUT	22—400 RA AUT	
		6,197—400 HO MAN	766—400 HO MAN	
		3,140—400 HO AUT	461—400 HO AUT	
		2,841—400 2BBL AUT	432—400 2BBL AUT	
		25,371—400 STD MAN	3,116—400 STD MAN	
		39,215—400 STD AUT	5,091—400 STD AUT	
				87,684

1969	(58,126 HDTP)	(7,328 CONV)	
	(6,725 HDTP JUDGE)	(108 CONV JUDGE)	
	549—400 RAIV MAN	45—RAIV MAN	
	151—400 RAIV AUT	14—400 RAIV AUT	
	6,143—400 RAIII MAN	249—400 RAIII MAN	
	1,986—400 RAIII AUT	113—400 RAIII AUT	
	1,246—400 2BBL AUT	215—400 2BBL AUT	
	22,032—400 STD MAN	2,415—400 STD MAN	
	32,744—400 STD AUT	4,385—400 STD AUT	
	64,851—TOTAL	7,436—TOTAL	72,287

1970	(32,737 HDTP)	(3,615 CONV)	
	(3,629 HDTP JUDGE)	(168 CONV JUDGE)	
	627—400 RAIV MAN	24—400 RAIV MAN	
	140—400 RAIV AUT	13—400 RAIV AUT	
	3,054—400 RAIII MAN	174—400 RAIII MAN	
	1,302—400 RAIII AUT	114—400 RAIII AUT	
	1,761—455 4BBL MAN	158—455 4BBL MAN	
	1,986—455 4BBL AUT	241—455 4BBL AUT	
	9,348—400 STD MAN	887—400 STD MAN	
	18,148—400 STD AUT	2,173—400 STD AUT	
	36,366—TOTAL	3,783—TOTAL	40,149

1971	(9,497 HDTP)	(661 CONV)	
	(357 HDTP JUDGE)	(17 CONV JUDGE)	
	476—455 HO MAN	21—455 HO MAN	
	412—455 HO AUT	27—455 HO AUT	
	534—455 4BBL AUT	43—455 4BBL AUT	
	2,011—400 STD MAN	79—400 STD MAN	
	6,421—400 STD AUT	508—400 STD AUT	
	9,854—TOTAL	678—TOTAL	10,532

1972	134	HDTP CPE	
		5,673	
	3—455 HO MAN	310—455 HO MAN	
	7—455 HO AUT	325—455 HO AUT	
	5—455 4BBL AUT	235—455 4BBL AUT	
	59—400 STD MAN	1,519—400 STD MAN	
	60—400 STD AUT	3,284—400 STD AUT	
			5,807

1973	494	SPT CPE	
		4,312	
	25—455 4BBL AUT	519—455 4BBL AUT	
	187—400 4BBL MAN	926—400 4BBL MAN	
	282—400 4BBL AUT	2,867—400 4BBL AUT	
			4,806

1974	COUPE	HATCHBACK	
	5,335	1,723	
	2,487—350 4BBL MAN	687—350 4BBL MAN	
	2,848—350 4BBL AUT	1,036—350 4BBL AUT	
			7,058

Total GTO Production 514,793

APPENDIX IV
Serial Numbers

A word about serial number prefixes: In some cases LeMans and Ventura models have been converted into GTO's, and 1969-71 GTO's have been given The Judge option. There is no way of telling from the serial number whether or not you have a GTO for the following years: 1964, 1965, 1972, 1973, 1974. The same is true for The Judge, 1969, 1970, 1971. For all the other years (1966-1971) the serial number prefix will indicate whether or not it is a GTO.

YEAR-BODY STYLE	SERIAL NUMBER PREFIX	
1964-CPE	22227	(Option—LeMans)
1964-HDTP	22237	(Option—LeMans)
1964-CONV	22267	(Option—LeMans)
1965-CPE	23727	(Option—LeMans)
1965-HDTP	23737	(Option—LeMans)
1965-CONV	23767	(Option—LeMans)
1966-CPE	24207	
1966-HDTP	24217	
1966-CONV	24267	
1967-CPE	24207	
1967-HDTP	24217	
1967-CONV	24267	
1968-HDTP	24237	
1968-CONV	24267	
1969-HDTP	24237	
1969-CONV	24267	
1969-HDTP JUD	24237	(Option—GTO)
1969-CONV JUD	24267	(Option—GTO)
1970-HDTP	24237	
1970-CONV	24267	
1970-HDTP JUD	24237	(Option—GTO)
1970-CONV JUD	24267	(Option—GTO)
1971-HDTP	24237	
1971-CONV	24267	
1971-HDTP JUD	24237	(Option—GTO)
1971-CONV JUD	24267	(Option—GTO)
1972-CPE	23527	(Option—LeMans)
1972-HDTP	23537	(Option—LeMans)
1973-CPE	2AF37 or 2F37	(Option—LeMans)
1973-SPT CPE	2AD37 or 2D37	(Option—LeMans)
1974-HTCHBK	2XY17	(Option—Ventura)
1974-CPE	2XY27	(Option—Ventura)

The preceding GTO production figures and serial number prefixes lists were compiled by the GTO Association of America from information provided by General Motors and Mr. Chuck Jones of Urbana, Illinois.

BIBLIOGRAPHY

"Auto Talk," Radio Program, WXYZ, Detroit (March 22, 1981).

Baker, C. J. "Pontiac's New Super-Duty 455," *Hot Rod* (October 1972), 60-61.

Baumann, P. D. "The Complete GTO," *Car Exchange* (November 1979), 8-17.

Brock, Ray. "LeMans," *Hot Rod* (December 1963), 26-31.

———. "Pontiac's Strongest," *Hot Rod* (April 1962), 76-77.

Burger, Gerry. "GTO Judge on Trial," *Car Exchange* (March 1981), 26-29.

"Car of the Year," *Motor Trend* (February 1968), 41-49.

Carroll, William. "Knudsen, The Man and His Car," *Motor Trend* (June 1958), 30-33.

Corry, Will and Rudolph Wurlitzer. "Two Lane Blacktop," *Esquire*, LXXV, iv (April 1971), 104-114, 142-144.

Dahlquist, Eric. "GTO," *Hot Rod* (July 1965), 31-33.

Davis, Jr., David E. "We Think it's Important," *Car and Driver* (January 1975), 52-54.

DeLorean, John Z. "Engineering the New Pontiacs," *Motor Trend* (February 1965), 68-71.

Dianna, John. "Poncho's Tunnel Port Four-Oh-Oh!" *Hot Rod* (May 1969), 36-38.

"GTO: A Tale of a Tempestuous Tiger!" *Car Craft* (March 1965), 22-25, 75-76.

Gunnell, John. "The Glorious 'Goat,'" *Special-Interest Autos*, #49 (February 1979), 38-43.

Humble, Wick. "1961 Pontiac Tempest," *Special-Interest Autos*, #48 (December 1978), 36-41.

Huntington, Roger. "GTO Trick Stuff," *Car Craft* (February 1967), 38-41, 78.

Jedlicka, Daniel A. "Gaining Respect on Woodward Avenue," *Esquire*, LXXII, iii (September 1969), 112-117, 44-58.

Kelly, Steve. "Here Come de Judge," *Hot Rod* (December 1968), 64-65.

———. "Lightweight, Hemi-headed . . . and Beautiful," *Hot Rod* (October 1970), 44-48.

———. "Pontiac's Answer to the GTO," *Hot Rod* (June 1971), 40-42.

———. "Testing the Tigers," *Motor Trend* (January 1967), 39-42.

Langworth, Richard M. "Look What's Happened to Grandma!" *Special-Interest Autos*, #48 (December 1978), 12-17.

Lienert, Paul. "Flexing Their Muscle on Woodward Avenue," *Detroit Free Press* (May 27, 1979), 5D.

Mandel, Leon. "Jim Wangers: Svengali of the North," *Car and Driver* (March 1968), 46-48, 86-87.

McGonegal, Roland. "Poncho Power, 1969," *Super Stock* (April 1969), 28-31, 74, 78.

Morehouse, Edward. "GTO: The Performance Years," *Car Collector* (March 1979), 27-32, 63-67.

Neumann, Bill. "Record Day for Thompson," *Car Craft* (October 1961), 15-19.

Pennington, Howard. "Mr. GTO," *Car Craft* (January 1967), 10-12, 74.

"Pontiac GTO: Blueprint for the Muscle Cars," Report of survey taken by MacManus, John and Adams, Inc. (1970).

"Project Car: Pontiac GTO 428," *Car and Driver* (February 1968), 25-28.

"Ram Air GTO," *Car Life* (October 1967), 87-91.

"The Royal Pontiac Story." Two brochures published by Royal Pontiac including reprints of road tests and articles. 21 pp. Undated; one pre-dates the GTO, the other covers the GTO.

Sanders, Bill. "GTO The Hot '70s," *Motor Trend* (September 1969), 60-62, 99.

Schmidt, Julian G. "King Mover of Motor City," *Motor Trend* (December 1968), 30-31.

"Showdown for Spoilers," *Car Life* (June 1969), 20-27.

Smith, LeRoi. "Snap for the Tiger's Tail," *Car Craft* (April 1965), 60-63.

"The Teenagers," *Newsweek* (March 21, 1966), 59-ff.

Wright, J. Patrick. *On A Clear Day You Can See General Motors*. Grosse Pointe, Mich.: Wright Enterprises, 1979.

Yates, Brock. "The Macho Machines," *Playboy* (April 1974), 158-162, 188-194.

_____ . "Street Racing," *Car and Driver* (September 1967), 62-65, 92-93.

INDEX

MORE GREAT READING

American Car Spotter's Guide 1940-1965. Covers 66 makes—almost 3,000 illustrations. 358 pages, softbound.

American Car Spotter's Guide 1966-1980. Giant pictorial source with over 3,600 illustrations. 432 pages, softbound.

The Production Figure Book For U.S. Cars. Reflects the relative rarity of various makes, models, body styles, etc. Softbound, 180 pages.

Pontiac: The Postwar Years. One of America's most exciting makes of automobile is described in this factual 33-year history. 256 photos, 205 pages.

Chevy Super Sports 1961-1976. Exciting story of these hot cars with complete specs and data. 176 pages, 234 illustrations, softbound. Large format.

Son of Muscle Car Mania. 176 pages of more great ads from the 1962-1974 muscle car era. All U.S. makes represented. Softbound, 250 illustrations.

Muscle Car Mania. A collection of advertisements for muscle cars 1964 through 1974. 176 pages, 250 illustrations, softbound.

Fearsome Fords 1959-1973. Over 250 photos of these great cars accompany 182 pages of interesting information. Softbound, large format.

Mighty Mopars 1960–1974. The story of these great muscle cars is told through text and over 175 great illustrations. 176 pages, softbound.

Auto Restoration From Junker to Jewel. Illustrated guide to restoring old cars. 292 pages, 289 illustrations, softbound.

Shelby's Wildlife: The Cobras and Mustangs. Complete, exciting story of the 260, 289, 427 and Daytona Cobras plus Shelby Mustangs. 224 pages, nearly 200 photos.

Classic Motorbooks Chrysler 300 1955-1961 Photofacts. Over 125 photos accompany lots of info on these cars. Softbound, 80 pages.

Classic Motorbooks Pontiac Trans Am 1969-1973 Photofacts. Over 125 great photos help tell the story. 80 pages, softbound.

Bob Bondurant on High Performance Driving. World-famous instructor teaches secrets to fast, safe driving. Over 100 illustrations, 144 pages, softbound.

Restoring Convertibles. Great tips on restoring post-WWII convertibles. 242 pages, 222 illustrations.

Classic Motorbooks Mercury Cougar 1967-1973 Photofacts. Covers all these models with over 150 illustrations. Softbound, 80 pages.

Porsches For The Road. Beautiful photo essays on 12 models. In the Survivors Series. 128 pages, 250 illustrations, 125 in color.

Automotive Fuel Injection Systems: A Technical Guide. Thorough analysis and description of current gas-engine technology. 173 illustrations, 182 pages, softbound.

The Art and Science of Grand Prix Driving. Complete analysis and discussion by World Champion Niki Lauda. Over 150 photos, 23 in color, 245 pages.

Autocourse. Large-format racing annual. Coverage of each Grand Prix and other major racing events and series. Over 200 pages with lots of color.

Illustrated Corvette Buyer's Guide. Includes 194 photos and lots of info on all these cars 1953-1982. 156 pages, softbound.

Illustrated High Performance Mustang Buyer's Guide. Covers the 1965 GT, the Shelby, through the 1973 Mach 1. Softbound, 250 illustrations, 176 pages.

Harley-Davidson Motor Company: An Official Eighty-Year History. More than 250 photos plus 8 pages of color tell the complete story of the company 1903–1983. 288 pages.

Illustrated Camaro Buyer's Guide. Covers models from 1967 to 1985 with lots of information and nearly 200 illustrations. 156 pages, softbound.

Supertuning Your Z-28 Camaro. Hands-on guide to tuning, supertuning and race prepping a Z-28. 148 illustrations, 160 pages, softbound.

Engineer To Win. Latest info on racing materials technology, prevention of fatigue failure and other fascinating subjects. 280 pages, over 250 illustrations, softbound.

The New Formula One: A Turbo Age. Twice World Driving Champion Niki Lauda on aerodynamics turbos, ground effects, suspensions, racing developments and much more. 252 pages, 135 illustrations including 12 pages in color.

Corvettes For The Road. Lavish pictorial coverage, in the Survivors Series. 128 pages, over 250 photos, 100 in color.

The Ford Y-Block: Origin, Maintenance, Rebuild. Step-by-step guide to tearing down and rebuilding. Softbound, nearly 200 illustrations, 120 pages.

Restorer's Model A Shop Manual: Complete and Illustrated. Step-by-step instructions of best methods to restore these cars. 224 pages, 143 illustrations, softbound.

Mustang Performance and Handling Guide 1964–1985. Easy-to-use tips on getting more power and better cornering from your Mustang. Softbound, over 200 illustrations, 165 pages.

Pontiac GTO Restoration Guide 1964–1970. 1,000-plus authoritative photos, drawings and year-by-year text cover all components for a restoration. Softbound, 480 pages.

Motorbooks International
Publishers & Wholesalers Inc
Osceola, Wisconsin 54020, USA